PIETER BRUEGEL

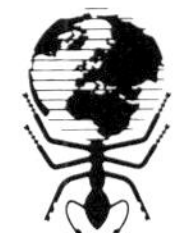

Books in the RENAISSANCE LIVES series explore and illustrate the life histories and achievements of significant artists, rulers, intellectuals and scientists in the early modern world. They delve into literature, philosophy, the history of art, science and natural history and cover narratives of exploration, statecraft and technology.

Series Editor: François Quiviger

Already published

Artemisia Gentileschi and Feminism in Early Modern Europe *Mary D. Garrard*

Blaise Pascal: Miracles and Reason *Mary Ann Caws*

Botticelli: Artist and Designer *Ana Debenedetti*

Caravaggio and the Creation of Modernity *Troy Thomas*

Donatello and the Dawn of Renaissance Art *A. Victor Coonin*

Erasmus of Rotterdam: The Spirit of a Scholar *William Barker*

Filippino Lippi: An Abundance of Invention *Jonathan K. Nelson*

Giorgione's Ambiguity *Tom Nichols*

Hans Holbein: The Artist in a Changing World *Jeanne Nuechterlein*

Hieronymus Bosch: Visions and Nightmares *Nils Büttner*

Isaac Newton and Natural Philosophy *Niccolò Guicciardini*

John Donne: In the Shadow of Religion *Andrew Hadfield*

John Evelyn: A Life of Domesticity *John Dixon Hunt*

Leonardo da Vinci: Self, Art and Nature *François Quiviger*

Leon Battista Alberti: The Chameleon's Eye *Caspar Pearson*

Machiavelli: From Radical to Reactionary *Robert Black*

Michelangelo and the Viewer in His Time *Bernadine Barnes*

Paracelsus: An Alchemical Life *Bruce T. Moran*

Petrarch: Everywhere a Wanderer *Christopher S. Celenza*

Piero della Francesca and the Invention of the Artist *Machtelt Brüggen Israëls*

Pieter Bruegel and the Idea of Human Nature *Elizabeth Alice Honig*

Raphael and the Antique *Claudia La Malfa*

Rembrandt's Holland *Larry Silver*

Rubens's Spirit: From Ingenuity to Genius *Alexander Marr*

Salvator Rosa: Paint and Performance *Helen Langdon*

Titian's Touch: Art, Magic and Philosophy *Maria H. Loh*

Tycho Brahe and the Measure of the Heavens *John Robert Christianson*

PIETER BRUEGEL

and the Idea of Human Nature

ELIZABETH ALICE HONIG

REAKTION BOOKS

For Deb

Published by Reaktion Books Ltd
Unit 32, Waterside
44–48 Wharf Road
London N1 7UX, UK
www.reaktionbooks.co.uk

First published 2019
First published in paperback 2022

Printed and bound in India by Replika Press Pvt. Ltd

A catalogue record for this book is available from the British Library

ISBN 978 1 78914 675 2

COVER: Pieter Bruegel, detail of *Children's Games*, 1560, oil on canvas; akg-images.

CONTENTS

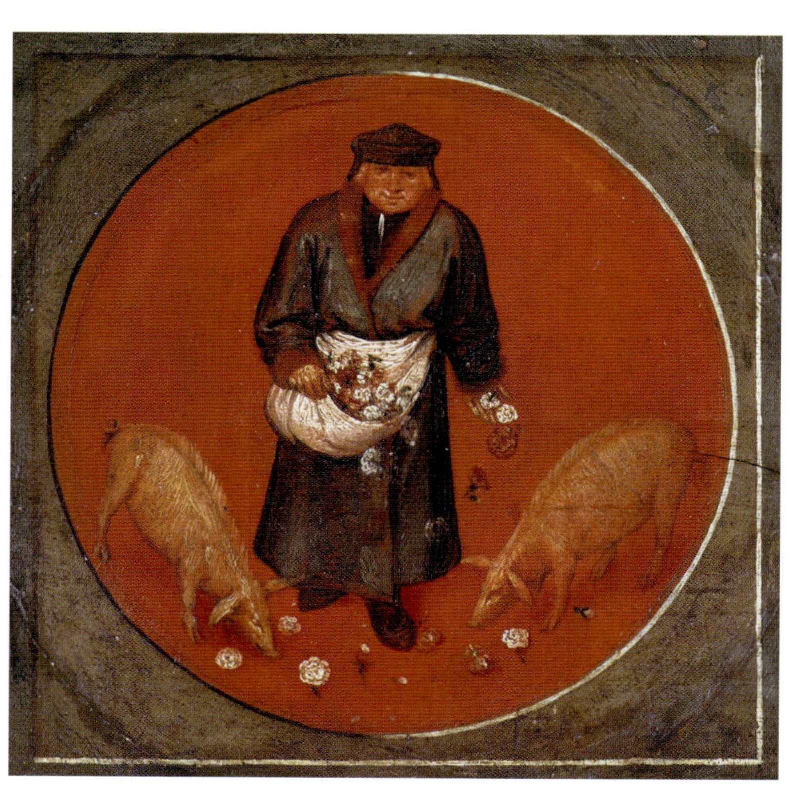

ONE

Humanity and Self-knowledge

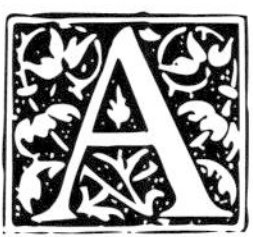A DINNER PARTY IN Antwerp around 1560, with twelve guests. Some of them, and perhaps their host, are officers of the Antwerp mint, the city's money-makers in a most literal sense. The group is well-to-do, and most are educated but not intellectual; they are politically informed but not partisan.[1] The food has been abundant and the talk convivial, and everybody has enjoyed themselves. As the banqueters finish their sugar desserts, each one picks up his small round wooden trencher, or *teljoor*, and flips it over.[2] On its reverse side is a single figure painted by Pieter Bruegel: a peasant, a merchant, a peddler, a housewife, a soldier, a scholar. Local, familiar types. But the actions they are engaged in seem absurd, quite unlike the usual doings of soldiers and housewives. The merchant is strewing flowers in front of two pigs (illus. 1); the housewife carries a pail of water and a burning coal; the soldier, missing a key piece of leg armour, is tying a bell around the neck of a cat, while another man with one bare leg is walking headlong into a wall (illus. 2).

The images are puzzles, challenging the guests to make sense of what they show. Since the time of this dinner party,

1 Casting roses before swine: detail from Pieter Bruegel, *Twelve Proverbs*, 1558, oil on panel.

the twelve plates have been set together into an elaborate painted panel, and each given a simple rhyming couplet that provides in words the proverb that Bruegel had visualized (illus. 3).[3] Thus the flower-throwing merchant is revealed as a man who casts roses before swine, a version from local folk culture of the biblical 'pearls before swine', while the woman with fire and water is revealed as two-faced. In some cases the couplet extends the proverb with a brief explanation of its significance, remarking for instance that the rose-strewer is a man whose work is wasted. But none of this guidance is available to the original dinner-party guests. At first, perhaps, they don't even recognize that the nonsensical activities they see relate to proverbs at all: they have encountered proverbs before as inscriptions on dinnerware, but not as visual images.[4] Then somebody says, 'Wait, my man is banging his head against a brick wall!' and the next declares that his is filling the hole after the calf has drowned – we would say, closing the stable door after the horse has bolted. Laughing at the cleverness with which common parlance has been made visual, the guests continue to work out what is being illustrated, sometimes understanding that not one but several common sayings are referred to within a single image, like the man who falls between two stools and also lands in a pile of ashes.

Once the basic proverbs have been discovered, the party begins to discuss the implications of all these sayings, their common themes and unexpected interconnections. Proverbs that look and even sound quite dissimilar share the same insights into human behavioural tendencies. People are inconstant, the guests agree, always trying to play two sides at once or following the shifting winds. They waste their best efforts in useless endeavours. Hypocrisy is common, as are envy and anger and deceit. And these failings cannot be isolated to some group defined as 'other', be it peasants or women or soldiers. The commonalities that knit one proverb to another, the bare legs and watery pits as well as the metaphorical failings, move the company to acknowledge that what they are discussing is simply human nature, our common flaws and the things these flaws make us do. As the evening progresses, laughter intermingles with more serious conversation as the guests acknowledge the consequences of humanity's failings and ponder which weaknesses they most need to remedy within themselves.

The year 1558 is inscribed on one of these proverb plates, and a date of 1557 found on another single-proverb roundel, also originally part of a set, makes it Bruegel's earliest surviving painting.[5] Before this stint as a *teljoor* painter, he had been working for about three years as a print designer for the important Antwerp publisher Hieronymus Cock. Bruegel had originally come to the booming commercial metropolis from his home town, possibly Breda, some time in the 1540s. In Antwerp and then in Brussels, he was apparently trained by Pieter Coecke van Aelst, a designer whose diverse talents and interests included creating magnificent tapestries for Europe's wealthy and powerful, translating the architectural treatises of Vitruvius and Serlio into Flemish and journeying to Turkey to sell tapestries and observe local customs.[6] Coecke's work and thought were marked by a deep understanding of Italian as well as local artistic traditions, and although Pieter Bruegel's

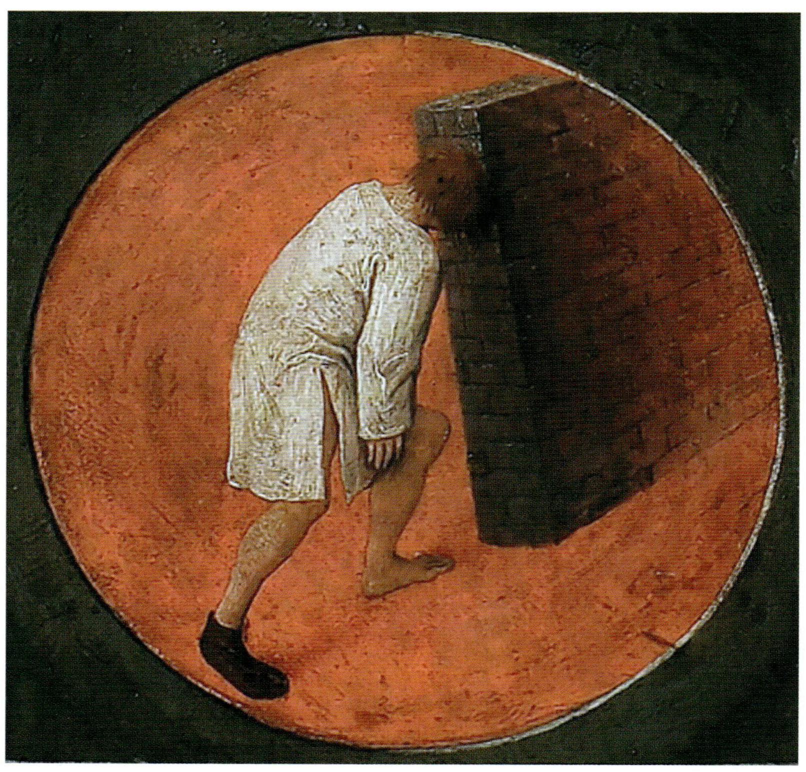

art bears little trace of the former, his teacher's intellectual internationalism was important. Perhaps it was what inspired him to travel to Italy himself after Coecke's death in 1550, journeying as far south as Naples, collaborating with the great miniaturist Giulio Clovio in Rome, and making the vivid Alpine landscape drawings that would form the basis of his prints for Hieronymus Cock upon his return to Antwerp.

Heroic bodies, grand gestures and memorable individual deeds clearly interested Bruegel not at all: in what contemporaries saw as a contest between a more Italianizing manner

2 Banging head against a wall: detail from Pieter Bruegel, *Twelve Proverbs*, 1558, oil on panel.

of painting and one that attached itself to a local tradition, Bruegel was the hero of the latter cause.[7] His vernacular images used that style to articulate ideas that were much more broadly shared among the literate public of early modern Europe. In particular his art was well suited to presenting a perspective, or opening up questions, on the subject of human nature. Bruegel's very choice to focus much of his attention on the most common, ordinary people of his day meant that beholders were viewing characters who were untutored, not fully formed by the precepts of civil society, so that the essentials of humanness made themselves more keenly apparent. Bruegel furthermore rarely seems to care about a single individual. Even in pictures where he depicts a narrative with key actors,

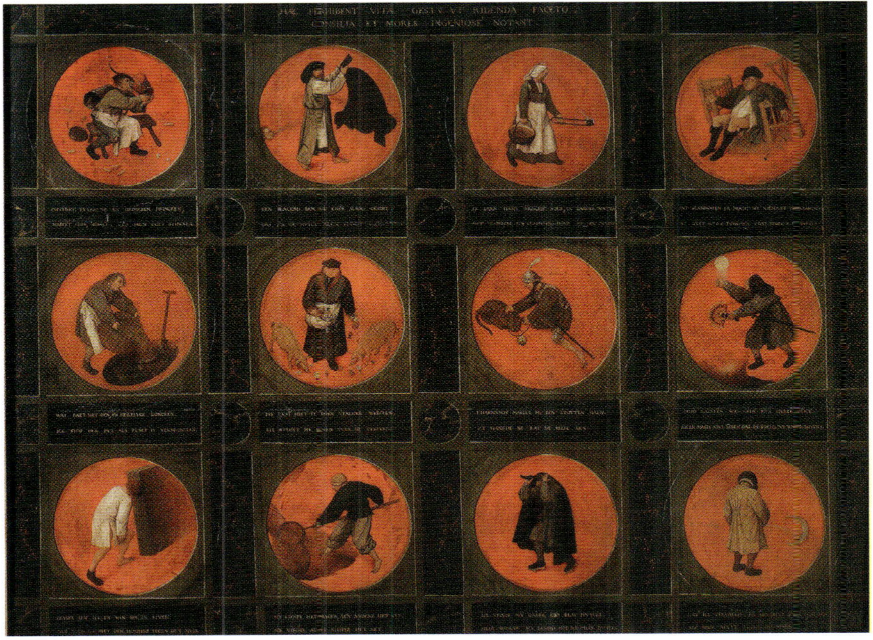

3 Pieter Bruegel, *Twelve Proverbs*, 1558, oil on panel.

and even when those actors express clear emotional states, they are only rarely characterized as singular persons: usually, they are treated as types. The viewer is not asked to identify or empathize with an individual in a given situation, but to contemplate and understand a state of being. We are allowed to connect to Bruegel's paintings on the level of shared humanity.

Pieter Bruegel is a participant in a larger conversation about human beings, their position in the cosmos and how their habits and acts contribute to the nature of civil society. This conversation was being carried on by theologians and Humanists writing in Latin, but equally by urban merchants talking in Flemish. In this book I will often set Bruegel's viewpoint into dialogue with famous thinkers, particularly the great scholar Erasmus of Rotterdam, Bruegel's countryman. Erasmus, who died in 1536 when Bruegel was just a child, influenced thinking all over Europe, but nowhere more than in his homeland, where his key works reflecting on human nature were frequently translated into the vernacular and reissued.[8] Erasmus himself was deeply knowledgeable about classical authors, more than a little familiar with Italian Humanists, and a correspondent of the German Gregor Reisch, whose popular *Margarita philosophica* of 1503 had gathered together and synthesized the ideas about the human soul, inherited from medieval theology, that most writers of his time and long after took as common knowledge.[9]

Bruegel's pictures entered into this ongoing conversation by inviting others to regard his perspective and, from there, to take one of the two routes I have imagined above: to enter into social discussion, perhaps deploying their own knowledge of written arguments, or to look inward and consider their own selves. Bruegel has certain expectations of his viewers' nature and sets up situations of spectatorship for the individual based on those expectations. He often structures his pictures so that they insist upon a detached perspective on the world, on humanity, on history – a viewpoint that can also promote self-questioning or what we might call introspection. At the same time, though, his works are perfectly geared to allowing each beholder to partake in discourse with others. As opposed to the tightly knit symbolic ensembles of Jan van Eyck's generation, rigorously pieced together so that every element adds its part to the larger sense of the work, Bruegel's paintings are dense with meaningful details that do not cohere to form a single argument. They are, therefore, endlessly discussable. At the Kunsthistorisches Museum in Vienna, where many of his paintings hang today in a single gallery visitors are constantly seen to point, discover, share and talk before these rich works. Bruegel's original audience had quite different social and philosophical contexts for their discussions, but the structure of stimulus was the same.

The debate over human nature was certainly not the only context in which Bruegel's contemporaries viewed his pictures. I believe, however, that it was a framework that would have informed many of the other themes and issues that those first beholders might have discussed, over dinner perhaps. In this chapter I will therefore sketch out some of the key issues that reasonably educated sixteenth-century people considered when they thought about human nature in general and about their individual selves within that context.

Bruegel's proverbs, like those of Erasmus in his *Adages*, offered early modern audiences access to knowledge, or perhaps better, to wisdom, that would help in understanding humankind in general and also enable individuals to contemplate themselves. In both cases, beholders were rendered better equipped to function in society, to be actors after they had been contemplators.

HUMAN NATURE: THE SHARED AND THE SELF

Nosce te ipsum, know thyself. In his *Adages*, a massive compendium of annotated proverbs from antiquity, Erasmus tells his reader that this is one of the most famous sayings left to us by the philosophers, a maxim of universal application.[10] Cicero, Juvenal, Ovid, Socrates, Plato, Diogenes and more all cited and commented upon it. The Delphic oracle, Erasmus notes, once claimed that the way to true happiness could be found 'if you have learned to know yourself'. But a few pages earlier, Erasmus had been citing proverbs that despaired of self-knowledge: nobody is really willing to search within and contemplate their own, innermost faults.[11]

In the same year that he was painting plates, 1558, Pieter Bruegel joined Erasmus and the ancients in articulating a view on self-searching, self-seeking and self-knowledge. Published by Cock after Bruegel's design, the engraving depicts Everyman in search of himself (illus. 4).[12] Carefully labelled 'ELCK', or Everyman, this figure, repeated eight times over, is searching in a number of different ways. Often he looks actively into the world around him: he wears glasses in two iterations and carries a lantern in three. This is Everyman

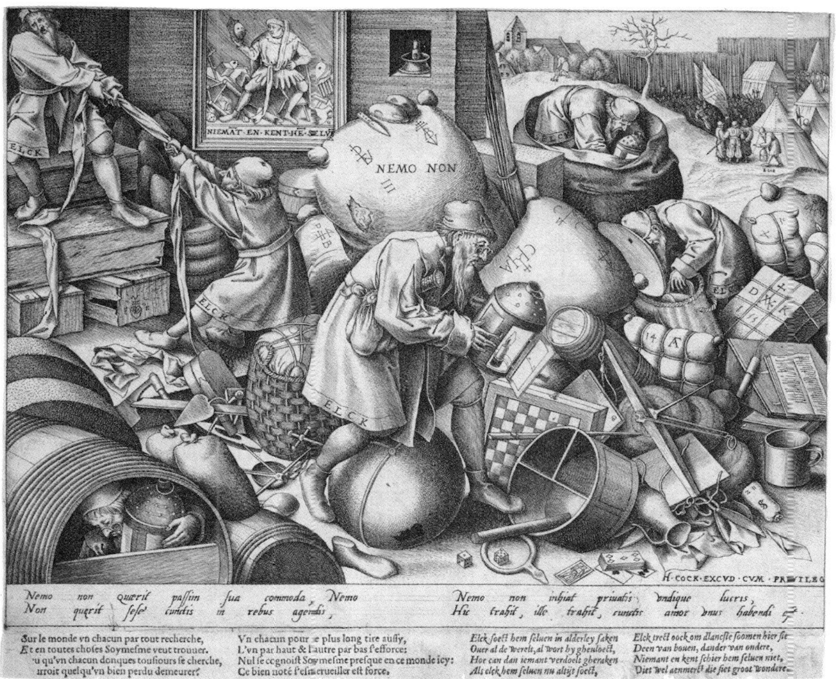

hoping to define himself through the visible, material things of the world, through bales and barrels and bundles of saleable commodities. One box at the left is even inscribed with the trademark of Bruegel's publisher Cock, but neither artists' pictures nor (at the right) scholars' books are ultimately going to provide Elck with the knowledge he needs. Other professions are referenced and rejected here as well, in the form of the builder's trowel, the salesman's scales, the tailor's cloth and shears and the shoemaker's last, whose anonymity and promise of universality neatly echoes the nearby foot of 'Everyman'. Men have individual tasks in the world, but they are not the way an individual can understand himself.

4 Pieter van der Heyden after Pieter Bruegel, *Elck* (*Everyman*), 1558, engraving.

Everyman, in the distance, drifts off to visit an army encampment and also a church, but neither one is a site of self-knowledge. He also tries 'self-seeking' in another sense: at the left, around Cock's box, two of the figures tug furiously at a length of cloth, each seeking his own advantage; as the proverb had it, 'every man pulls for the longest end.' For the picture is at once a compendium of many proverbial sayings and a direct illustration of none of them as it turns words into images and layers them over each other. The primary sayings are 'Every man seeks himself', cited in the Flemish inscription, and 'Nobody knows himself', written in block letters beneath the picture on the back wall, which shows a fool contemplating himself in a convex mirror. Is the fool then nobody? Does he know himself? Perhaps yes to the first, and surely no to the second, for only a fool thinks to know himself by looking at his outward appearance. 'Nobody' appears again in Latin on the large central bale, but now it's a double negative: NEMO NON, no nobody. This probably points to a proverb, also cited by Erasmus, that complains how 'no one, no, not one, seeks to get down into himself.'

What would it be, in the Renaissance, to 'get down into' yourself? I have been using terms like individuals and self-knowledge, but it is not so easy to say what a person in Bruegel's time understood by a 'self', or how he (or she) would have related that self to the larger scope of human nature — how one man related to everyman, as it were. There was, for most people, a self that was bound to community, to a trade, even to the very material things Bruegel rejects as the locus of self: this was part of what John Jeffries Martin calls the 'social or conforming self', where the beliefs and attitudes of the individual are pretty much in accord with those around them, and identity is formed as part of community.[13] Next to this Martin places the 'prudential' self, a self that feels in conflict with the values of his or her community and is more attached to what it identifies as an internal world. In a time of increasing religious conflict, this self was coming to play a larger role in a greater number of people's self-understanding. A third Renaissance self that Martin describes is the 'sincere' self, one that feels ethically obligated to reveal its inner beliefs and convictions to the world. Martin lists other early modern understandings of the self as well, but these three are the ones I find most useful for understanding Bruegel and sixteenth-century Northern Europe in general.

If we look at Martin's three self-types that I have listed, it is striking that in two cases the self is recognized as having different levels — one that is naturally given to the world and another that must be 'got down into', whether it will then be hidden or shared. Bruegel was not alone in thinking that such a project of self-discovery was seldom undertaken and difficult to achieve. The necessity, and the difficulty, of self-knowledge is central to the writings of Erasmus, in particular to his *Enchiridion*, a handbook for the 'Christian Soldier'. This slim book, first published in Latin in 1503, was soon translated and went through fifteen editions in Dutch before 1600.[14] Intended as a guide to living for people operating in the world, decision-makers and actors rather than cloistered thinkers, it was a book that appealed to people because of its insistence that the internal self, rather than external religious performances, was what constituted a worthy individual: Elck will not find himself in that distant church, but must keep getting down into himself. The *Enchiridion*'s enduring popularity also reflected the fact that it accommodated a view of human nature in general that felt right to its sixteenth-century readers.

Near the beginning of his book, Erasmus promises his reader that he will 'set before you a kind of likeness of yourself, as in a painting, so that you may have a clear knowledge of what you are on the inside and what you are skin deep'.[15] The picture he then paints is of a person under siege. Attack is constant and comes from two sources: the external world and our human nature. To resist these attacks we must arm ourselves, mentally, through a wisdom that is based on self-knowledge. As the individual comes to understand the flaws and impulses of their soul, they can restrain those impulses by reason and redirect them towards virtue.[16] The person who remains ignorant and blind to themselves is incapable of this.

Conspicuously absent from this picture of the human self and its conflicts are notions like sin, or the Devil, that might have played a part in earlier generations' picture of the travails of mankind. Erasmus does accept that mankind is corrupted by original sin, and this is the origin of our failings. But that corruption is only one side of human nature; Erasmus locates it in the body, which pulls us downward. The spirit, on the other hand, tends upward, and has 'such a capacity for divinity that we can soar past the minds of angels and become one with God'.[17] The basic idea here, of mankind divided between a corrupted body and a spirit closer to divinity, was nothing new: it had developed in the long history of debate over the meaning of Genesis 1:26–7, in which God says that

he will make man 'in our image, after our likeness . . . So God
created man in his own image.'[18] In this context there emerged
an idea that it was the soul or spirit that was created in God's
image, and therefore that this side of humans might aspire
to higher things.[19] It was the enlarged sense of man's capacity
developed by Humanism, a sense that human beings were
capable of very great evil but also extraordinary achievement,
that led to the more extreme view put forth by Erasmus
and, before him, by Italian thinkers like Marsilio Ficino or
Giovanni Pico della Mirandola, who proclaimed that of all
beings, man alone has no limits and does have free will.[20]

Pico goes further than Erasmus in his immense optimism
about human nature. Where they agree, though, is that human
beings are uniquely capable of self-transformation, that
they have the freedom to make a choice about what they will
become. Freedom is the quality that puts human beings between
animals (who lack potential) and the angels (who lack constraints).[21] In order to use our freedom wisely, to fend off
attacks from the world and from our base nature and so
elevate ourselves, we need to cultivate reason. Reason can
control the lower parts of our nature; to do so, it needs
self-knowledge to identify weaknesses that need control. Lust,
anger, ambition, avarice – Erasmus works through these pas-
sions, urging the power of reason to overcome each of them.
Not every person has the same flaws, or has them to the same
degree, but that is exactly why we need self-knowledge. A
really heroic individual is one who successfully combats the
greatest flaws.

Erasmus presents a powerful view of the individual self,
the 'Christian Soldier', engaged in a struggle against his own

lower nature. Although Bruegel's pictures usually tend to avoid such strong individualism, giving a sense of what is shared in humanity rather than how a single person separates from that common nature, they at the same time always allow for individual responses and judgements. His play between the general and the specific is perhaps close to earlier, less Humanistic writers like Gregor Reisch. Reisch explains that we have a shared specific *nature* which is human, but also what he calls an individual *degree*, a kind of Gregor-ness.[22] It is the individual degree, to him, that must strive to perfect nature. Reisch's human being is therefore more in need of understanding collective nature than his own, but Reisch also emphasizes the power of reason and the freedom of choice: these were the bedrock principles of ideas about human nature during Bruegel's time.[23]

Around 1559–60 Bruegel designed a set of prints to be published by Hieronymus Cock, illustrating the Seven Virtues. They followed on another successful set of seven – showing the Seven Deadly Sins – that had been produced a year or so earlier.[24] The sins had standard iconographic features, and in his designs Bruegel had also been able to follow the example of Hieronymus Bosch, a marketable brand in the 1550s. The virtues did not have a strong visual tradition and required much more invention. In them, Bruegel offers us his view on the side of human nature that, if not flawless, can be culti-vated to a higher level of perfection. One particular virtue is positioned suggestively between the sins – what Erasmus would have termed weaknesses or vices – and the very possi-bility of virtue, and that is Fortitude (illus. 5). As in the other prints in the series, a single female figure in the centre of the

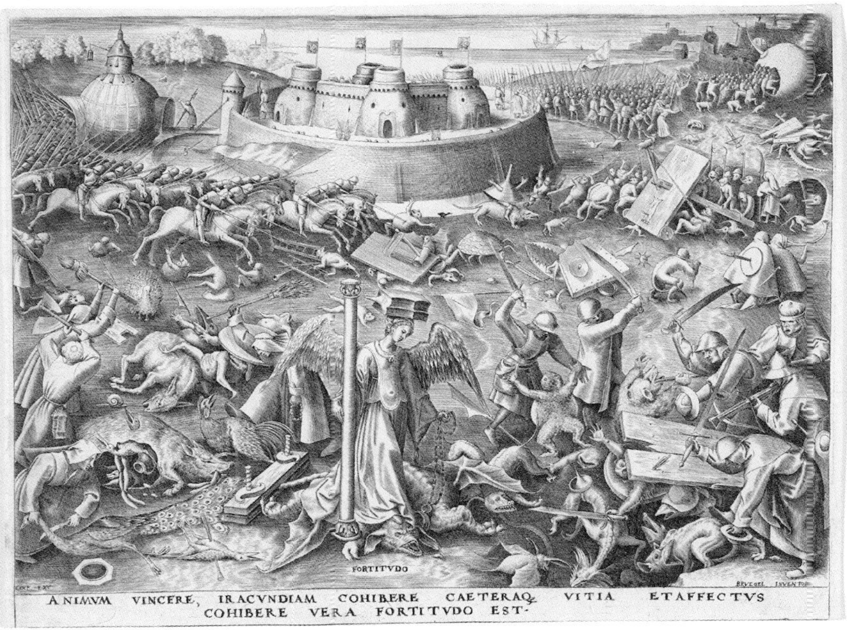

image embodies the totality of the virtue. Fortitude stands upon a dragon, representing evil, which she has conquered and chained. On her head she balances an anvil that does not falter under many blows, while her column is another sign of her steadfast nature.

Around Fortitude swirls a scene of desperate conflict. The flashing swords and armed figures momentarily convince us that this is an ordinary battle, but we quickly perceive that it is nothing of the kind. The fighters on the left are all women; their weapons, spindles and brooms; their victims, animals. Even the men at the right do combat with non-human creatures, and many of those creatures can be identified with, almost cross-referenced to, the animals that

5 Philips Galle after Pieter Bruegel, *Fortitude*, c. 1560, engraving from the Seven Virtues series.

signified individual sins in the Seven Deadlies. The toad had denoted avarice and the bear, anger, failings considered particularly common to men; while women are vanquishing the donkey of sloth, the pig of gluttony and the peacock of pride. Fortitude, we understand, is the virtue necessary to take on any and all of humanity's failings. Different sorts of people, as Erasmus had also said, incline to one or another vice, but all need the same kind of strength to overcome their vices. In the background of Bruegel's scene, angels have been aiding a fortress in withstanding attack from external forces in the world, but in the foreground humanity does battle with its own demons. We are witnessing there the artistic externalization of an infinity of internal battles, battles that we ourselves must enter with equal fortitude.

PROVERBS: HUMAN NATURE
AND THE GETTING OF WISDOM

To the Renaissance, the past was a trove of wisdom to be retrieved, examined and learned from, and this certainly included wisdom about the nature of man. Not everybody was going to read the classics and the Church Fathers with the intensity of an Erasmus, though. For less scholarly people, one source of past wisdom lay in proverbs: pithy, often witty, always memorable, they were the ideal way to build up a bank of knowledge that could be deployed at dinner parties or in making judgements and decisions about actions in lived experience. Proverbs and popular sayings were familiar to everybody from folk culture, which Bruegel had drawn upon for his dessert plates, but they derived a special kind of authority from their long history in literary form, from the Bible and especially from classical antiquity. Erasmus made it a lifelong project to gather thousands of classical proverbs, or adages, and, in the course of numerous and ever-expanding editions, to make these snippets of ancient advice and insight available to a proverb-hungry public: the first enlarged edition of his *Adages*, published in 1508, was the work that really spread his fame.[25] Adages, as Erasmus says, can reveal 'the behaviour, the natural qualities of any race or individual' and are useful in both the conduct of life and the pursuit of philosophy, for, as Aristotle had said, they contain the vestiges of the most ancient wisdom of humanity.[26]

But Erasmus also warns that proverbs are simple neither to use nor to understand.[27] His commentaries on the proverbs he gathers, sometimes brief and sometimes extremely extensive, may simply clarify a saying, but more often they enlarge upon its flexibility to bear multiple meanings in various situations, to shift in implication according to context. Erasmus first presents a saying and explains its original literary or cultural context: for instance, 'cut to the quick' is, according to Erasmus, an adage that originates with hairdressers and refers to their needless precision. Next, since authority matters, it is important that the adage was used by Cicero.[28] Erasmus goes on to note that proverbs about shearing are also used by Plautus and others to imply deception: a single real-life context generates multiple insights. This kind of insertion of related adages by a range of authors into the entry for a single proverb is something Erasmus often does, but the relations he constructs are of different sorts. Sometimes a second proverb is just a small variation on the original words of the first, but there can also be similar-sounding proverbs that mean quite different things because they each come from a different context. In other cases Erasmus joins together adages whose meanings extend one another: Plutarch's 'no fox is caught twice in a trap' is about cunning, but Gregory of Nazianzus uses 'to trip twice over the same stone' to mean something that only fools do. Thus the repeating of a mistake generates one adage about the folly of those who do it, and another about the savvy of those who avoid it.[29] Moreover, many proverbs, as Erasmus had noted, can mean completely opposite things depending on how they are deployed. Irony is one easy way to twist your wise saying into implying something completely different from its original intent. A gentle generalization about human nature can become a sharp criticism of an individual's behaviour and can even carry a politically subversive suggestion.[30]

The unstable nature of proverbs is just one of the reasons why Bruegel's famous painting, usually called *Netherlandish Proverbs*, feels like chaos (illus. 6).[31] The twelve proverb plates set into action at a dinner party seemed so neatly contained and comprehensible, each saying assigned to one of the individual guests and open to comprehension, exchange and comparison with the bits of folk wisdom held by the other diners. In the painting of only a year later, proverbs have taken over an entire world. Everywhere we look, human beings are behaving madly in ways that appear nonsensical even as they claim, proverbially, to be entirely humanly typical. The most basic question, of how many proverbs are visualized here, is not securely answerable: a handout from the Gemäldegalerie in Berlin, where the painting now hangs, assures visitors that 118 proverbs, and possibly 119, are present, while a card provided by the Frans Hals Museum, which owns an exact copy by Bruegel's son Pieter the Younger, tells its visitor that they can discover just 72 proverbs. The range given in scholarly books is similarly great.[32] In the plates, Bruegel had occasionally compounded proverbs, like the man falling between two stools and into ashes, but in the painting we have no idea where the boundary of 'proverbness' ends. When things look abnormal or absurd we take it that a proverb is being visualized, but what of, say, the boat sailing away towards the horizon? There are many proverbs about sailing in the Low Countries: how to know which, if any, is involved here?

The fact that Bruegel's proverbs can normally be pinpointed by the absurdity of their visual depiction is important. Proverbs themselves, in condensing wisdom, often sound peculiar or paradoxical – nobody literally casts pearls (or roses) before swine – although the implications of the proverb can apply to many real acts of extravagance or, indeed, to unappreciated words of wisdom. But the literal visualization of any metaphor is an essentially nonsensical move. It takes that which was profound and makes it comical. There are few passages in high art more simply hilarious than the 'pillar-biter' (religious hypocrite) in the bottom left corner of Bruegel's scene, adjoining the woman fiercely tying the Devil to a pillow (spiteful stubbornness), although each refers to a well-known saying that its original viewer would have used perfectly seriously (illus. 7). Bruegel takes common, vernacular language and, through visualizing it, estranges it. In some senses this is the opposite of Erasmus' careful gathering of

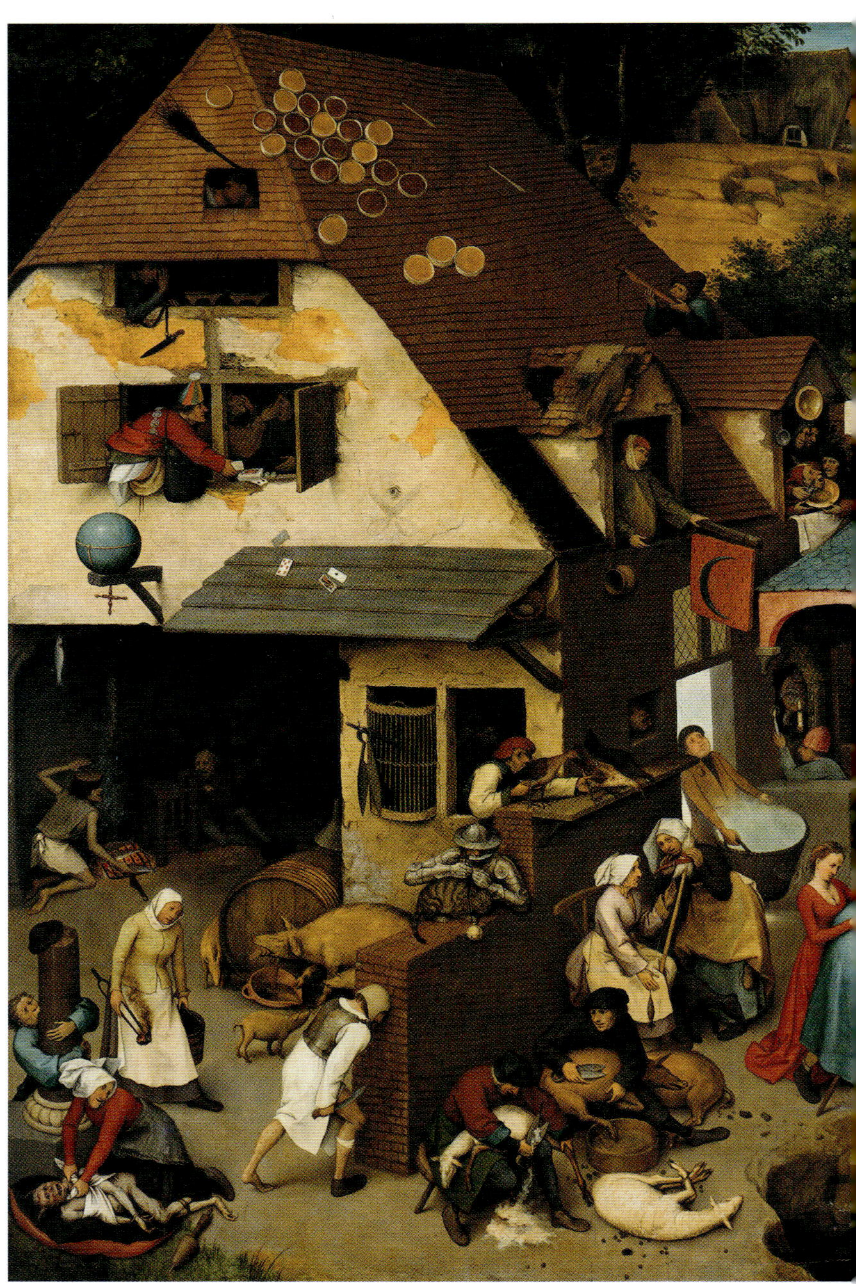

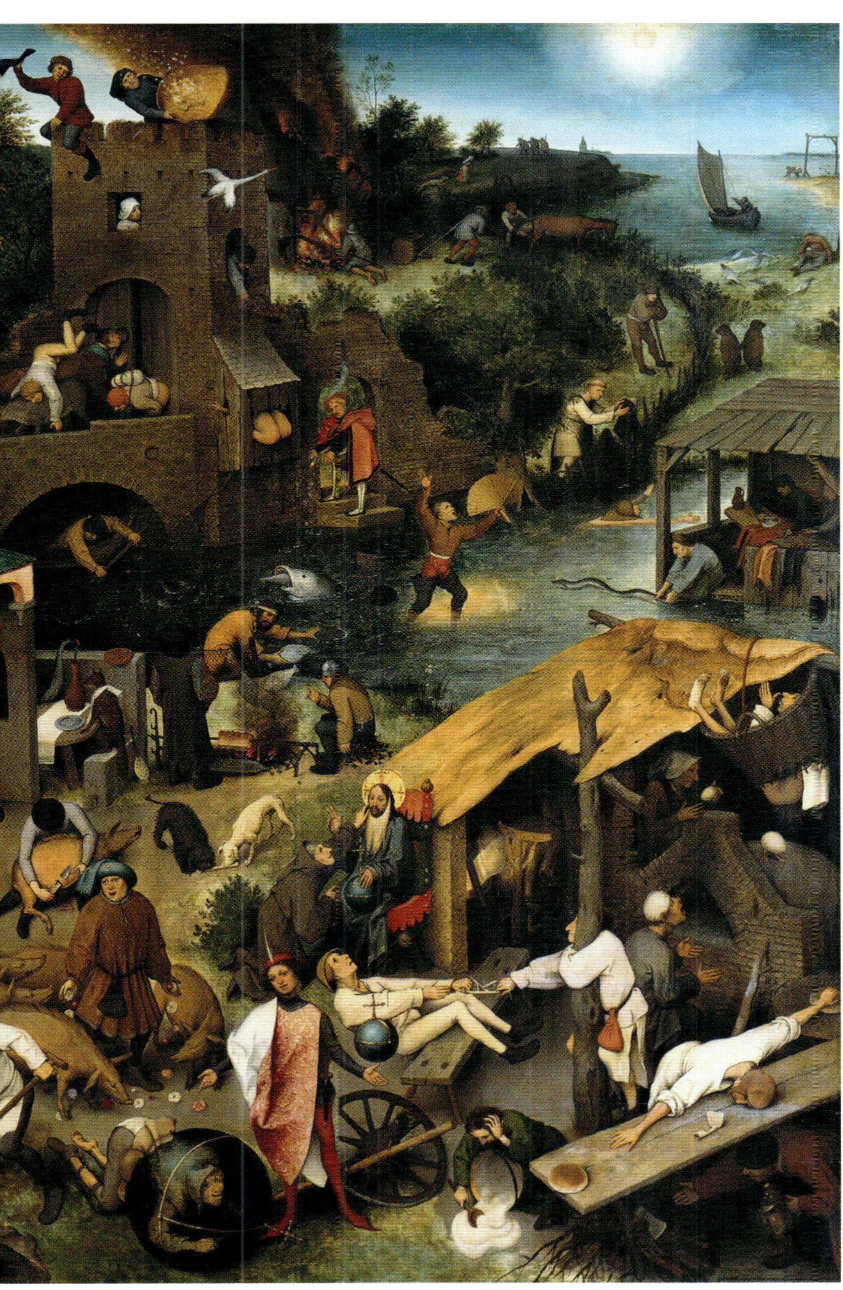

6 Pieter Bruegel, *Netherlandish Proverbs*, 1559, oil on panel.

ancient wisdom, for in Bruegel's hands, things his audience already very much knew, and very much believed, are rendered nonsensical.

Over the past century, many scholars have tried to suggest an order or guiding principle that could make sense of Bruegel's picture, and none of their solutions has really been wrong. The proverbs are indeed loosely grouped around the buildings in this odd little corner of a village according to which human weakness they point to. For example, many sayings concerning wasted effort are clustered around the semi-ruined castle in the mid-ground. Here we see a man who throws his money into the water, another who tosses feathers into the wind and another who misses every opportunity because he 'fishes behind the net'. But the man who fills the well after the calf has drowned and the merchant throwing his roses before swine, both of whom had featured in the dessert plates, are in the centre foreground and far from the castle, even though these proverbs are certainly related to wasted effort.

On one side of the well-filler and the merchant, a woman puts a blue cloak on an old man, illustrating a folk saying about deceit; on the other side of them, a disabled man must crawl to get on in 'the world' while a princeling spins 'the world' on his thumb. The orb that is duplicated in these sayings about poverty and privilege reappears over the door of the inn at the left, where it is balanced upside-down below a man who is shitting on it (illus. 8). He is a fool (for fools, as the saying has it, also get the best cards), and the inn is filled with further examples of folly: two men who 'lead one another by the nose' or deceive each other; a man who, as on one of the plates, tries to piss over the moon; and, watched by 'two fools under one hood' (for folly loves company), a man who 'shaves the fool without lather', another barber-based proverb meaning to make a fool of somebody.

Both the world upside-down and the blue cloak of deceit have been proposed as master tropes that might generally explain the image, as has the notion of folly. But really, there is far too little order to this painting's chaos to sustain a claim that one or another critique gives us the key to the painting's message. We could think instead that Bruegel allows his viewer to chart an itinerary through a world gone mad, a world in which common persons do ridiculous things; in an era before genre painting even existed, the extraordinary nature of this depiction would have been even more vivid. To become sensible and meaningful, the painting, like the plates, has to be activated. It needs a beholder who stands before it – perhaps in the company of others – and speaks. Moving a saying from its ludic visual form back into the original verbal one re-endows it with the wisdom it originally contained, while keeping the edge of the comical that visualization had brought out. Reconnecting received wisdom to its literal visualization renders the saying more memorable, but also more open to further argument.

To create itineraries through the land of folk wisdom, Bruegel offers the beholder many options. Some rely on compositional structure: for instance, the fool shitting on the world upside-down has his mirror figure at the opposite end of the main spatial diagonal where, in the far right-hand distance, another fool 'shits on the gallows', meaning that he has no care about death. Other itineraries rely on similar visual

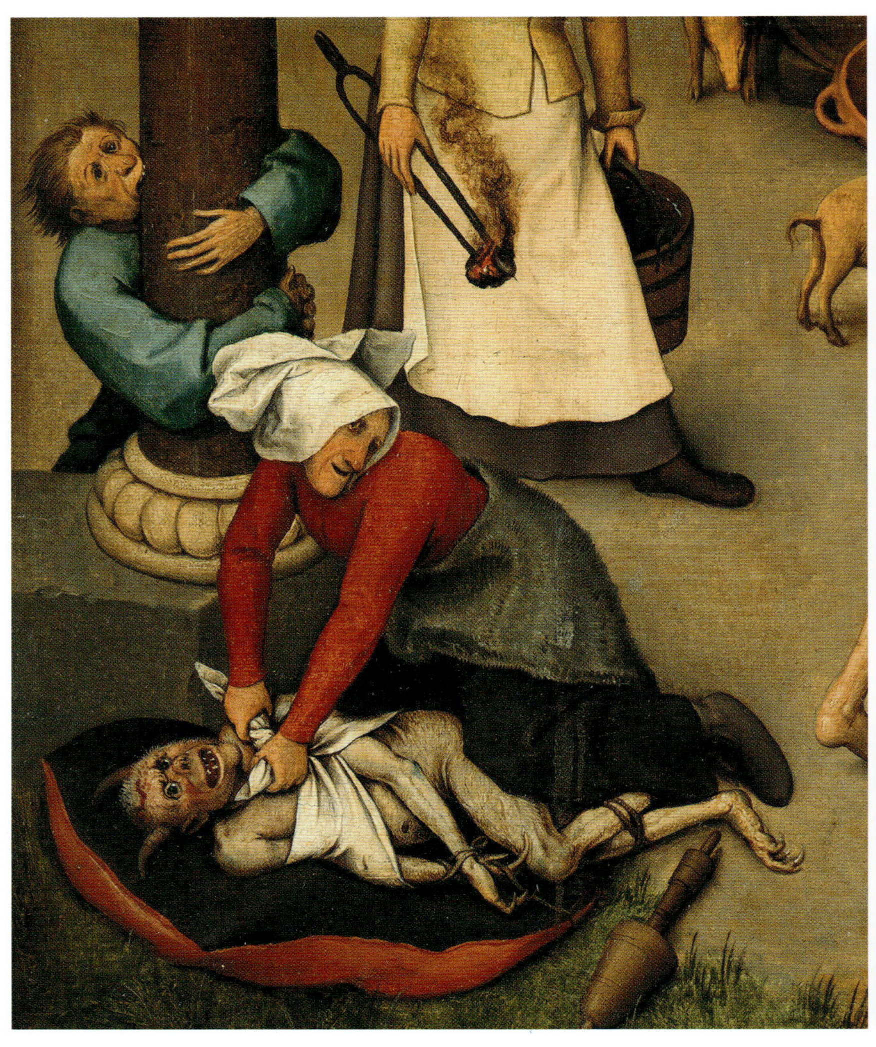

7 Pillar-biter, tying the Devil to a pillow: detail from Pieter Bruegel, *Netherlandish Proverbs*.

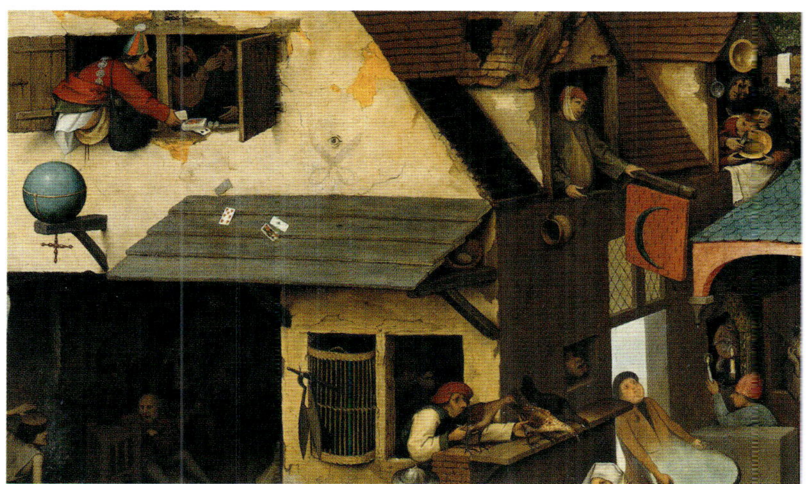

forms, as the man at the bottom right corner who cannot reach from loaf to loaf (we would say, can't make ends meet) is linked to the inn whose 'roof is tiled with tarts' (it's the land of plenty). Ideas also repeat in random places and in unrelated visual forms, so that the religious hypocrite as pillar-biter is reiterated in the monk who ties a beard on Christ on the opposite side of the foreground. These are just a few pairs, but in every case between one and the other the eye has traversed dozens of sayings that may reinforce, or rebut, the two that were linked.

Between the bearded Christ and the prince with the world on his thumb, two men seek their own advantage, *Elck*-like, by pulling on a pretzel. But does anybody seek to know himself in this picture? None of the typecast figures within the painting engages in such an intellectual and self-reflexive enterprise, but it is one of the responses that may be performed before the work. The beholder who has studied their Erasmus

8 Shitting on the world, pissing over the moon, shaving the fool: detail from Pieter Bruegel, *Netherlandish Proverbs*.

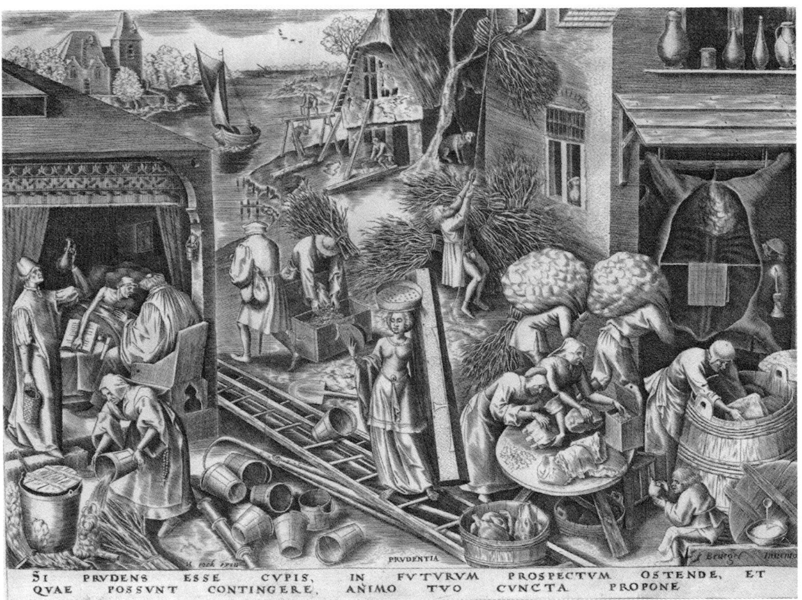

will add classical wisdom to the displayed folk knowledge, for any proverb that gives a true insight into human nature has its equivalent in many times and tongues. Some viewers may take certain proverbs to hint at social criticism (the whole world spins at the command of princes); other groups of conversing beholders will spend their time discussing human folly, mankind's tendency towards greed or wastefulness, deceit or hypocrisy. Bruegel has provided an encyclopedic picture of the weaknesses and proclivities of humankind, but it is also a world in which no individual viewer recognizes a self since every depicted actor is nothing but a type, an extremity, an absurd embodiment.

If the inhabitants of the *Netherlandish Proverbs* are entirely absorbed by their various foolish weaknesses, then their

9 Philips Galle after Pieter Bruegel, *Prudence*, c. 1559, engraving from the Seven Virtues series.

opposite or their antidote in Bruegel's logic lies not in the besieged virtue of Fortitude, but in Prudence (illus. 9).[33] Bruegel's original drawing for this print is dated 1559, the same year in which he painted the *Proverbs*, and the print too shows a kind of village-corner assemblage – not a place one could imagine as existing, but one that recalls reality in order to contain significance. This place is less densely populated than that in the painting, and the figures are somewhat less comically awkward, but the scene appears equally nonsensical. That effect is produced by the complete lack of unity or even logical congruity of action. At the right foreground a woman is dousing a fire with a bucket of water, while on the opposite side, a group of women and men have butchered a large animal and are working to preserve its meat. Behind them, a man hoists bundles of twigs to a friend who stores them in the attic. Near the twig-gatherer, a man empties coins into a chest. Unlike the miser criticized for his avarice in Bruegel's Seven Deadly Sins series, though, this man is merely foresightful: as Erasmus said, a virtue and a vice can sometimes be very close together, the latter a corruption of the former, and this man's actions are motivated by virtue.[34] He is thus interconnected in his nature with the other villagers, for each individual here is behaving in a manner that early modern people would have described as prudent.

Prudence is a form of practical wisdom, a virtue fundamental to living one's life well. It involves remaining always aware of the future, and thinking of what must be done to prepare for it. Prudence can be a social virtue – in the background of Bruegel's print, a group of men repair a dyke so that when storms come, the sea will not inundate their land.

But most of all it is cultivated by the self-aware individual who, like Erasmus' Christian soldier, knows themself, recognizes their own motives (avarice? prudence?) and acts accordingly. Thus Prudence, the allegorical figure in the centre of Bruegel's composition, gazes at herself in a convex mirror. Unlike the mirror of the fool in *Elck*, hers signifies a self-examination that reveals the truth, enabling the prudent person to separate good motives and impulses from bad ones, as indicated by the sieve of discernment on Prudence's head. With her other hand, the figure embraces a coffin. This brings our thoughts to the dying man in the cut-away room to the left. A monk is hearing his final confession. But this man, a crucifixion hanging above his deathbed, has been prudent and death holds no fear for him, for reasons precisely the opposite of the fool who shits on the gallows in the *Netherlandish Proverbs*. A prudent man has always thought of death, and the afterlife that Christ's sacrifice promised us, and has prepared himself for that future as the living prepare for winter storms.

Fortitude and prudence are inward virtues. The former encourages us to stand firm, like Erasmus' Christian soldier against our weaknesses; the latter provides a kind of guideline to be followed in making decisions, both practical and moral, in the course of life. Both must be cultivated, and both draw upon a combination of understanding human nature and examining the individual self. In his own contemplation of human nature, particularly in the *Netherlandish Proverbs*, Bruegel produces and offers to his beholders a superficially comical view of humanity that highlights human folly and distances the beholder by estranging received wisdom and presenting ideas in the form of extremes, stereotypes, adages. By turning verbal ideas into visual humour, Bruegel insists upon the engagement of beholders who must re-endow absurd forms with the wisdom that originated them. From our distanced, individual vantage point, we speak of the nature of man.

TWO

Mankind in the Cosmos

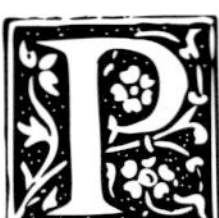IETER BRUEGEL WAS a traveller, and this informed the way that he understood and represented the relation between humanity and the natural world. At a time when travelling over long distances was rare, uncomfortable and often dangerous, he made a journey of several years between about 1552 and 1554 that took him through France via Lyons and then to southern Italy, at least as far as Reggio Calabria (the toe of Italy's 'boot') and possibly to Sicily as well. He spent a period in Rome, where he befriended and collaborated with the famous miniaturist Giulio Clovio, and also passed through Bologna. On his way home, he crossed the Alps. It is possible that he had travelling companions, or at least met up with friends from Antwerp while he was in Italy: the painter and print designer Maerten de Vos, the sculptor Jacques Jonghelinck and the cartographer and geographer Abraham Ortelius – all young men of around Bruegel's age – were there during the same period.[1]

Bruegel and his cohort were exceptional in their time, but in later generations, a trip to Rome would become a crucial step in the training of ambitious artists determined to study the works of great ancient and modern masters. A handful of Netherlandish artists, notably Bruegel's own master Pieter Coecke van Aelst, had made that journey even earlier. Bruegel, though, seems to have had a different agenda from all the others. The only artwork we are sure that he studied in Italy was a landscape drawing by Venetian draughtsman Domenico Campagnola.[2] Rather than heading towards a particular cultural goal, Bruegel's interest lay in what was to be seen along the way – the journey itself, instead of its endpoint. What principally absorbed his attention was the strange and exciting world through which he travelled, a landscape viewed, experienced and eventually transformed into images.

The numerous drawings made on this Italian trip, Bruegel's earliest remaining works, are a surprising lot. Only two are directly from nature. Some seem to depict the Flemish countryside back at home with unusual, intimate plausibility, while others are mountain views that have clearly been composed. This is also how Bruegel's earliest biographer, Karel van Mander, understood the artist's work: writing in 1604, he reported that while in Italy, Bruegel drew from life, but that 'it is said that when he was in the Alps he swallowed all those mountains and rocks which, upon returning home, he spat out again onto canvases and panels, so faithfully was he able, in this respect and others, to follow nature.'[3] What mattered for Bruegel's depiction of nature was not the drawings, but the memories stored within himself, interpretations ready to inform new compositions. Those memories were not just from an artist's eye, but from a traveller's feet.

ABOVE THE WORLD

The drawing of a mountain landscape executed while Bruegel was in Italy, now in the British Museum, is an invented scene (illus. 10). It offers not the record of a specific site, but a general sense of place and, moreover, a place through which one could travel. It is at once coherent and incredibly detailed, a combination that allows its beholder to imagine visual itineraries through it.[4] The natural terrain is diverse, encompassing flat farmlands, gentle hills and rocky mountains. Signs of human presence and human making are seeded into it everywhere we look, from mountaintop castles and towns to farmhouses and fields lower down, inviting the wayfarer to turn their steps – or eyes – in this or that direction. A group of travellers, including a peddler with his pack, have paused by a roadway on the left, while several mounted travellers are moving on another road that leads from the centre foreground over a ridge, projecting them into the distant world. Even on the river, snaking through the land towards the horizon, boats are moving people from place to place. Bruegel's landscape is energized both by the multiplicity of his own quick, vigorous pen strokes and by the human motion that it contains.

Upon his return to Antwerp in 1554, Bruegel quickly monetized the powerful vision of landscape he had developed while drawing in Italy. Over the following years he worked for Hieronymus Cock, proprietor of the great Four Winds press, designing the set of twelve prints now known as the 'Large Landscapes'. These works are indeed large at 32 cm (over 1 ft) high, a scale that, in a Bruegel print, demands a particular kind of looking: leaning bodily over the table, bringing eyes close to the surface, exploring intently the myriad of detail that the landscape offers (illus. 11). Compared to the drawing, edges have been sharpened and, even in the distance, individual items stand out more, the result of the printmaker's labour after Bruegel's original design.[5] We can now easily trace multiple roadways, paths that meander through valleys and crawl up steep hills, past farm and city and castle. Individual figures can even be picked out as they struggle along the road up the central mountain mass, but what is their destination? Two human monuments stand on outcroppings there: to the left, a gallows from which hangs a single body, and to the right, a cross. It would have been perfectly plausible to pass either of these on the roadside in Bruegel's time, but their paired appearance here is striking. Even more striking is the group of angels nearby, raising a woman above the earth. This is Mary Magdalene, who experienced regular elevations during her thirty-year life of penitence in a cave in the Sainte-Baume

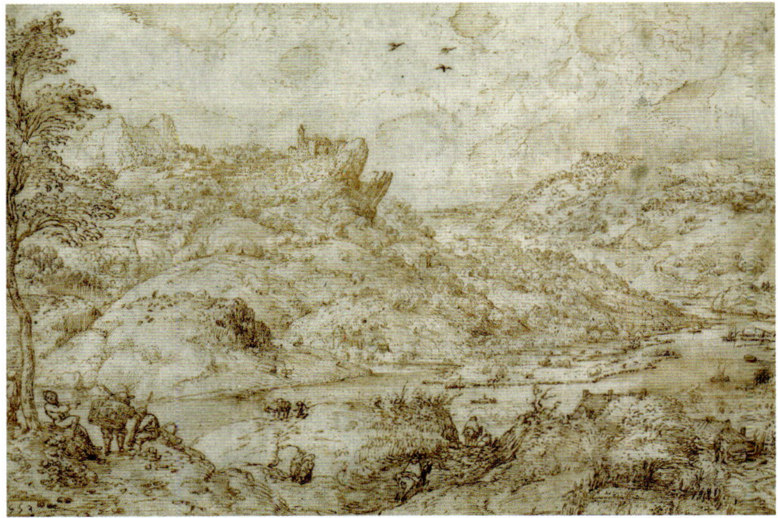

10 Pieter Bruegel, *Mountain Landscape with River and Travellers*, 1553, drawing, pen and brown ink.

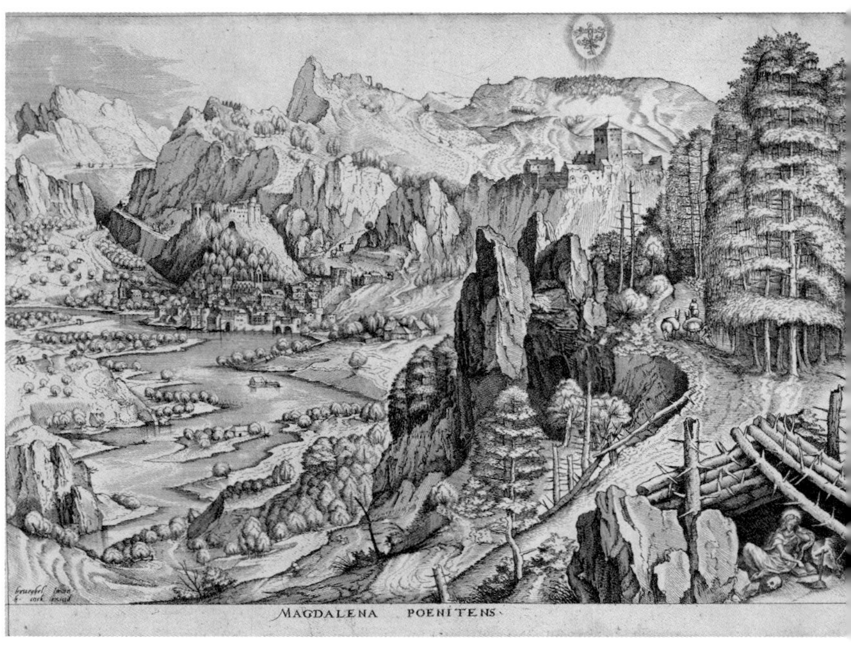

mountains in France. And indeed, if we search, we can easily find her in the cave as well, at the bottom right corner of the print. Her retreat has been reinforced with harsh pine logs, which, along with natural rocks, assure that she will never see the remarkable landscape that we have traversed unless she is above it.

Bruegel's Large Landscapes present the visual traveller with several models for assessing a human relationship to the natural world, and with some suggested evaluations of that relationship, so that the journey we make may be less neutral than in the Italian drawings. Passage through the world is a universal baseline, but withdrawal and rejection, like Mary Magdalene's, is offered in the foreground of several prints.

11 Joannes and Lucas van Doetecum after Pieter Bruegel, *Penitent Magdalene*, c. 1555–6, etching with engraving, from Large Landscapes series.

A print titled *Rustic Care* (*Solicitudo rustica*) presents, also in the lower right corner, two more possibilities (illus. 12). A pair of farmers with their scythes have paused beneath a tree by a hilltop roadway. One is occupied with hammering the blade of his scythe; like Mary, his back is to the world, but he is preparing himself to engage with that world as a labourer, to harness nature and to put his mark on it. His companion, though, stands with his back to us, and, leaning on his scythe, gazes out over the same vast world as we do. He sees other labourers working the fields and driving wagons laden with goods; he sees villages and cattle and many boats on the impossibly winding river. The mountains are forbidding, but a church nestles in a high valley; and in the flatlands, if we look very closely, we can find a wayside cross, a gallows and several wheels for the exposure of criminals' corpses. It would be possible to pick out one detail and build an interpretation of the scene around it, but this doesn't seem to be what Bruegel expected from the viewers who would eventually see his printed image. Judgements have occurred below, but from the hilltops in Bruegel's foregrounds, the world is too distant for that kind of investment. The print's title – a very unusual thing for a landscape or genre image at this time – might also ask something of us. 'Rustic care' is often taken to refer to the first farmer's attention to his scythe, but it could equally apply to his companion's care, even uneasiness, about the world he contemplates.

The relationship that Bruegel constructs between human-kind and the world we inhabit moves back and forth between engagement and detachment, the sense of a journey ahead and refusal of that invitation. In this, Bruegel is negotiating

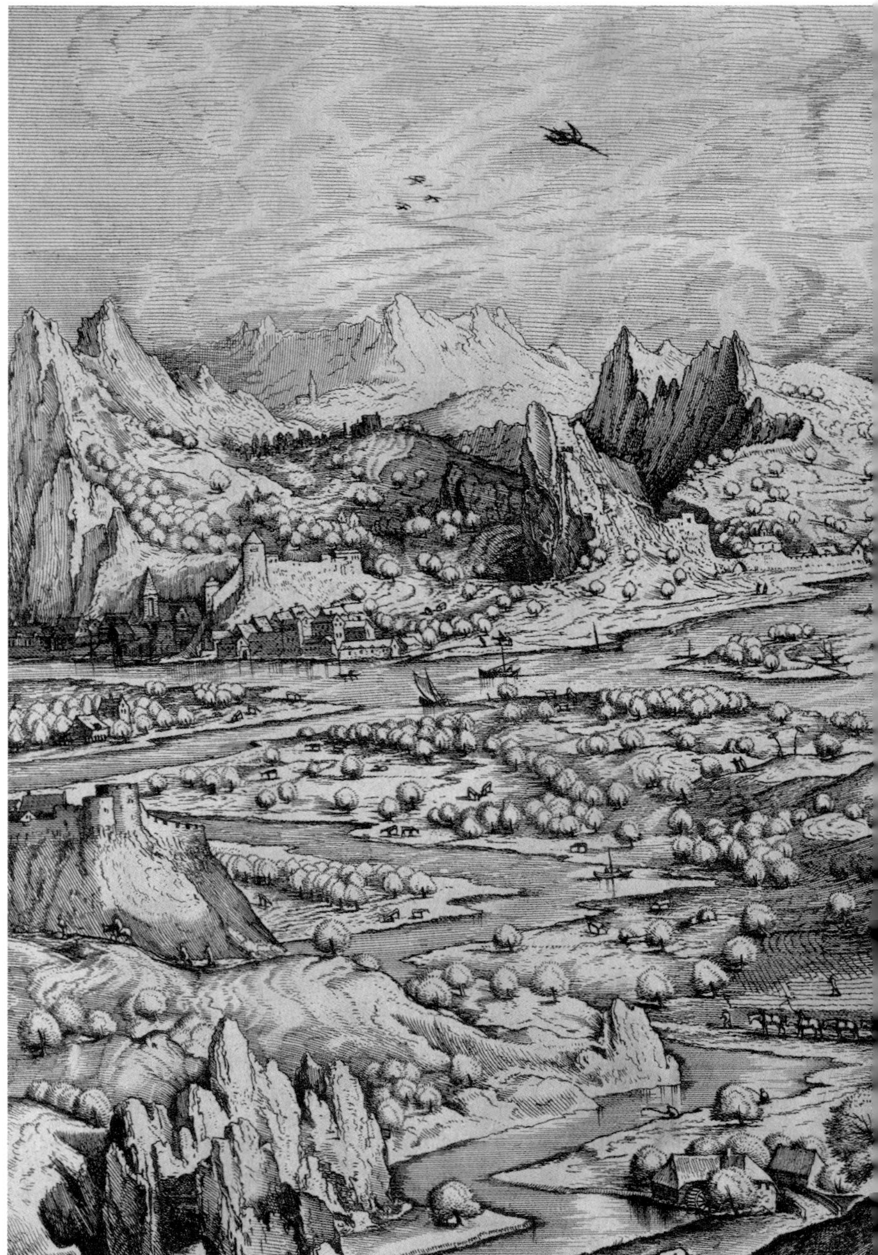

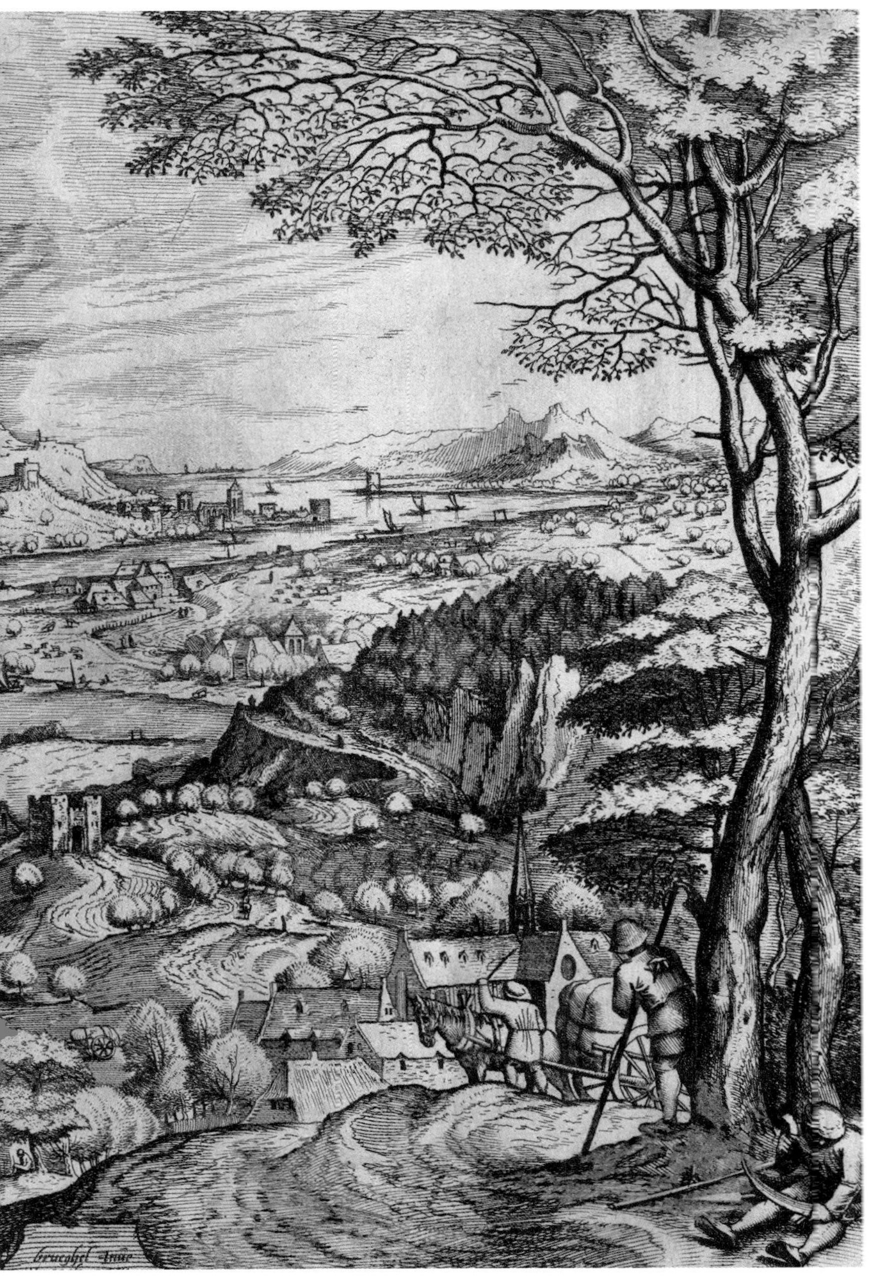

12 Joannes and Lucas van Doetecum after Pieter Bruegel, *Solicitudo rustica* (*Rustic Care*), c. 1555–6, etching with engraving, from Large Landscapes series.

between several possible ways of thinking about how mankind relates to the greater world: in particular, between a perspective that sees humanity as deeply embedded in the cosmos, indeed as a microcosm of its very macrocosmic essence, and a view that sees mankind as somehow apart from other living things and distinguished by, precisely, the capacity to have a view on the rest. These two models were less opposed to one another than they might sound to us today, because people of the early modern era saw what we now conceptualize as an infinite universe as a closed system.[6] That system, the cosmos, was perfectly ordered through its creation by God, so that in each part of it the same meaningful structures could be discerned.[7] The human organism, and likewise human society, reflect and repeat these same structures of natural order, so that when Erasmus declares that our reason is like the king of a people, this is not a mere analogy but a strong point of argument, stating a truth about the political cosmos and human nature.[8] Thinking about the world and man's place in it as a harmonious system of such correspondences was an old idea, but one still utterly commonplace during Bruegel's lifetime.[9]

But while human beings are part of the cosmological system, their place in it is, uniquely, unfixed: we alone have a choice between growing downward into lower nature, or upward towards the divine. Moreover, the self-knowledge necessary to make that choice is always embedded in cosmological knowledge, so that in some sense contemplating the natural world, like Bruegel's resting farmer on his hilltop, is a form of contemplating the self. In this the farmer's perspective has a Humanist tradition. Two centuries earlier, Petrarch had climbed Mont Ventoux in search of a view; he had been inspired by Philip of Macedon's view from Mount Haemus, as described by Livy.[10] But, his own view attained, Petrarch immediately whipped a copy of Augustine's *Confessions* from his bag and turned to its pages for help in examining himself, asking whether his physical ascent of the mountain had been met, internally, by a similar ascent towards virtue.

Bruegel's possible travel companion, Abraham Ortelius, provides a somewhat different way of imagining the philosophical results of a mountaintop view such as those the artist constructed. Whether or not the two shared their Italian journeys, Ortelius had joined the Antwerp guild just a few years before Pieter Bruegel, and recorded his own friendship and admiration for the artist after Bruegel's death.[11] In his *Theatrum orbis terrarum*, the great atlas first published in 1570, Ortelius famously appended to his introductory world map a quotation from Cicero: 'Who can consider human affairs to be great, when he comprehends the eternity and vastness of the entire world?'[12] (illus. 13). In later editions, Ortelius added a series of further quotations from Cicero, and also from Seneca, that often dismissed the complete triviality of human affairs. Other sayings simply enjoined readers to be contemplators of the whole vast earth, but always from a distance. 'The purpose of the horse is to carry, the ox to plow, the dog to hunt and guard. Man, however, is born to contemplate the universe,' says Ortelius' Cicero, a sentiment closely echoed by the Italian Humanist Pico della Mirandola when his figure of God tells man, 'we have set thee at the world's centre that thou mayest from thence more easily observe whatever is in the world.'[13]

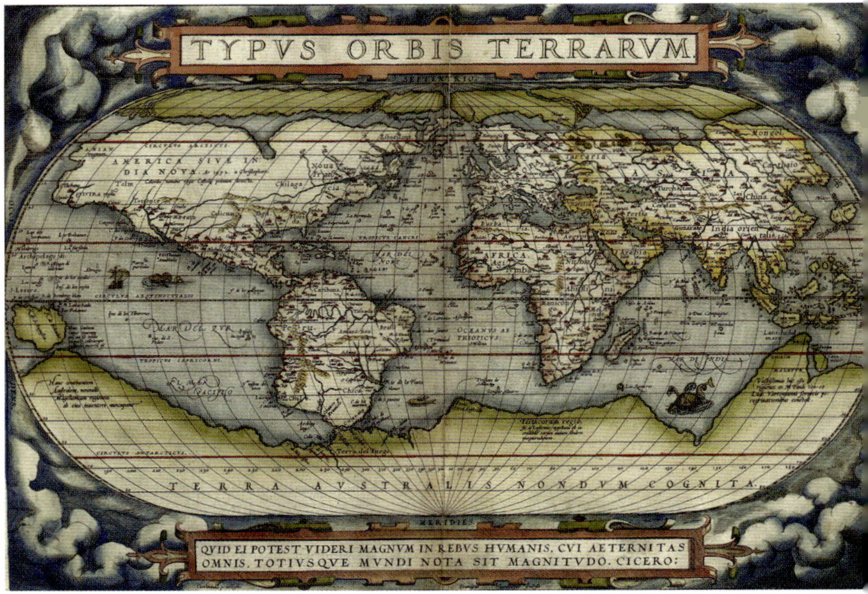

Cicero, Pico and Ortelius all reflect a thread of Stoic and, later, Christian neo-Stoic thinking in Europe. This was a set of ideas, a view of man's place in the cosmos, shared by Erasmus – he edited the works of both Seneca and Cicero – and, most likely, by Pieter Bruegel as well.[14] The classical Stoic view was easily reconciled with Christianity because it understood the cosmos as a rational creation which humankind, endowed with reason, was uniquely able to comprehend; Christianity's God added purpose and meaning to the created cosmos, and demanded a different kind of cosmological reading.[15] And whereas classical Stoicism recommended contemplating the world as a detached observer, separated by distance from human and natural turmoil, Christianity tended to change this to a potentially more engaged stance.[16]

13 *Typus orbis terrarum*, from Abraham Ortelius, *Theatrum orbis terrarum* (1570).

The Humanists' growing sense of mankind's transformative and self-transformative power naturally embraced a more active role for even the contemplating person. For Humanism, the world was an entity set apart from us, and to behold it was a kind of philosophical and even moral activity, but with an ultimate goal of self-shaping through cosmological knowledge, leading to ethical actions and choices in a life lived, of course, at the centre of that contemplated world.

Bruegel's Large Landscapes, with their sweeping views over a vast landscape seen from an elevated, distanced viewpoint, create a viewing experience that would have operated well for art-buyers whose sense of their place in the cosmos had been shaped by neo-Stoicism. But that is not to say that Bruegel was committed to this relationship of humans and nature: the views he constructs are not those of Ortelius. When Ortelius promotes his *Theatrum orbis terrarum* using the words of ancient philosophers, he is urging a kind of viewing that is far more distanced and, in fact, far less travel-oriented than the kind that interested his friend Pieter Bruegel. Ortelius offers us maps, and in this period, maps generally did not function to enable actual journeying. They allowed you to form a mental image of the enormity of the Earth, or some part of it, but not to travel through it. To Ortelius this was a positive benefit, for his maps permitted a completely neutral contemplation, whereas travel would embed a person too deeply in the world of human affairs.[17] Journeys, in the mid-sixteenth century, were navigated by means of simply asking for directions. The first published route guide appeared in 1552, for travel through France – the year that Bruegel journeyed there – so he could actually have known this new phenomenon.[18] But he would not have utilized a map. And as a maker of images, what he offered to his buyers was not map-like either, but a unique compromise view of the world, informed by experience as well as by philosophy and allowing for imagined engagement after contemplative distance. Bruegel enables the lofty thinker to eventually leave the mountaintop, informed by an understanding of cosmos and self, and to rejoin those whose life journeys are through the material intricacies of the world.

IN THE WORLD

The three hunters at the hill's edge in Bruegel's *Hunters in the Snow* of 1565 do not stop to contemplate the world before them, stretching out over a broad, populated river valley to distant, forbidding crags. Bending their heads against the cold, laboriously lifting every footstep through the heavy snow, they are determined to make their way home to display their trophy to friends in the village, for they have caught the fox that was killing the hens: it was an important task, and the villagers will be thankful. Behind them, at the hunters' inn of St Hubert, members of the innkeeper's family are likewise too busy to gaze at the landscape. Like the hunters, they are concerned with food supply, building a fire to singe a pig before using the table-block to butcher it. Food and fire are concerns of the winter months that occupy many people in Bruegel's scene. Down the hill from the inn, at the last house in this row, a trap has been set up – a tilted board with a cord, reaching into the house, that a hidden watcher can yank to smash the unwitting birds that have come to feed there. Fire, the second winter concern, has turned from tool to tragedy in the distance, just to the left of the village church, where the chimney of a house is ablaze. Neighbours are rushing in with ladders to help the homeowner avert catastrophe. In this painting, neither travel nor detachment are possible relations between mankind and the greater world: rather, we see involvement, as well as work that is demanded by or cooperates with the season of the year or, we might say, with the time of the cosmos.

Bruegel's winter landscape was one of a series of six paintings that represented either the months or the seasons of the year. Either way, the division was uneven and not entirely orthodox. These works had been commissioned from Bruegel by Niclaes Jonghelinck brother of the sculptor Jacques with whom Bruegel may have travelled in Italy. When he painted them, Bruegel had recently moved from Antwerp to Brussels, but the cities were only a day's easy journey apart and clearly the artist kept up with patrons whom he had been cultivating in Antwerp: Jonghelinck had previously bought two of his paintings, a *Tower of Babel* and the *Road to Calvary* discussed below. They all formed part of a major collection of contemporary art Jonghelinck was amassing, which included allegories and mythologies by Frans Floris and landscapes by Gillis van Coninxloo.[19] These works hung not in Jonghelinck's city home but in his luxurious newly built suburban villa, 'Ter Beke', located just outside the town walls. It was a place for cultivated leisure and entertaining: here, it has been suggested, he probably hung his Bruegels around the dining room, as did other Antwerp collectors of the artist's works.[20] Thus the pictures would have been subjects of conversation, like the dinnerplates discussed in the last chapter: images of labour, people embedded in the natural world, but viewed from a more philosophical perspective by wealthy and educated men distanced from such toil.

In some ways this is a correct description, but it is only a partial one. Even as the paintings allowed nature to sweep around the room in which Jonghelinck and his guests sat, absorbing them in its relentless cycle – making them the centre of the cosmos even while they beheld it – they also demanded careful visual examination, engagement with detail. Did Jonghelinck allow his guests to discover details, or point them out himself before they sat to eat? If so, he would have been interacting with images of nature in a manner much like the host in Erasmus' colloquy 'The Godly Feast', first published in 1522. Here, Eusebius welcomes guests to his country villa, possibly modelled on one near Brussels where Erasmus had spent much of the previous year. Before they enter the house proper, they are treated to a lengthy tour around a garden loggia decorated with natural imagery, for, as Eusebius says, 'nature is not silent but speaks to us everywhere and teaches the observant man many things.'[21] You could examine these pictures, we are told, for days on end, for they are filled with a great variety of things; and so it is also with Bruegel's scenes. But of course Bruegel's works show not just a speaking nature, but one in which humanity is deeply embedded, and they speak about the state of mankind in the world.

Of the original six paintings, five remain today (four of them shown as illus. 14, 15, 17, 18), and they take us not just through the full scope of the seasons but also over a whole variety of terrains. Bruegel matches earth to weather, so that the times of bitter cold occur in places with harsh mountains, while harvest scenes are set among rolling hills: the cycle connects to the 'world landscape' tradition of a previous generation of Flemish painters, but it divides that geographical encyclopedism among the whole series of images, knitting them together as a portrayal of the cosmos. Even the quality of light and the weather change, from the thin, icy clarity of the *Hunters in the Snow* (December/January) to the heavy, damp turbulence of *Gloomy Day* (February/March) to the lucid, bright calm of *Hay Harvest* (June/July), the hazy, sultry heat of the *Harvesters* (August/September) and finally the dimming cold, balanced between threat and promise, of the *Return of the Herd* (October/November). This emphasis on weather, almost unknown in painting not only before Bruegel but even for many decades after his death, adds another layer to the sense of time, stressing that mutability is not just predictably cyclical, but random and unpredictable.[22]

Weather was certainly not part of the crystalline atmosphere of the world landscape tradition, nor was it shown (apart from winter's snow) in the other visual tradition Bruegel draws upon here: the depiction of labours of the months, seen in the calendar pages of late medieval books of hours and in the printed almanacs of Bruegel's time.[23] Seasonal labour is foregrounded in his paintings, but is also counterbalanced in nearly every image by evocations of particular forms of play appropriate to each season, or of festivity linked to the human calendar. The interaction between work and play complicates our sense of how humanity fits into the cosmos. Labour alone can be read as the ordained fate of Adam and Eve's descendants after leaving Eden, and thus wrapped into a neat biblical view of the world. But play is voluntary. It implies

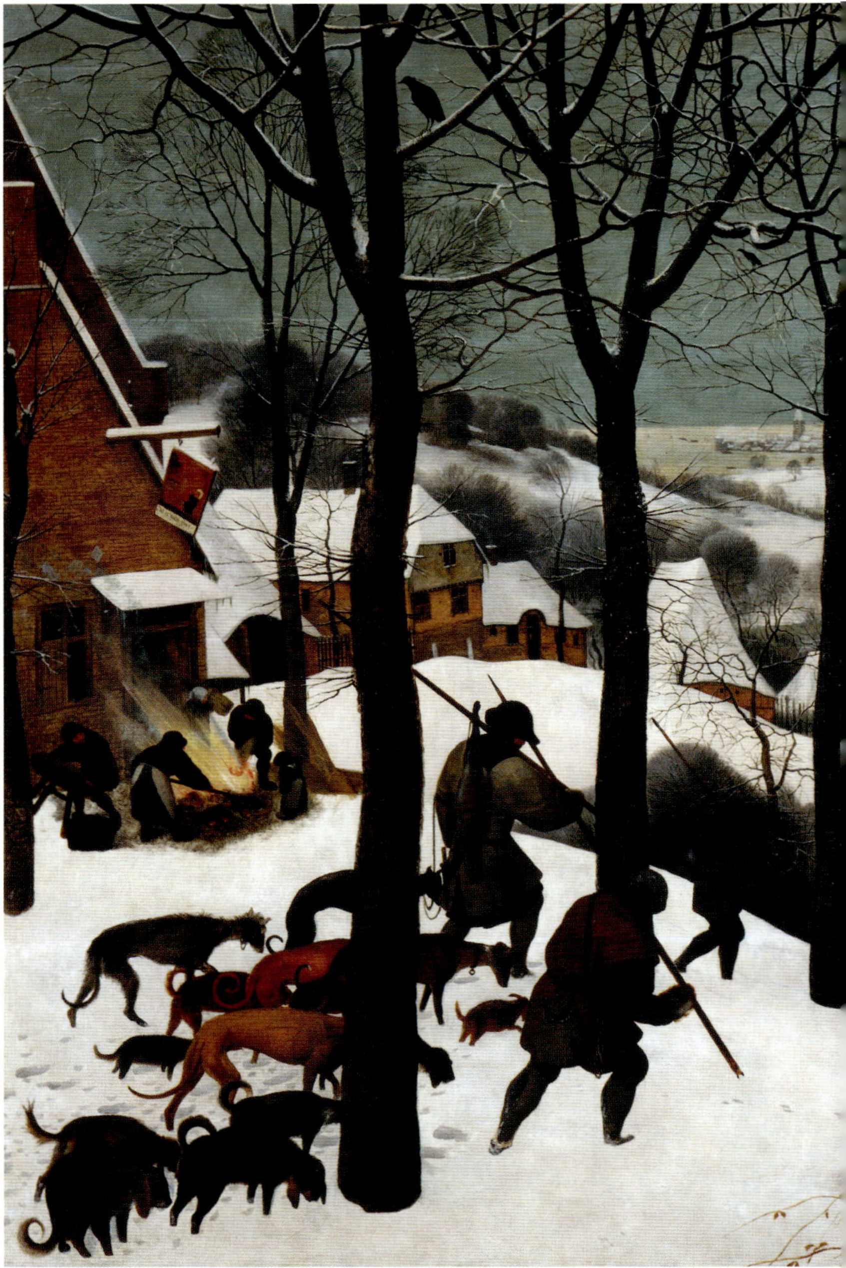

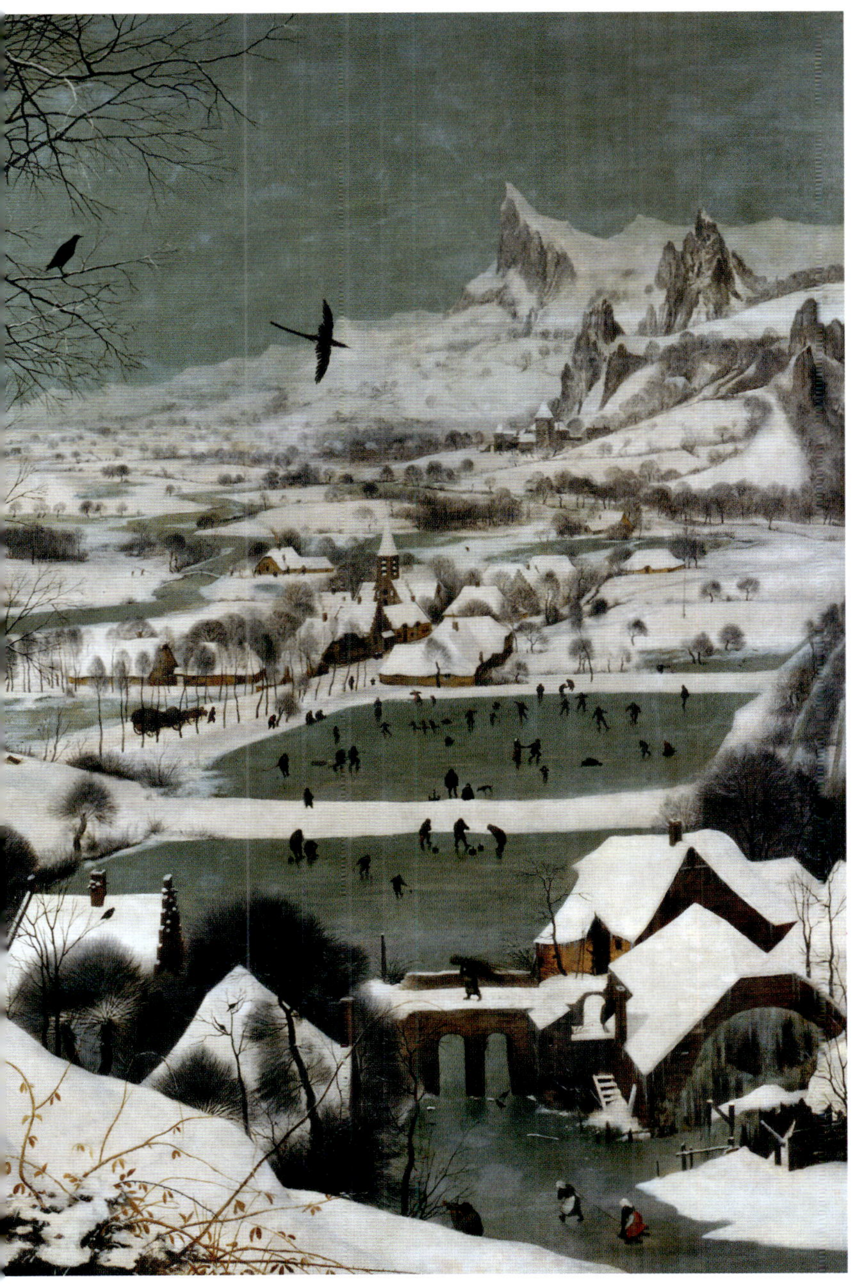

14 Pieter Bruegel, *Hunters in the Snow* (December/January), 1565, oil on panel.

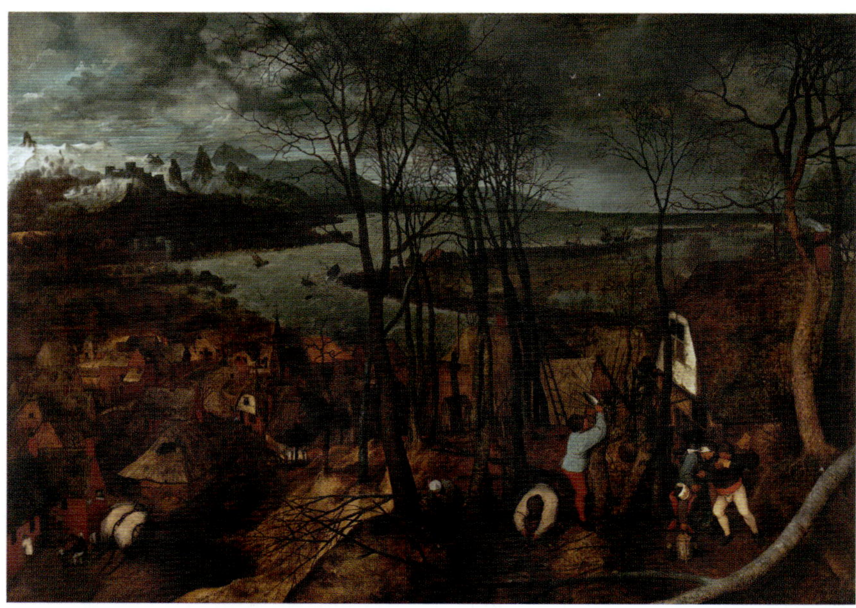

choice and a human acknowledgement of the world's greater natural opportunities. Within the Christian cosmos, play is less simple than work.

Play is most obviously shown in *Hunters in the Snow*, for the visual trajectory leading downward from the hunters' path takes us straight to a pair of frozen artificial ponds or reservoirs where dozens of villagers amuse themselves on the ice (illus. 14). The winter of 1564–5 in Antwerp had been exceedingly cold and the river had frozen hard and thick, so games on the ice were familiar to Bruegel's audience.[24] The ice-players, like the labourers on the hill, tend to operate in groups: one pulls another on foot or on a makeshift sled, four children play some kind of tag or follow-the-leader game, while several others play a form of ice-hockey (kolf). Others

15 Pieter Bruegel, *Gloomy Day* (February/March), 1565, oil on panel.

are alone and are having less fun. Several have fallen over and at least one seems to just lie on the ice, unaided. In the right foreground, a man is using the branches of an overhanging tree in his struggle to stand up. And near two background kolf-players lurks real danger: a hole has opened in the ice. Like the birds flying blithely to snack on bait near the trap, the skaters are in more peril than they realize. This was a parallel Bruegel had set up in another, independent winter landscape of the same year, and it is emphasized by the fact that the bird trap, though rather distant spatially, is very near the centre of the panel's surface, a favourite ploy of Bruegel's in these years.[25] The ominous threat to the skaters suggests that man's position in the cosmos is far more precarious than we might usually recognize. Care must be our watchword, and even the butcher's family should be careful with their fire, for above them their inn-sign is about to fall into the flames. In the cruel months of winter, we learn that we are not as different from the birds, or even the fox, as we like to suppose.

In *Gloomy Day* (illus. 15), the distant mountaintops are still snow-covered but in the rest of the world a thaw has come, and the flat farmlands across the river from the mountains are waterlogged. The river itself, like the wider sea beyond, is filled with drama: evidently a highly localized storm, not affecting the labourers in the foreground, is churning its waters and driving the ships into the shallows, where the waves break them up. Shipwreck was a vivid and immediate fear to a sixteenth-century city such as Antwerp whose wealth was based on maritime trade, and Bruegel had drawn upon that fact in his engraving of *Hope* from the Seven Virtues series (illus. 16). Four ships, one of them a large ocean-going vessel, are being pushed towards disaster at the shore. Desperate sailors stretch their arms to Heaven, where their hope lies. Meanwhile, on shore, a group of neighbours have brought ladders to help douse a fire, a theme Bruegel would use again in *Hunters in the Snow*. One man pauses to offer his prayer to an urban roadside shrine. Hope, to Bruegel, is a response to the perilous, unpredictable position of mankind in the cosmos, the workings of what his contemporaries would have called *fortuna*.[26]

Fortune's vicissitudes are balanced, in *Gloomy Day* as in *Hunters*, by the virtue we can cultivate to guard against disaster: Prudence (illus. 9). The activities in both of these scenes of harsh weather have their equivalents in this print: butchering meat, bundling twigs, patching the house after a storm (at

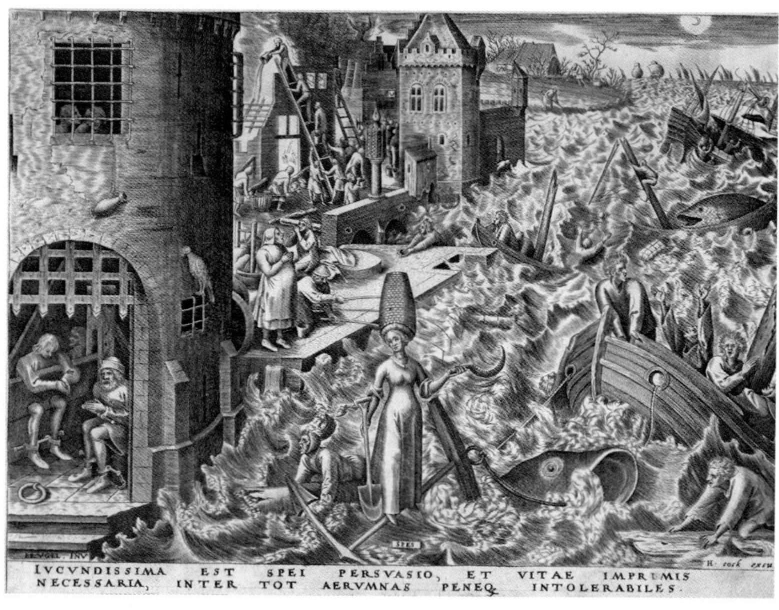

16 Philips Galle after Pieter Bruegel, *Hope, c.* 1559, engraving from the Seven Virtues series.

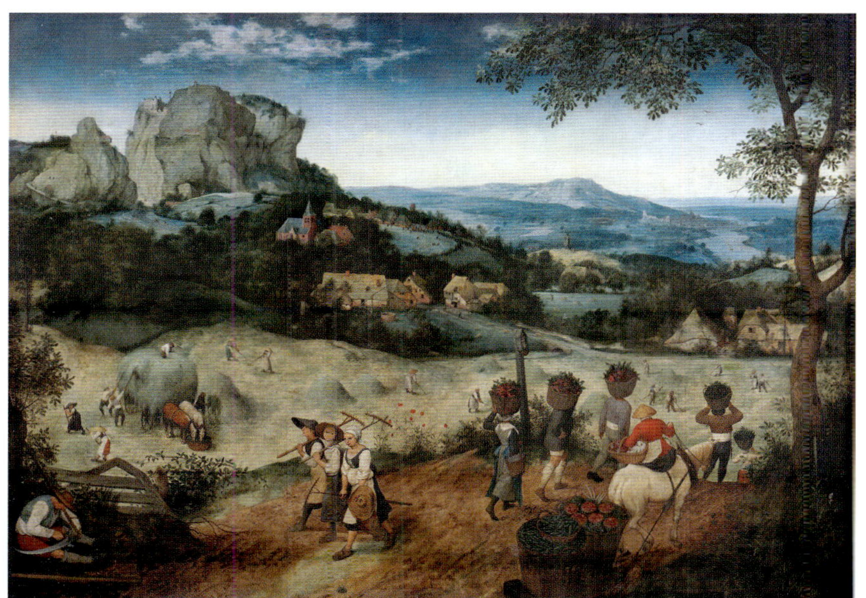

the right of *Gloomy Day*, and also in its village behind the two
parked wagons), and even dousing the fire after it has served
its purpose. Prudence, which guided the Erasmian person
though life's moral pitfalls, also enables Bruegel's farming folk
to prepare for, and recover from, the physical dangers that
bedevil the cosmos.

It is the calendar's festivity of carnival in *Gloomy Day* that
balances out the prudent tasks of early spring: at the right,
the little carnival king in his printed paper crown watches
the adults happily eating waffles, while in the opposite corner
of the scene, down in the village, another family dances in the
street outside an inn. In the next remaining scene of the series,
Hay Harvest (June/July, illus. 17), the festive moment is very
distant and yet, characteristically, fairly central on the panel:

17 Pieter Bruegel, *The Hay Harvest* (June/July), 1565, oil on panel.

on a village green, people have gathered for a competition involving shooting at a popinjay on a pole. This pole also stood in an empty, snow-covered village green beyond the frozen ponds in *Hunters*, one of the echoes in the series that gives a sense not that we see the same place, but that every place we see is somehow archetypal, universal. In *Hay Harvest* Bruegel gestures to the universality of the view by structuring his composition as a clear echo of the 'world landscapes' of Joachim Patinir, some forty years earlier, with the colour scheme moving carefully from foreground brown to green to distant blue, the rather choppy sense of space where roads fail to connect individual features, and the great inhabited rock formations jutting suddenly upward from pleasant farmland.[27]

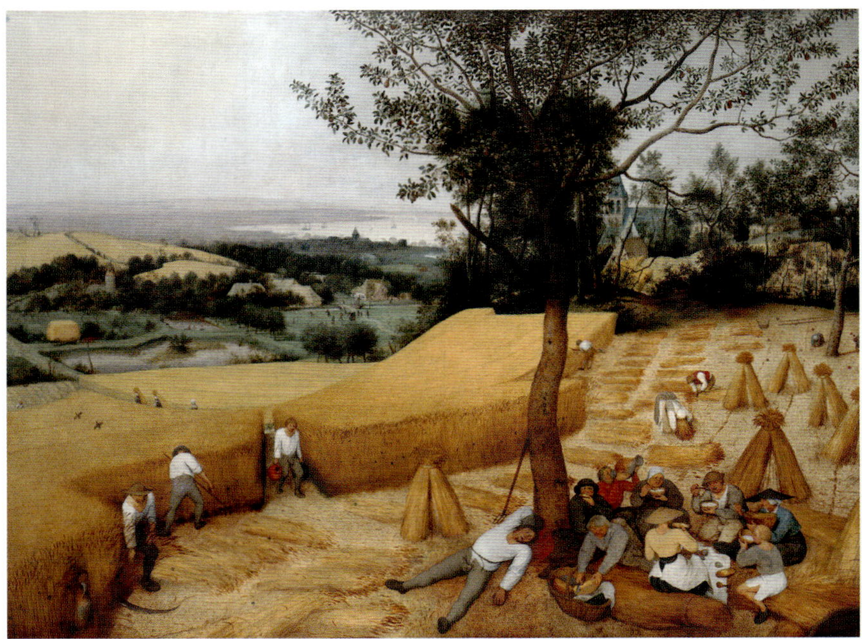

18 Pieter Bruegel, *The Harvesters* (August/September), 1565, oil on panel.

The labourers of *Hay Harvest* work more in concert than those in the winter months, as befits a season when all energy is exerted to bring in the crops, which includes both hay and produce. Fully absorbed by the tasks set them by their season, they have no inclination to pause and consider the world in which they toil. Bruegel seems to emphasize this with the figure in the lower left corner, who bends himself to caring for his scythe blade, an exact analogue of the corner figure in *Rustic Care*, a print Jonghelinck would certainly have known. A second scythe lies on the ground beside him but now there is no peasant companion to lean on it and contemplate the world. In the *Months*, only Jonghelinck and his guests are privileged to contemplate both nature and human nature together; the labourers, no longer our surrogates but our objects, bend their bodies and their eyes to the world whose demands absorb them.

The figures bringing in the produce, moving rightwards on the foreground road, bear fruits and vegetables of such abundance that they are nearly consumed by them. None has a visible face and for several, the basket of food they carry visually occupies the place where their head ought to be. They march right past the roadside shrine, their thoughts far from the God who created and ordered the cosmos that they inhabit.[28] And yet, their place in the order of things is still one of necessary virtue, for in this scene in particular they are bound to the land's plenty, the assistants or even collaborators in nature's provision of bounty to humankind. Farmers were lauded in Bruegel's and Jonghelinck's Antwerp for performing this role diligently and without complaint; and while one woman in the foreground trio of hay-rakers does look less than content with her lot, there is a humour to her grievance, which the second woman seems to invite the beholder to share.[29]

The next harvest scene, the *Harvesters* (August/September), brings us to the end of the crop-growing season and thus typically to a time of celebration, for nature's promise has been fulfilled (illus. 18). In the background of the print of *Hope* (illus. 16), Bruegel had depicted farmers preparing the fields to receive seeds, reminding us of how precarious food provision could be in early modern Europe, how dependent on the whims of weather, so that the *Harvesters* represents the happy culmination of a year of hope and prayer. There is more sustained play in the background here, as the squared ponds that hosted skaters in winter now open their waters to bathers. On the village green, people hurl sticks at a live goose hanging from a pole, one of several goose-torture games popular in the early modern Netherlands. In the field beyond the houses, cattle graze contentedly in the meadow: they had not appeared in any of the earlier *Months* but would feature prominently in the following scene, *Return of the Herd*, being driven back to their winter quarters inside the village.

Meanwhile, in the foreground fields of August, the bodies of the labouring workers bend and twist under the weight of the wheat, or fold over to gather fruit being shaken down from a tree, registering difficulty and even exhaustion in contrast to the light, almost graceful work of the *Hay Harvest*. One man trudges down a path between fields with two jugs to quench the thirst of his companions, who are pausing from their work beneath a tree. They are eating foods of the simplest sort – porridge, bread, cheese and a few pieces of fruit – the basic products that these labourers themselves have produced. By showing them consuming the products of their own labour on their own soil, Bruegel emphasizes how fundamentally they are embedded in and open to the natural world. These people, with their round, flat faces, staring eyes and lumpen bodies, have little in common with Jonghelinck and his urban, educated guests. The sleeping peasant, stretched out on the mown field, is an element of nature more than of the higher, human order. In a literal, physical way, the farmers' relation to the cosmos depends on how they *use* it, not how they traverse it or how they view it.[30] They cannot have a philosophical or aesthetic perspective upon the world because they are too much a part of it; in Humanist terms, they fail to cultivate the qualities that would elevate them, and remain earth-bound.

OF THE WORLD?

Hanging in Niclaes Jonghelinck's collection, only slightly larger than each of the *Months*, was another landscape dating from the year before and very differently configured from the way the seasonal cycle would be (illus. 19).[31] No sweeping river, no mountains, just a single high horizon line that allows a large, but not immense, territory to spread out before us. There is weather, however: placid over the city on the left and then transformed by ominous clouds that are moving in above the small village on the right. But what most differentiates this landscape from Bruegel's others is its population density. Dozens, scores, hundreds of people are in this place. They have emerged from the city gates, the dark-clad stragglers still running along the road in the distant left. The procession's trajectory swings around across the sodden ground of the

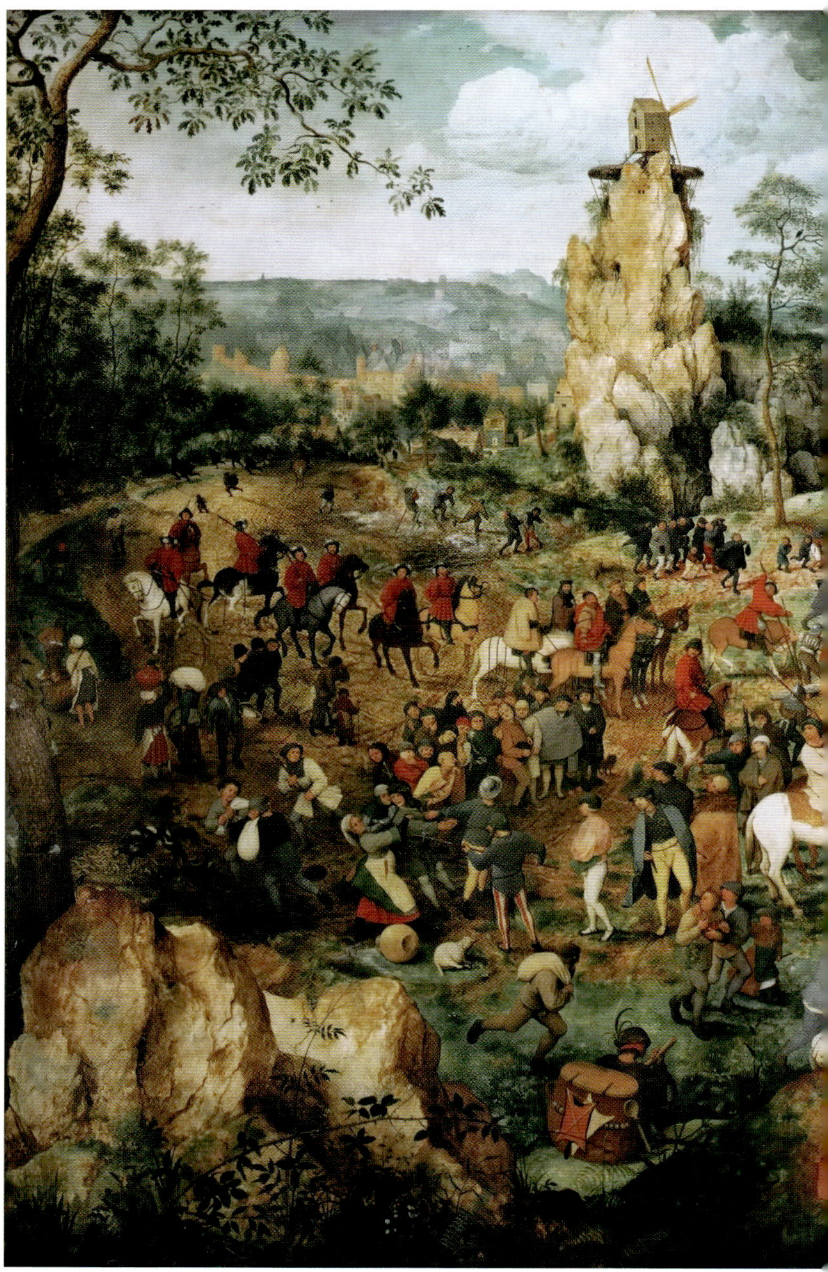

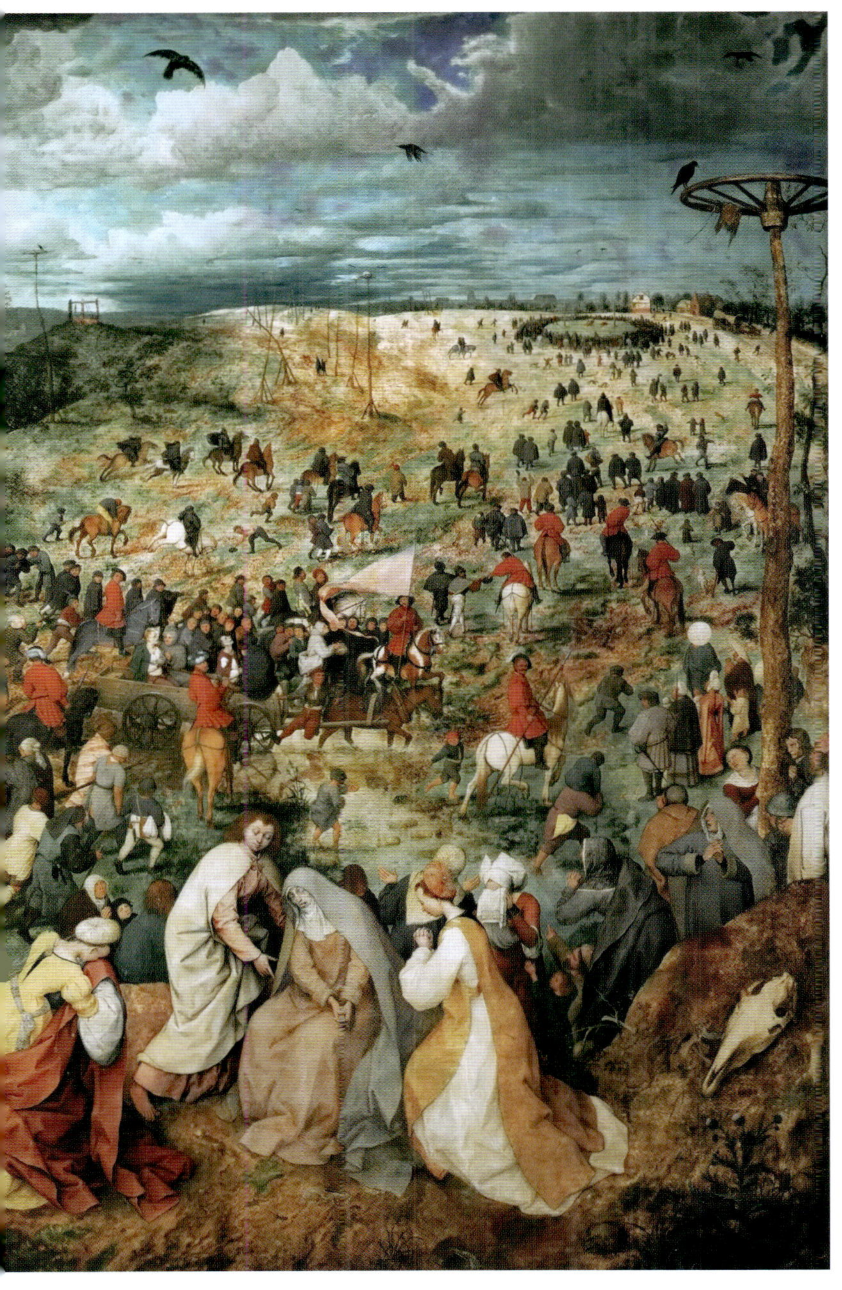

19 Pieter Bruegel, *Christ Carrying the Cross*, 1564, oil on panel.

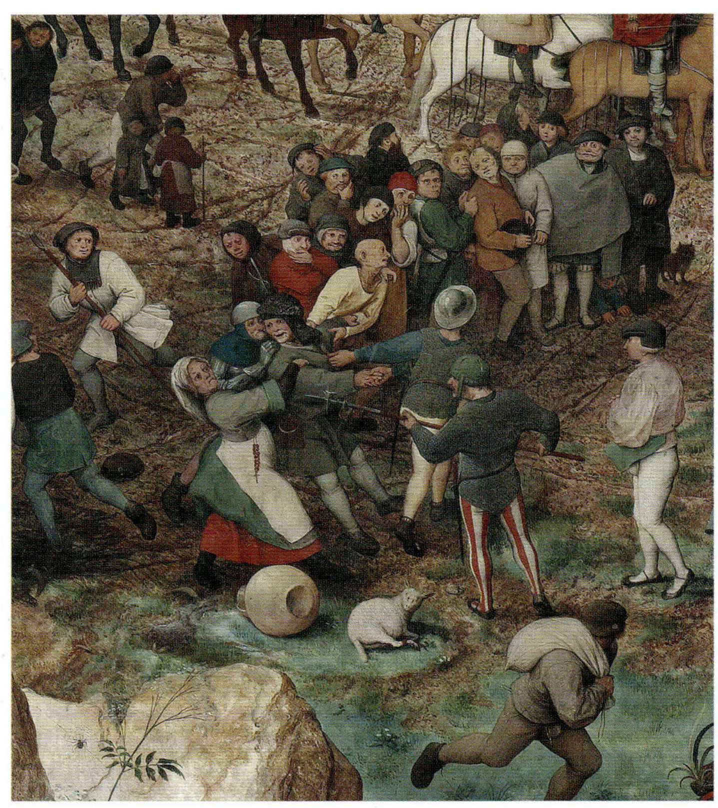

field at the picture's centre, over the creek at its right, and then makes its way slowly upward to the village under a clouded-over sky, where a crowd of men has already created a circle on the green. Instead of a single pole for festive play in this town, though, two crosses have been erected and the hole is being dug to receive a third. In fact, as our gaze sweeps with the travelling crowd towards this destination, we recognize that this village is commonly a place of execution, its surroundings planted with the paraphernalia of state-ordained death: at

20 Soldiers with Simon of Cyrene: detail from *Christ Carrying the Cross*.

least two gallows still bear hanging bodies, but more frequent are the wheels, mounted on tall, twisting tree trunks, upon which corpses have been and in some cases still are exposed for consumption by the carrion birds. One stands near to us on the right, balancing the still-living tree that frames the scene on our left. On the wheel, a lone scrap of the clothing of somebody long dead still flutters, and a raven awaits the next victim.

Moving against the current of this urban crowd are a few farmers in the left foreground, carrying sacks and bundles and pushing a cart holding a pair of calves in a basket. In the farmers' minds, it is simply market day, and, oblivious to whatever event occupies the others, they are set upon their proper task of provisioning the city. But one couple has encountered some trouble. Three soldiers, and a passer-by, are dragging Simon of Cyrene away to help in the procession while his wife fights fiercely to keep him by her side, although the rosary she wears suggests that she ought to be a willing helper herself (illus. 20). In the heat of the struggle she has dropped her jug of milk and the fat lamb they were bringing to market. But it is the Lamb of God that her husband is being called upon to help: deeper within the landscape, Christ has fallen under the cross he is being forced to carry with him, the cross that will fill that third hole on the village green. Bowed under its impossible burden, he barely even tries to rise and walk as, around him, some men deliberately add to the cross's weight while others attempt to help move it along (illus. 21). Travelling in the wagon in front of him are the two soon-to-be-occupants of the crosses already erected on the village green. Each man has, anachronistically, been given a small crucifix, and each is being ministered to by a priest. The red-headed criminal is sceptical, but the man in the front of the wagon throws his head back and looks to Heaven: like the praying people in Bruegel's print, he has Hope.

I have not yet touched on several of the most important elements of this painting and yet, in two paragraphs, its main subject – Christ – has barely emerged. And so it is also in Bruegel's composition. While the figure of Christ is almost exactly at the midpoint of the panel's surface, spatially he is far from the foreground and, in particular, he is lost amid the crowd.[32] So many figures, of such fascination, demand our attention before he does: the merchants in the costumes of many nations, the group of village idiots being brought out to watch the excitement, the Roma women with their characteristic flat, white headgear, the local children with their snacks and games, the riders who cannot control their horses . . . the list is almost endless. There are figures of humour and ones who are expressive, but few who are in fact as still and calm as Christ himself, despite the horror of his situation. He knows things that the other people do not. He knows, for instance, the place of himself and his story in the greater sweep of time in the cosmos: perfect centrality. And yet, in the kind of paradoxical twist at which Bruegel excelled, we experience him as visually insignificant.[33]

The Stoics, who advocated taking a distanced, detached view of the world, could do so because they also believed that human affairs in that world were, precisely, insignificant. Cicero famously described how Scipio Aemilianus dreamt of looking down onto the Roman Empire from a place high in the heavens and learning the lesson of the puniness of his own possible accomplishments and ambitions, for even the greatest fame a man can achieve on earth is as nothing in the scale of the cosmos.[34] To the ancient Stoics, the corollary here was that the gods were disinterested in humanity's feeble struggle against the arbitrariness of nature. But the Christian cosmos had a greater, God-given plan that provided humanity with a very particular temporal framework stretching from creation, to the original sin, to Christ's incarnation, death and resurrection and eventually to his second coming, a cosmic linearity that enfolded within itself the cyclical time of months and seasons that was humanly comprehensible.[35] Nothing in this greater set of events is puny, and God's interest in it is paramount. And at the very heart of this eschatological temporality is the momentous event depicted by Bruegel in his painting for Jonghelinck.

Competing with Christ for centrality in Bruegel's world is the singular rock formation rising abruptly from the earth just to the left of the painting's centre, forming the axle around which the moving wheel of the procession to Calvary turns. It is topped by a windmill built upon an odd circular platform, a cousin of the wheels of death and decay surrounding the nearby village. Those wheels, though, are horribly stable, as death is forever until it is not, until time's end that is also death's end. The mill, on its own wheel, measures impermanence on a much smaller scale, for it is a type of windmill whose body turns to catch the wind that will move its sails, responding to the micro-changes within a single day, even an hour. Its cruciform sails, a paradoxical formal reiteration of a more permanent cross, are eternally mobile.[36] Spinning its multiple rotations at the centre of the painting's great swirl,

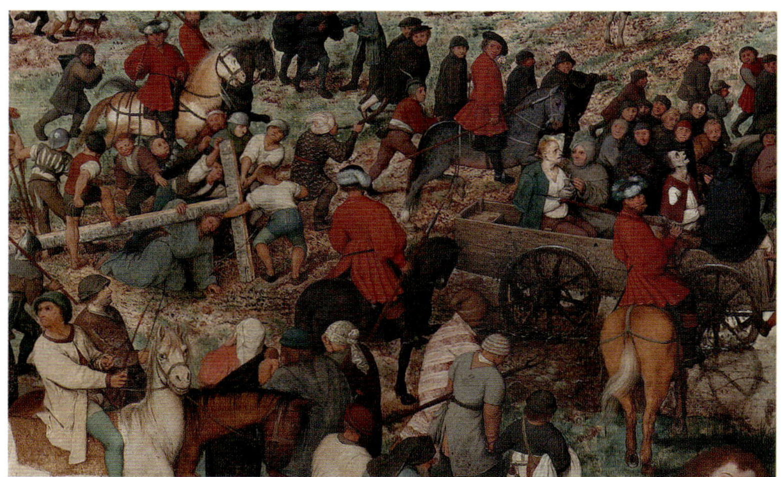

the mill is grandiose yet obviously inadequate, for although it rises above the earth, fundamentally it is earthbound and of the moment. The wheel of human fate that is spun around it is of massively greater consequence than this, yet who but Christ himself recognizes that fact?

Some figures know, at least, that a terrible thing is occurring. Apart from one man at the painting's right edge, gripping with clenched fingers the trunk of the dreadful wheel above him (illus. 22), they are mostly women, for in early modern paintings it is often women's job to model emotional responses, particularly grief. Two white-scarved women, the nearest figures to Christ on our side, cover their faces in horror. But most of the grieving figures are gathered in the right foreground, and among them four stand out vividly: they are of a different scale to the rest, are posed more gracefully and wear non-contemporary costumes that would have been most familiar to Bruegel's audience from earlier

21 Christ and the two thieves: detail from *Christ Carrying the Cross*.

Netherlandish religious art, particularly from the mourners in images of Christ's death by Rogier van der Weyden and his followers. And this is precisely what they are for Bruegel: figures of mourning, calling forth compassion from the beholder and bringing the powerful emotive force of Weyden's work into the midst of a strangely ordinary and very contemporary scene of execution. Anachronisms in artistic terms, they also point to the anachronism of everything else in this picture apart from themselves, who in some sense more truly belong with Christ in a time that is past. By this gesture, along with the thieves' crosses and Simon's wife's rosary, Bruegel threads together the layers of time in his image.[37] Past and present can meet because they are part of the same greater divine plan for human time, a plan that always stitches together our moment and the key events of past and future.

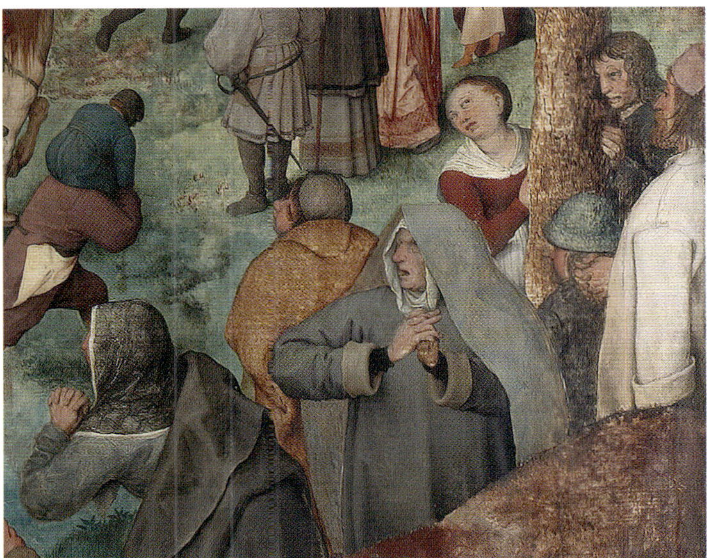

22 Onlookers at right: detail from *Christ Carrying the Cross.*

One person neither participates in nor (as far as we can judge) reacts to the unfolding drama: a peddler, who has taken his seat on a grassy bank near the foreground just to the left of centre, and turns away from us so that we can see the pack of wares he has been carrying on his journey. The peddler was often used as an everyman figure in sixteenth-century art, but at the same time he is the quintessential traveller.[38] Indeed, he is everyman precisely because he always travels, as every man is a perpetual traveller on the journey through life. In the generation before Bruegel this metaphor had often been the structuring trope in landscape paintings that represented spiritual wayfarers being asked to decide between the virtuous, difficult climb or the sinfully easy way, a kind of passage through perpetual moral choices that Erasmus' *Enchiridion* also described.[39] But Bruegel's travelling peddler here is peculiar in that he has ceased moving, and in fact is the only figure in the entire busy painting who is seated and entirely still. He has stopped on his journey to contemplate the world, not from high above it but from just at the edge of the action. From here, he needs to understand the moral value of what he sees: an ordinary day's justice under civic laws, or a massive turning point in the cosmic order of time? The judgement he eventually makes from this vantage point will not be detached. His own forward movement through life, as an actor in the temporal world, will depend on his acknowledging the same truths about the cosmos as does the man falling under the cross.

THREE

Ambition and Authority

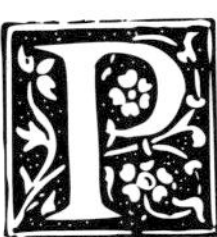AUL HIMSELF TELLS the story no fewer than three times in the New Testament book of Acts (Acts 9, 22, 26). An early, avid and voluntary Jewish persecutor of Christ's followers, originally named Saul, he set out with a group of companions to arrest Christians in Damascus. But as he neared the city, a bright light shone around him so that he fell to the earth, and a voice rang out: 'Saul, Saul, why persecutest thou me?' In one version he says his companions also saw the light, in another that they heard the voice and in the third that they all fell to the earth with him; but in any case Saul, on the ground, was now blind. Helped by his friends, he stumbled to Damascus, where he would pray, regain his sight and become the great Apostle Paul.

This is, and is not, what Pieter Bruegel showed in his painting of 1567 (illus. 23). His persecutor travels not with a few companions but with a vast army. Helmeted men with pikes, a standard-bearer in foppish green, soldiers in armour and short hose, and others wearing the long, loose breeches characteristic of sixteenth-century Swiss and German mercenaries. The men wrapped in blankets, and sometimes barefoot, are not soldiers but members of the travelling army's retinue.

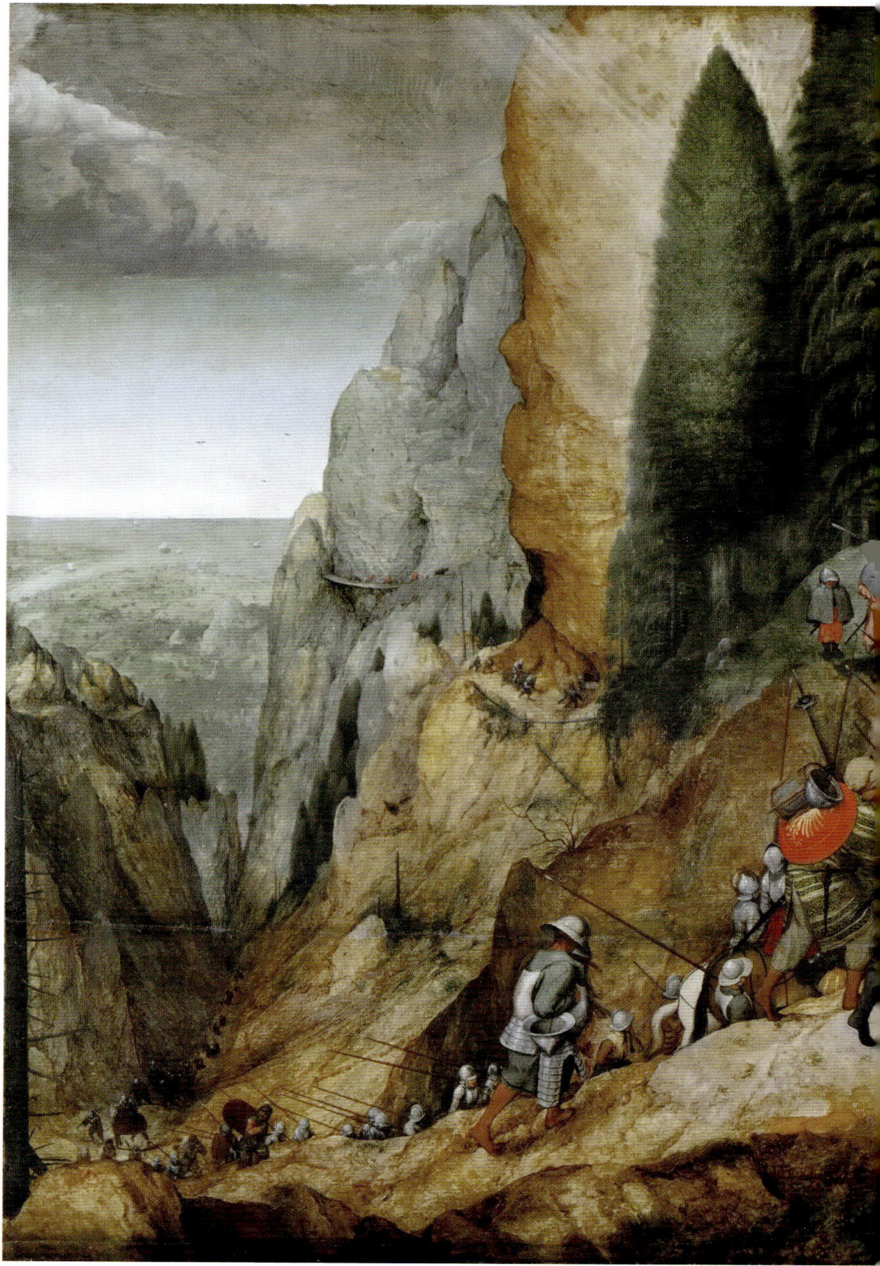

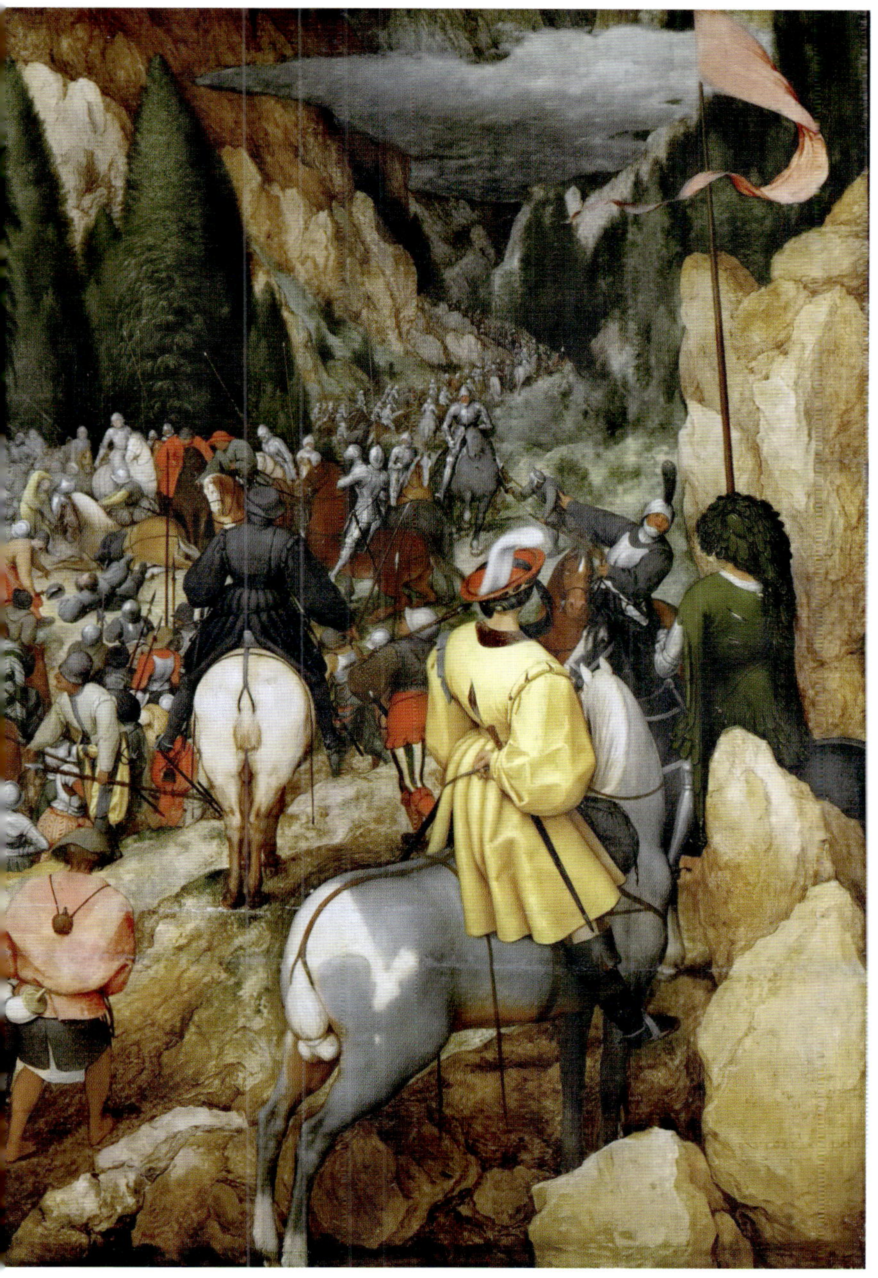

23 Pieter Bruegel, *Conversion of Paul*, 1567, oil on panel.

The company fill the road in their hundreds, from deep down in the valley at the left to the furthest visible part of the mountain pass at the right, disappearing ant-like into the distance. And then, that pass. Narrow and steep, it climbs from a broad seaside plain upward to the clouds, only a few hardy pine trees clinging to the rocks along its way. None of this accords with Paul's historical journey. Yet there he is, near the geometric midpoint of the panel but rather far back spatially, in a place where the path widens amid a cluster of tall trees, nature's exclamation points around his momentous experience, their dark forms pierced by a shaft of miraculous light.

THE TUMOUR OF PRIDE

Paul's story is one of revelation and conversion. But in Pieter Bruegel's day, it carried a second crucial meaning. According to a long tradition of biblical exegesis, Paul the persecutor had been a proud man; Christ's miracle 'cured Paul of the tumor of pride, offering him the depths of humility, not the heights of majesty', as the *Golden Legend* put it.[1] Pride was one of the Seven Deadly Sins as illustrated by Bruegel in his print series (illus. 24), and Paul on the road to Damascus was one of the standard exemplars of that sin. Once this is recognized, Bruegel's *Conversion of Paul* takes its place within a core group of his works: *Fall of the Rebel Angels*, the *Fall of Icarus*, two versions of the *Tower of Babel* and the *Suicide of Saul*. In fact, nearly every narrative painting by Bruegel that is not illustrating the life of Christ or the Virgin Mary treats a theme commonly associated with pride, ambition and the contestation of authority or hierarchy. Some are also open to

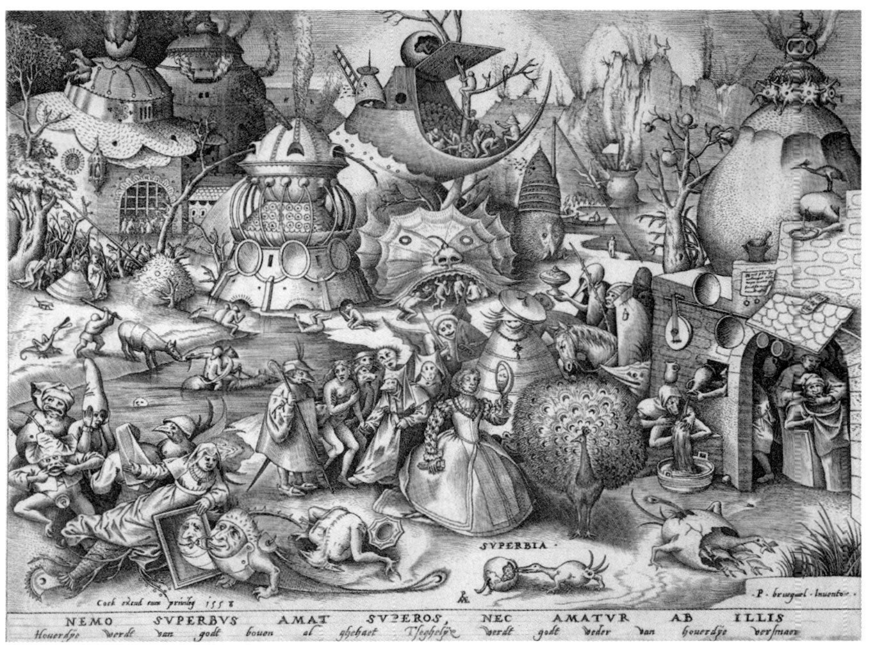

alternative interpretations, but in Bruegel's day every one of these works would have been seen as primarily treating the 'tumour of pride'.

Pride is a trait we tend to value and even foster today, and its opposites in the modern thesaurus are negatives: shame, self-doubt, humiliation, melancholy. But in the sixteenth century, pride's opposites were among the most valued human and social goods. Within the canon of virtues and vices, pride's inverse was faith, because pride was associated with a disdain for God and, as the inscription on Bruegel's print notes, was therefore a human characteristic particularly hated by God.[2] Other positive oppositions to pride included humility, obedience, wisdom, contentment with one's lot in life,

24 Pieter van der Heyden after Pieter Bruegel, *Pride*, 1558, engraving from Seven Deadly Sins series.

and care for the common good. Pride was labelled as chief among the vices by Church Fathers from Gregory to Aquinas, a fundamental corruption of the soul. It meant excessive focus on the self: hence its association with physical vanity, the main way it is illustrated in Bruegel's print. But far worse and more insidious was social or behavioural self-absorption, putting your own desires and achievements first and believing yourself to be worthy of such primacy.

The way to avoid what Erasmus calls 'haughtiness and arrogance of mind' was, according to him, quite straightforward: self-knowledge. The figures who look into their mirrors in Bruegel's *Pride* are performing the vain, external form of the inward self-examination that would actually end their folly. Keep your reflective focus on your inner self, Erasmus counsels, and not on extrinsic things like money or, especially, status. Erasmus listed pride among five vices that the Christian soldier would need to be on special guard against: two, lust and anger, were bodily and even animal inclinations but the other three – avarice, ambition and pride – were particular to human nature and were closely interconnected.[3] All were linked to a desire for power and a tendency not to be content with one's place in the social hierarchy, although princes and prelates – those already near the top of the pile – were particularly likely to be corrupted by pride.[4] Machiavelli, whose interests lay precisely in the nature and habits of men desirous of power, sees pride and its correlative ambition as fundamental to 'the envious nature of man'.[5] The nobles are the worst in this regard, and a successful tyrant will need to keep a close eye on them.

Bruegel's contemporaries, had they read Machiavelli's advice, would not have been surprised at all. For the years between 1559 and Bruegel's death, when he was producing these pride-themed paintings, were a time of intense political turmoil, and tensions between representatives of the Spanish king and the local nobility were roundly blamed, by both sides, on pride. It is easy, in retrospect, to see these years as a time of growing religious division, as Protestant ideas took hold in the Netherlands and provoked suppression from rulers based in Catholic Spain, and this is certainly not untrue. But at the time, many saw the simmering unrest as being largely caused by personalities and ambitions. Of the religious divide itself, Bruegel's friend Ortelius would write: 'All this we have deserved through our sins; for we are motivated by pride and ambition . . . every one wishes to teach others, but not to humble himself; to know much and to do little, to dominate others, but not to bow under God's hand.'[6] Really, the only question was whose pride was more to blame. Major contenders for that honour were William of Orange, later the hero of the Dutch Revolt but in Bruegel's time just one of several local noblemen entitled to considerable say in the affairs of state, and Antoine Perrenot de Granvelle, an important representative of the Spanish crown. After King Philip II's permanent departure from the Netherlands for Spain in 1559, Granvelle had swiftly risen to a position of immense governmental power at the expense of the local nobles.[7] He was a cultured man who served as a kind of art agent in the Netherlands for the king; in this area, as in more political ones, he controlled immense potential patronage.[8] One of the artists whose work he purchased was Pieter Bruegel. Granvelle had been nakedly and notoriously ambitious in his earlier days, and was insufferably arrogant now that he had the power he had so craved. The pride that others saw in him, he saw in William of Orange and the other great nobles. To him, they were trying to undermine royal authority; to them, he and his allies were usurping ancient local rights and privileges.[9] Both sides made these views widely known, so that accusations of excessive pride as a threat to hierarchy became a staple of political discourse.

Usurped privileges were a cause for complaint, not yet for actual rebellion; but by the beginning of the 1560s, there was a sense that the potential for civil unrest was very real. At the 1562 competition between 'Chambers of Rhetoric', groups of writer-performers from Flanders and Brabant, Holland and Zeeland, the government-approved question that each group was to address asked by what means unrest could best be kept away. Pride and ambition were obvious culprits according to many respondents, whose answers focused on obedience and love of God – pride's great opposites – and made regular reference to the very narratives Bruegel would represent in paintings.[10] Relatively few chambers wrote at any length about religious division as the cause of unrest, for those that did were treading a fine line between urging, and opposing, rebellion. However, to argue that as long as a government ruled with the fear of God, or in obedience to God's will, that government itself commanded obedience, allowed for the possibility of legitimate rebellion against a ruler that was not doing so.[11] This was precisely what the Netherlandish nobles came to argue in the 1560s: while obedience was a divine command, disobedience was necessary if those in authority, in government, ceased to obey God themselves.[12] Thus the petition that three hundred nobles delivered to regent Margaret of

Parma in 1566 at once asserted their local rights, opposed the Inquisition as tyrannical, blamed everything on the proud ambition of unnamed foreigners advising the king, and accused them of having no care for God.[13] It was, as she recognized, a preliminary recipe for justifying rebellion.

Perhaps this entanglement of pride, religion, inquisition and rebellion is the reason why Pieter Bruegel's print of *Justice* is the only one in his series of Seven Virtues upon which his name has been carefully omitted, even though its preliminary drawing had been clearly signed (illus. 25). It is also the only virtue that is depicted as purely social: that is, while *Fortitude* or *Prudence* or *Hope* (see illus. 5, 9, 16) present models that would allow the individual to cultivate these traits, *Justice* seems to relate entirely to the doings of a society. Crucial information that would have allowed viewers to position themselves as just judges is conspicuously lacking. We have no idea of what crimes these men have been accused, nor how their guilt has been determined; and without that knowledge, our trust in the virtue of justice is hopelessly compromised. The process by which ordinary courts obtained evidence, decided on arrests and employed torture varied greatly from those procedures in the inquisitional courts.[14] It matters hugely, in particular, whether the man in the left foreground is a guilty criminal being tortured to extract a confession so that he can be hanged, or if he is suspected of heresy and is being tortured to determine what he believes. The former, if carried out with proper moderation, virtuously rids the social body of evil; the latter, however, is infinitely problematic. In a land characterized (to the continual annoyance of its Spanish rulers) by a rather flexible, 'enlightened' Catholicism, and increasingly

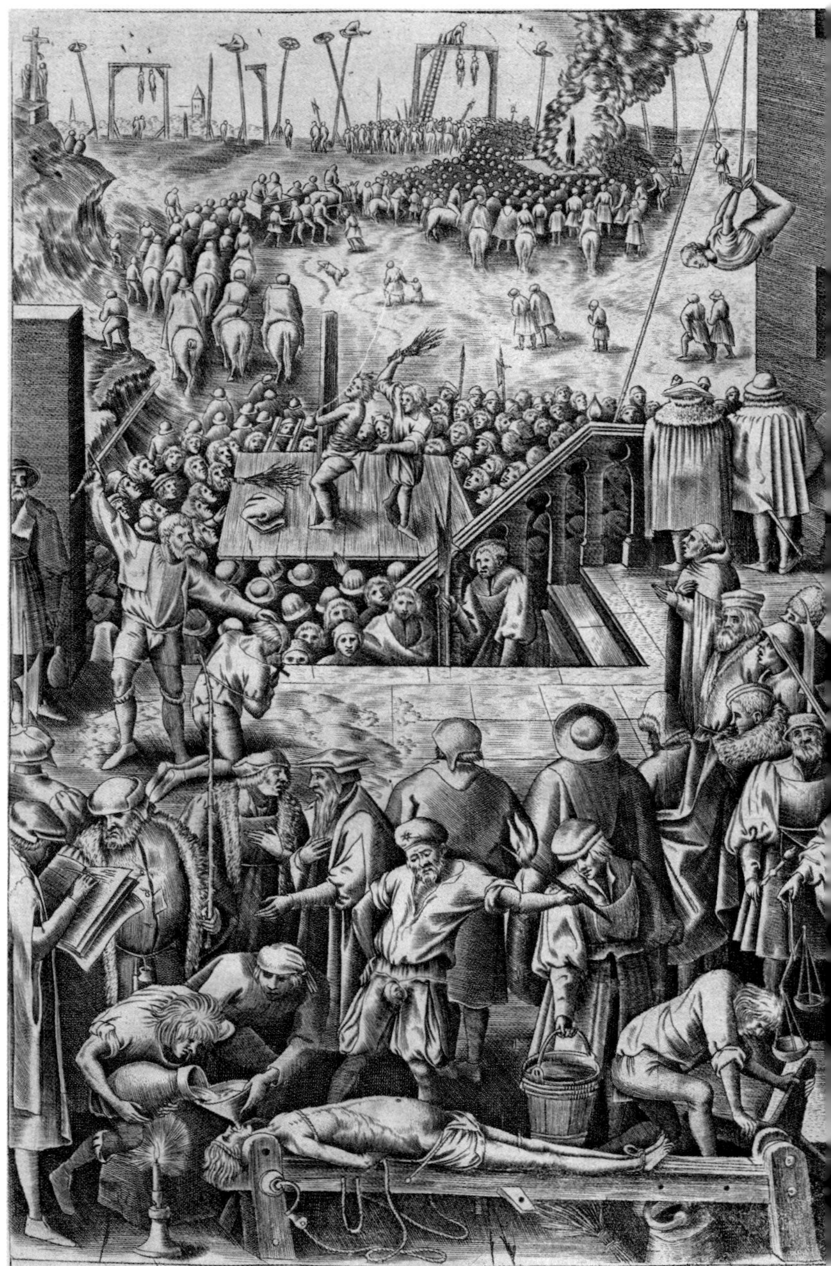

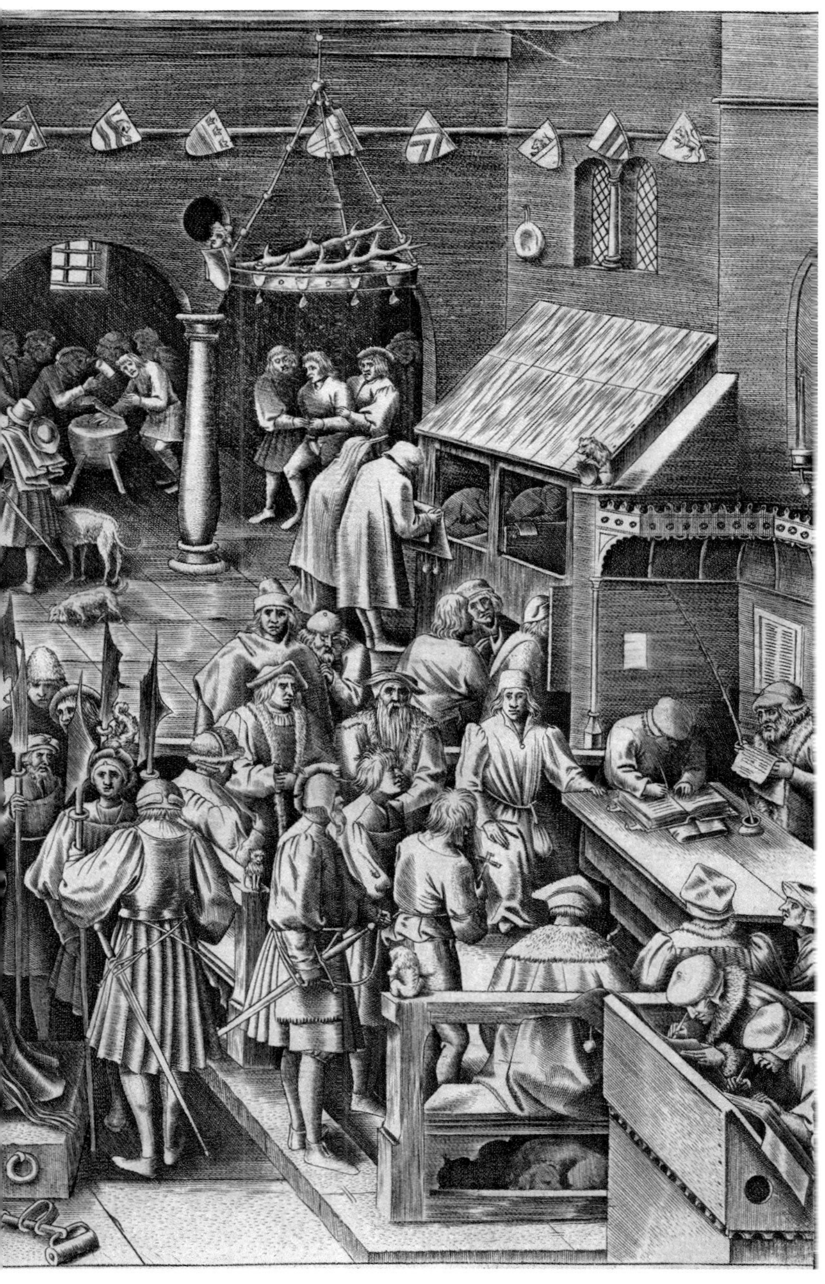

25 Philips Galle after Pieter Bruegel, *Justice*, *c.* 1559, engraving from Seven Virtues series.

open to reformed ideas, the notion of policing internal, personal faith through punitive external means was markedly unpopular.[15] Indeed, some wondered: does authority extend at all over an individual's beliefs and thoughts?[16] By the 1550s, these questions were leading local magistrates, even the Council of Flanders, to gently obstruct the work of the Inquisition.[17]

Bruegel's print of *Justice* presents an orderly spectacle of civic arraignment, trial and punishment, arranged in a carefully constructed and rational space that recalls, to some degree, the actual High Tribunal of the Counts of Brabant located in Antwerp.[18] By the standards of the mid-sixteenth century, all seems to proceed according to the correct implementation of the law. And yet, almost unnoticed in the scene's upper left corner, a sculpture overlooking the gallows field depicts John and Mary weeping at the foot of a crucifix, grieving at history's greatest injustice. Condemned men in the present die 'good' deaths, clutching their small versions of that crucifix while attendant priests pray; but how can we judge the judges here? At a historical moment when questions of obedience and authority were being contested in particular around this very point, Bruegel's missing signature sends a message. While everybody would have known who made this print – it is, after all, part of a series – his name's conspicuous absence seems to say that the image's author cannot himself perform judgement any more than his beholder can. Can – should – the authorities acting here be obeyed? The proud may rebel out of ambition and destroy social order, but a social order that disobeys God has destroyed itself.

When Bruegel painted the curing of Paul's pride in 1567, the political situation was changing rapidly. In 1564, the arrogant Granvelle had been forced to leave the Netherlands, his excessive pride followed by a swift fall. But the ensuing efforts of both great and lesser nobles to assert their rights had only led to further destabilization. Growing crowds at Calvinist preachers' sermons, the forceful demands of the nobility and finally the iconoclastic riots in the summer of 1566 prompted Margaret of Parma to beg for help from her half-brother, Philip II, in Spain: things were, she reported, spiralling out of control. She needed to make concessions, or she needed an army, and Philip swiftly resolved to send an army. Under the leadership of the Duke of Alba, 10,000 troops would march the 1,100 km (700 mi.) from Milan to the Netherlands, arriving in August of 1567. His mission: to forcibly eradicate Protestantism and restore proper civil order. The disobedient nobles would be executed, along with many hundreds of others, and while the extent of the brutality could not have been anticipated, people in the Netherlands knew of Alba's intentions. And they knew that he was coming, with not only 10,000 men but also their servants and family members, a massive company marching over the Alps. Like Bruegel's Paul.

The *Conversion of Paul* draws a careful yet ambiguous analogy between contemporary events and one of the great historical exemplars of pride. Alba was on a journey whose end was persecution; he would enter a situation in which pride and ambition were thought to be motivating players on all sides, human traits that, unchecked, produced social instability. The Duke himself, however, had not been part of this series of accusations and counter-accusations, so at what level does Bruegel's analogy bring him into events in the Netherlands? The painting, poised at a moment when much was feared from the powerful traveller and his army, seems to be a prediction or even a warning: those who arrogantly assume the power to persecute will be humbled. From the heights of power, of pride, they will be cast down, as God humbled Paul. Siting Paul's revelation in the heights of the mountains is more than a gesture towards the Alps being traversed by Alba; it intensifies the sense of self-elevation that stems from arrogance but that makes the fall into humility all the more dramatic. It is the mighty who fall the furthest.

PRIDE GOES BEFORE A FALL

It all started with pride. 'The beginning of all sin', the Bible calls it (Ecclesiastes 10:13), and throughout the Middle Ages there had been commentators willing to expound upon that definition.[19] For sin had to have begun somewhere, and among the Seven Deadlies, pride had a firm claim to originary status. Only avarice, often linked to ambition, gave pride any real competition. And in the greater Christian narrative of the world, humankind, our beginning and our end and our nature, pride had a crucial role to play. Because of the angels.

There they are, the rebels, in Bruegel's painting of 1562, tumbling downward in their multitudes out of a great, golden celestial light (illus. 26).[20] Hybrid, mutant creatures, they form a sea of monstrous absurdity, madly combining elements from the fish of the ocean, the birds and insects of the air and the animals of the land. A few still have human arms, remnants of their former state, and one blows his bannered angelic trumpet. Here and there, even a human face can be found, bearing an almost caricatural expression of shock or horror. Somewhere high up, in their original place, these creatures had once been beings physically like the dozen or so angels whose faces are eerily calm as they fly about, brandishing trumpets and swords and anachronistic crosses in order to help St Michael in this first great expulsion. For before the sin of disobedience that would lead to Adam and Eve's expulsion from Eden, there had been the disobedience of the proud angel Lucifer and his companions that caused them to be driven from Heaven. Lucifer had once been great, and beautiful, the very 'son of the morning'. But in his increasingly proud heart, Lucifer said: 'I will ascend into heaven; I will exalt my throne above the stars of God . . . I will ascend above the heights of the clouds; I will be like the most High' (Isaiah 14:13–14. See, too, Ezekiel 28:12–17). For this desire to climb above God himself, Lucifer was instead cast down to the lowest depths; according to some interpretations, he and his cohort went first to Earth, where they planted the seeds of all the sins that would beset mankind. Certainly in Bruegel's time Lucifer was the prime example of disruptive, rebellious pride: many Chambers of Rhetoric competing in Brussels in 1562, the very year of Bruegel's painting, wrote of how God had had to expel this arrogant angel in order to maintain peace in Heaven.[21]

The narrative of Lucifer's efforts to achieve godlike heights had a reverse echo in Renaissance notions of humankind's 'dignity', as Pico termed it in his call for a 'certain holy ambition' that would make people aspire to higher, near-divine achievements.[22] If mankind's greatest glory was the ability to

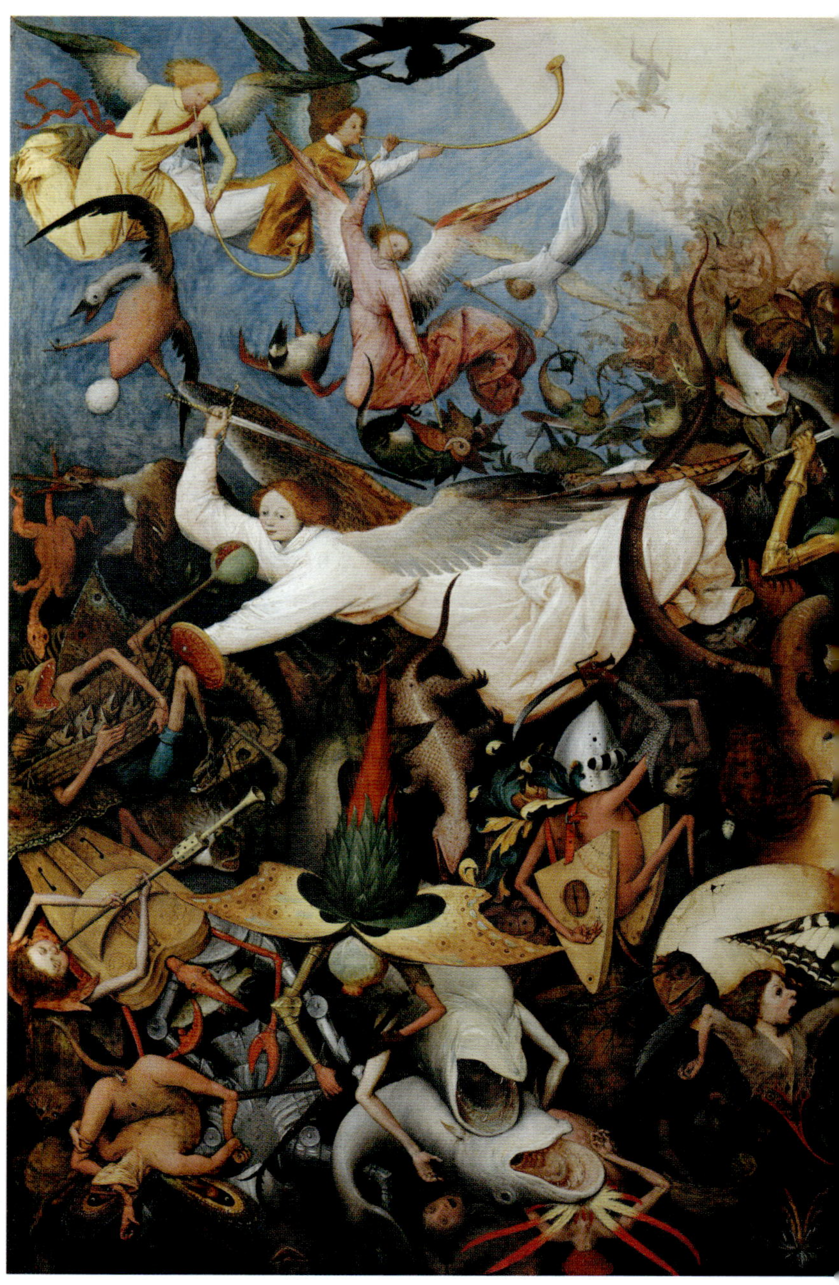

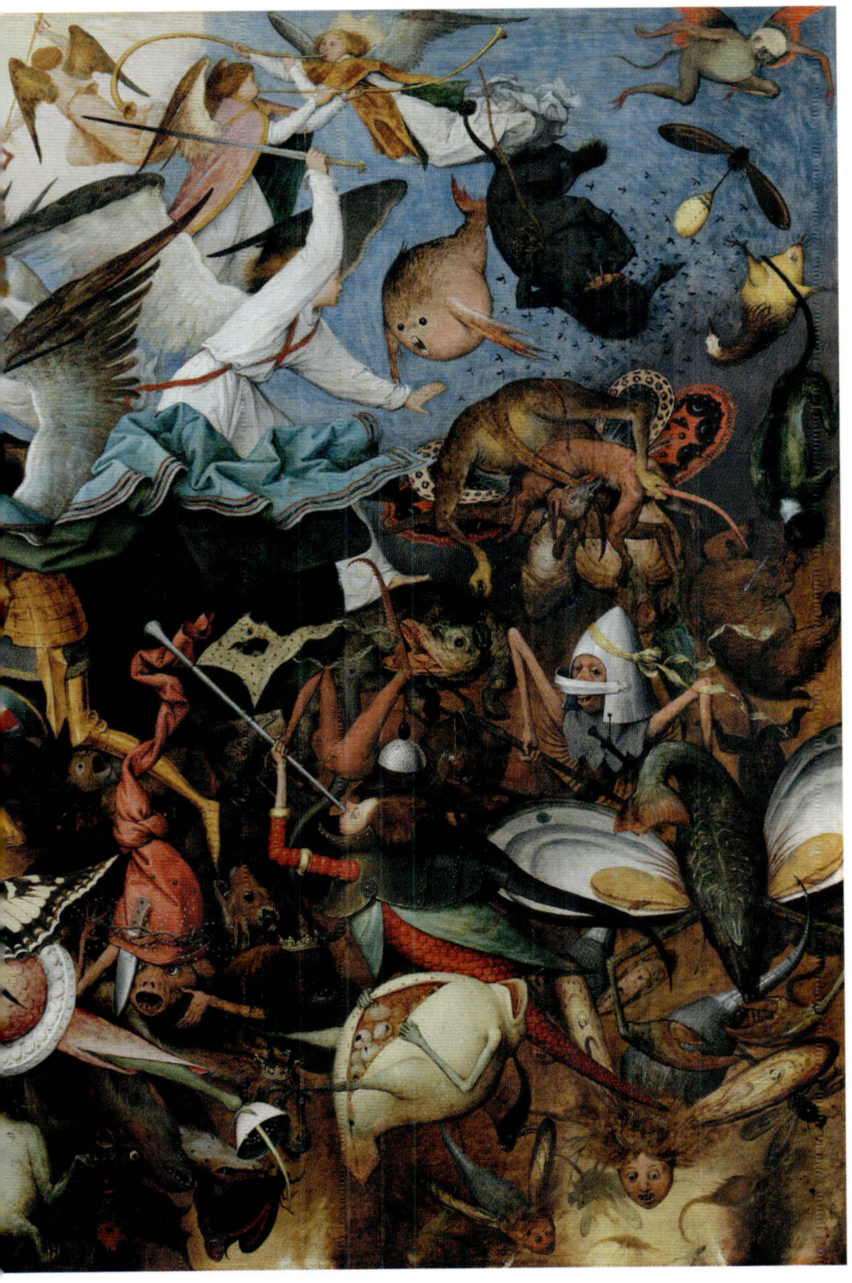

26 Pieter Bruegel, *Fall of the Rebel Angels*, 1562, oil on panel.

rival the angels, shouldn't that render pride – even that of the angels themselves – a lesser evil? Not really, because humanity's proud aspirations had to operate within particular constraints. As the Humanists insisted that it was mankind's free will, our ability to decide our own limits, that made us unique among God's created beings, so too were the angels said to have been particularly gifted with choice; and the fatal choice they made, inspired by pride, was to rebel against the wishes of God.[23] The choice and fate of the angels not only foreshadowed the Fall of Man, then, but was a permanent exemplar for the dangers of a pride that was unbridled and of ambitions rising in a way that would lead to a cataclysmic fall. In this construct, the antidote to pride was not humility, but reason, which would temper ambition. The angels' unreasonable ambitions had been in a certain sense political, operating against the celestial hierarchy, which made them particularly relevant to the contemporary situation even as the angels' fall lay at the heart of Christian cosmology, defining the entry of sin into the world.

Bruegel's painting extends the notion of pride at the beginning of earthly time to time's endpoint. For the fall of the angels was, in biblical and theological terms, a messy and imprecise story. Never exactly *told* in the Bible, but only referred to, it was often conflated with a second reference to Lucifer's defeat, one that would occur at the end of time (Revelation 12:7–9). The second defeat, as described by John, would involve Michael and the angels casting down a seven-headed, crowned dragon, and although it is difficult to disentangle the mass of creatures at the heart of Bruegel's painting, a cluster of crowned animal heads does appear just beneath

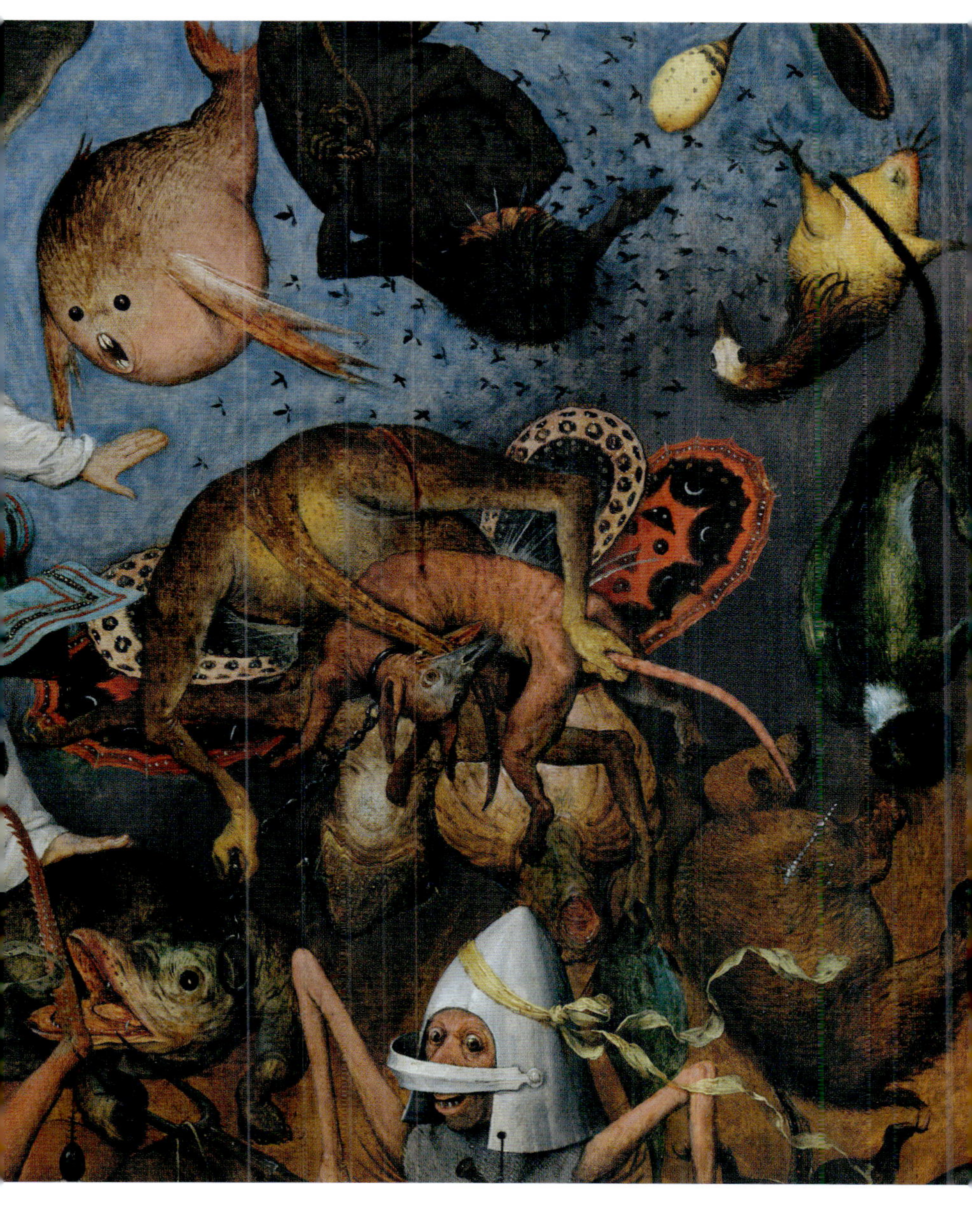

27 Beelzebub and other demons: detail from *Fall of the Rebel Angels*.

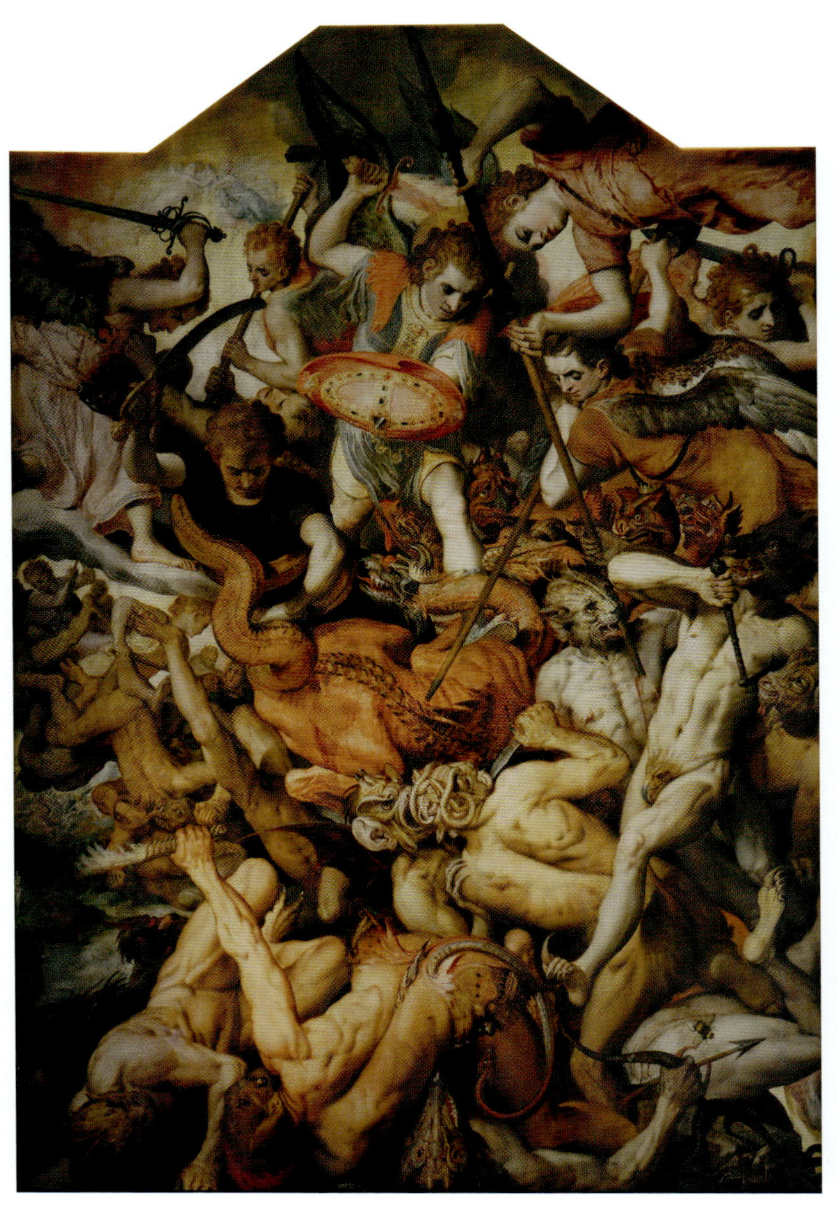

28 Frans Floris, *Fall of the Rebel Angels*, 1554, oil on panel.

Michael's left foot. The apocalyptic dragon's seven heads had, by numerological logic, become associated with the Seven Deadly Sins brought to humankind through the angels' fall. Bruegel takes up this connection and amplifies it, for among the mutations undergone by his plummeting angels, some have become the very creatures that signify the sins, familiar from Bruegel's series of prints from 1557 and cited more recently in his engraving of *Fortitude* (see illus. 5). A cluster of them appear just below Lucifer's chief agent, Beelzebub or 'Lord of the Flies', at the image's right edge: the bear of anger, the dog of envy, the ape of lust and – denuded of its finery – the peacock of pride (illus. 27). Bruegel thus definitively binds our sinful nature to the angels' fall.

And yet, just how dire is this connection? For both the overall impression of the picture, and the details that invite close examination, are simply not dark or terrifying. Even the fact of the angelic forces' triumph does not feel like a grand psychomachy in which the Good defeats the Evil. That is how the subject had recently been depicted in Antwerp, where Frans Floris's great altarpiece of 1554 for the fencers' guild showed an intense struggle between powerfully beauteous angels and muscled, Michelangelesque, monstrous rebels (illus. 28).[24] His was a painting in which the enormity of cosmic struggle was portrayed in starkly physical terms to create an analogy with the contemporary combat ability of an armed civic militia. Bruegel's picture is, perhaps deliberately, the opposite of Floris's.[25] It is anti-physical in the sense that hardly a single being corresponds to any actual creature. Even spindly Michael and his attenuated angelic assistants seem less human than angels normally do. The transfigured rebels are not fearsome, but ludicrous: we are invited to laugh at them, not to fear them. As epitomized by the pathetically plucked peacock, pride here is scorned and mocked. Like the Brussels rhetoricians, Bruegel treads carefully on the edge of political discourse, presenting a ludic version of the defeat of the proud without in any way identifying whose pride might be conflated with that of Lucifer.

To accomplish this particular transformation of the angels, Bruegel drew upon the way of thinking epitomized in an earlier generation by Hieronymus Bosch, whose monster-making he had referenced copiously in his early printed work for Hieronymus Cock (see illus. 24).[26] This is not to say he borrowed Bosch's forms, though. In Bosch's paintings, the nonsensical demons are often corporeally closer to humanity than are Bruegel's, or at least can interact intimately and easily with human beings; the sense of estrangement they produce derives from the way we can, and yet cannot, connect them to our humanity.[27] Bruegel's tangle of comic demonry lacks the bodily similitude that might bind the fallen angels, uncomfortably, to ourselves. They remain an oddly beautiful demonstration of how nature's diversity can be recombined by the imagination of man. In fact, the painting is a celebration of human inventive genius – Bruegel's own – even as it pokes fun at human pride and ambition through that of the angels.

The story of Daedalus and Icarus, also painted by Bruegel around this time, is another tale of pride and fall, hubris and nemesis, and also of inventive genius (illus. 29).[28] It concerns again the alteration of 'the natural order of things', as Ovid puts it, but now that disordering is the outcome of human invention, when Daedalus fashions two sets of wings that

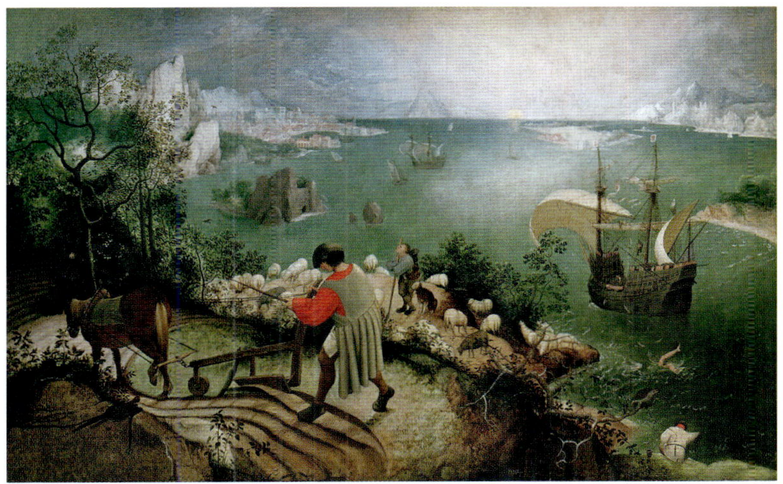

imitate the real wings of birds.[29] Indeed, Daedalus recreates himself and his son into hybrid beings, but with a utilitarian motive: to enable them to fly away from their exile on the island of Crete. Ovid dwells at length on the design and production process of these marvels of non-nature, how the ingenious artificer aligns feathers on a slant, fastens them with thread and with beeswax, and flexes the wings into a gentle curve so they will bear him and his son aloft, bird-like. Young Icarus pays little attention to the mechanics of invention, and equally little to his father's warning to him: when flying, take the middle path, avoiding heavy moisture too near Earth, or the heat too near to the Sun. The two rise high into the sky, to the amazement of a fisherman with his quivering rod, a shepherd leaning on his crook and a ploughman leaning on the handles of his plough, who all stand amazed by these godlike beings. Icarus, though, is lured by the pleasures of flight, 'drawn by desire for the heavens', and climbs too high:

29 Pieter Bruegel, *Fall of Icarus* c. 1560, oil on panel.

the Sun melts the waxen wings and he plunges into the sea, causing his distraught father to curse his own invention. The catastrophe causes mocking laughter from clever Talus, who, when his uncle Daedalus tried to murder him in jealousy at his brilliant inventiveness, had been turned into a partridge.

In his visual retelling of this story, Bruegel engages so directly with Ovid's vivid text that his divergences from it also stand out. The ploughman, a central figure in Bruegel's painting although incidental to Ovid, fails to pause in his work but continues to methodically turn over the earth, while the shepherd, a bit more distant, leans impassively on his staff and peers without much sign of wonder at the sky, where we presume he still sees Daedalus in flight although we do not. The third of Ovid's witnesses, the fisherman, is as oblivious as the ploughman – even though, not far from him, the legs of Icarus give a final desperate kick as he disappears beneath the waves. Between these two, perched on a branch, the once-ingenious partridge stays safely close to the ground. All of these details, and the setting in a sea dotted with islands, relate to Ovid, but Bruegel makes two important additions: in the bushes near the ploughed field we can glimpse the head of a dead man; and, near to Icarus, a great modern ship sails by, as oblivious to the youth's fate as is the fisherman.

Icarus' fall had rarely been painted before Bruegel, which probably explains why the artist drew so closely upon his poetic source. The subject, though, was well known in his time from moralizing emblem books, where Icarus was offered as an exemplar of disobedience, pride and ambition.[30] Erasmus mentions Icarus as a particularly obvious allegory of excessive ambition, teaching us that 'no one should rise higher than his lot in life allows.'[31] In this broader sense of ambition, one that applies to every man as a social being, Bruegel's ploughman provides a perfect counterbalance to Icarus' self-elevating folly. The humble farmer, content with his lot and unquestioning of the rightfulness of the social order, was a common topos at this time, and Bruegel has taken care to characterize his ploughman in accordance with that ideal.[32] Walking steadily across the field, he guides the plough with one hand and with the other uses a whip to urge his horse onward. His furrows are striped by shadows of his legs, his plough, his horse, binding the man and his labour close to the soil he works. Many times, already, he has passed by the dead man in the bushes, but the furrows there remain even and measured, for the farmer has paid no more note to this death than he does to that of Icarus. Neither the heights of human glory nor the depths of misery have altered his path: as the proverb had it, 'no plough stops for the sake of a dying man.'

The farmer ignoring death in his relentless focus on his proper task in the universal order of things is contrived as a contrast to Icarus, but Bruegel's other addition to Ovid – the great ship, equally ignoring the drama of hubris punished – is actually more parallel to the hero's weakness. Today such a ship appears quaint, but when Bruegel painted the ship sailing near to Icarus, it was a marvel of modern technical invention. The real-life equivalent of Daedalus' wings, it enabled human beings to travel over unimaginable distances: indeed, the wind-filled sails of this vessel seem to beg for that comparison, as they enable humanity to harness natural power in an extraordinary way. During the early 1560s, Bruegel designed a series of ten prints depicting ships, both vessels of war and of

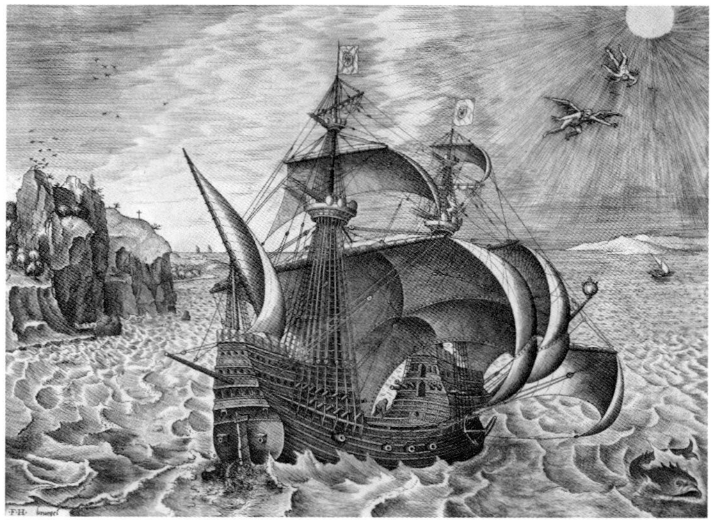

commerce, which were evidently produced in large quantities by his publisher Hieronymus Cock (illus. 30). Ships were fascinating and topical, their technology a source of pride to residents of Antwerp, for it was shipping that had enabled the city to become the economically powerful centre of world trade in Bruegel's day.[33] The riches of the artist, his neighbours and his patrons were founded at second hand, and sometimes directly, upon the circulation of goods passing through the city, brought from great distances on ships like the ones he depicts.

It is curious, then, that although Bruegel was living in Antwerp when he designed these prints, and had ample opportunity to study the vessels arriving at its wharf with their cargoes, his prints do not correctly represent ships he would have seen there.[34] They are not records of reality but artful inventions by the painter himself, proud rivals to the

30 Frans Huys after Pieter Bruegel, *Armed Three-master with Daedalus and Icarus*, c. 1561–2, engraving and etching.

work of naval architects. And in the print illustrated here, *Armed Three-master with Daedelus and Icarus*, two figures have been added in the sky: Daecalus, still flying aloft in the moderate zone, and Icarus, his wings disintegrating as he plunges headlong towards the sea. In the sky of a second print, another Ovidian figure appears: young Phaethon, who wrongly thought he could drive the chariot of the Sun, and fell to his death when he lost control. Another overly ambitious high-flyer, brought low through pride. Bruegel's ships celebrate human achievement while also hinting at its dangers and its limitations. They gesture towards his contemporaries' rivalries with the powers of God, and represent humanity's sense of its own boundless power. The ships' very status as brilliant constructions at the heart of Antwerp's current economic success makes this commentary on pride neither political nor individual: excessive pride is suggested as the precarious foundation of an entire culture's sense of itself. Beware. Ingenious humanity cannot truly construct its way to a glory beyond its natural place in the cosmos. That is a message also encoded in one of Bruegel's favourite subjects: the Tower of Babel.

BABEL: A CULTURE OF VAINGLORY

To have an overly high sense of your own self-worth was, in Bruegel's day, known as vainglory, and it was recognized as a serious human failing. Montaigne discusses the problem in his essay 'On Presumption', in which such false glory is contrasted with true glory, and humanity is found (in his estimation) to be much inclined to distorted self-imaging and hence also to the ambition that vainglory generates.[35]

This kind of prideful desire for fame seems, according to the Bible, to have characterized all of the early descendants of Noah (Genesis 11:1–9). Settled in the plains of Shinar, they took a group decision to 'make a name for' themselves by building a great tower that would reach as high as Heaven. God inspected their work and his response registers a sense of unease: 'this is only the beginning of what they will do; and nothing that they propose to do will now be impossible for them.' The biblical story implies that mankind does indeed possess a boundless ability to create, to indeed rise nearer to the heavens, but also that this is displeasing to God. To put an end to humanity's grandiose ambitions, God confuses their language so that instead of one universal tongue, they speak many. Linguistic fragmentation thwarts the cooperation on design and artisanship necessary for a great cultural endeavour; the tower project is abandoned.

This really rather odd tale was elaborated upon over the centuries, gaining a star figure – Nimrod, tyrannical king of the Jews, who cultivated in his people a contempt for God – and a location, Babylon.[36] By Bruegel's day, both person and place were established parts of the story in its now-standard association with vainglory and pride, and indeed had taken on lives of their own in signifying arrogance: Nimrod the very embodiment of proud impiety, figuring with other examples of extreme hubris in Dante's *Inferno*, and Babylon a city where pride had reigned supreme. In Bruegel's own circle, Babylon had been used by his teacher and father-in-law, Pieter Coecke van Aelst, as the setting for an allegory of the sin of pride in a tapestry series illustrating, at huge scale, the Seven Deadly Sins.[37] Pride, in Coecke's triumphal procession of sin, is

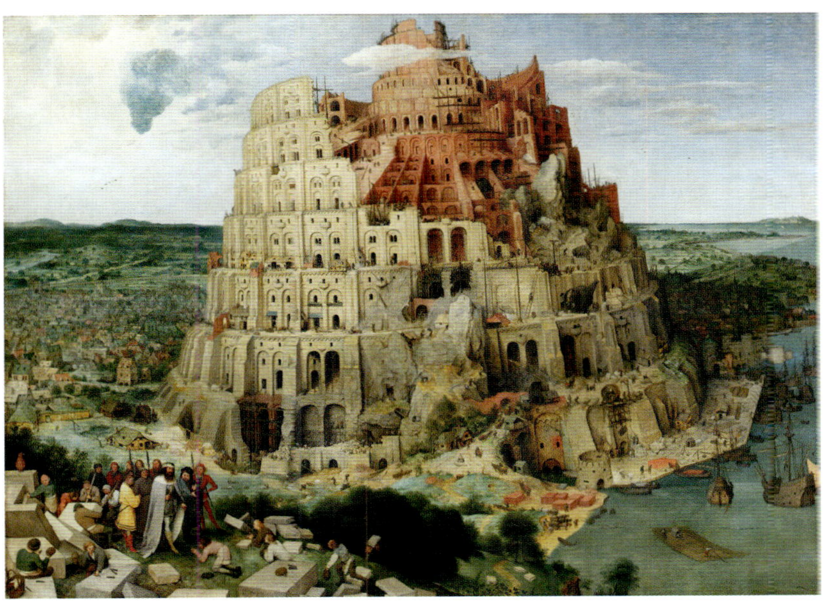

accompanied by the figures of sedition and ambition, and rides
a chariot pulled by the seven-headed apocalyptic dragon.
Alongside the dragon marches Nimrod himself, while the
procession is led by a personification of vainglory.

Like humanity after Babel, artists of Bruegel's day possessed
many languages in which to represent this story and its implications. At the opposite scale from Coecke's allegorical
tapestry, the Tower of Babel appeared regularly in illumina-
tions to Bibles or books of hours. It was at this small size that
Pieter Bruegel himself first engaged with the subject. While in
Rome in the early 1550s, he collaborated with the famous
miniaturist Giulio Clovio on a Tower of Babel painted not
in a book but upon ivory: Clovio had their little work in his
possession when he died.[38] Then, a decade later and living

31 Pieter Bruegel, *Tower of Babel*, 1563, oil on panel.

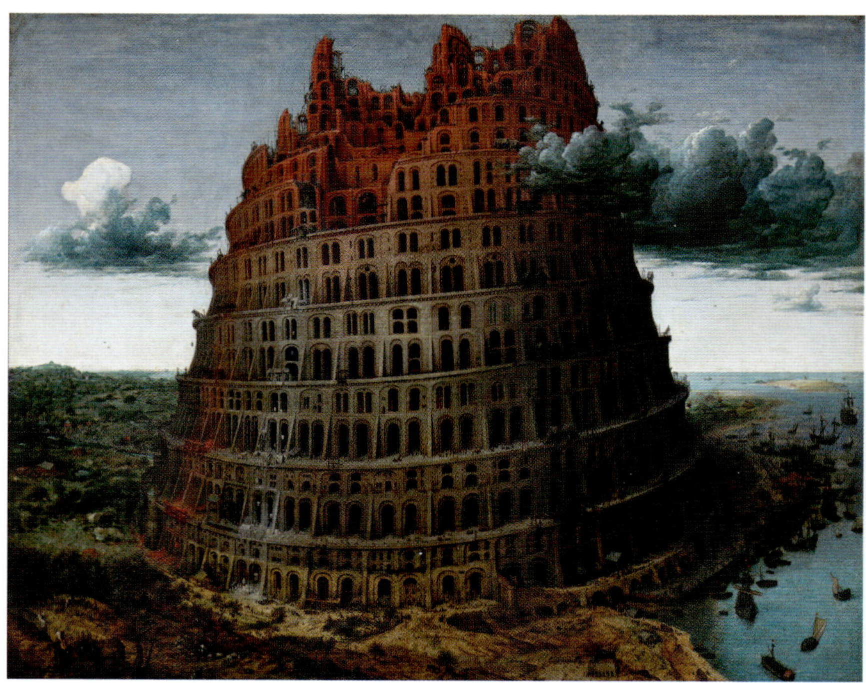

in Antwerp, Bruegel painted two full-scale works showing this subject. The earlier of the two, dated 1563 (illus. 31), was destined for the same collection as the *Months* and the *Christ Carrying the Cross* – that of Niclaes Jonghelinck – and hung with them in Jonghelinck's suburban villa. Bruegel's *Babel* is similar to those works both in dimensions and in being incredibly packed with visual incident. Its surface is worked with an immense amount of very small but fascinating detail. The picture expects to be examined slowly, closely, intimately. This is paradoxical for in fact it is miniatures, like Bruegel's work with Clovio, that usually call for intimate and hyper-detailed viewing, while large paintings like the *Babel* expect us to step

32 Pieter Bruegel, *The Tower of Babel*, oil on panel.

back and view them in their entirety. But what Pieter Bruegel produced in his *Babel* for Jonghelinck is a strange hybrid that combines the large (in terms of the work's dimensions), indeed the monumental (in terms of its subject), and the tiny and intimate (in terms of its detailing and the viewing it constructs). Perhaps it is only by demanding such protracted visual absorption from the beholder that a painting can succeed in conveying the monumental folly that is Nimrod's tower to Heaven.

Babel's tower is an unwieldy, impossible monument, a thing of beauty and also a monstrosity. European cities did often have a single structure – the cathedral – that dwarfed every other building within the city walls, and Bruegel surely intends his viewer to recognize this parallel, for his tower sits at the heart of a walled Flemish city, a perfectly familiar-looking place. The difference is, of course, that a cathedral's purpose is to reify a cosmic structure in which mankind is puny and God is great, and to contain ceremonies that constantly repeat that recognition. Babel's tower does not glorify God's greatness: it rivals it. It stretches to Heaven to enable its builders to 'make a name for themselves'. In creating this mad rivalry with God, the Flemish Babylonians have also consumed their own city. All energy here is directed towards one end: reaching higher into the heavens. Every type of human labour that we can identify is geared towards some aspect of this building, every boat in the harbour appears to be bearing construction material, and there is no sign of any other trade or activity. On the right side of the painting, a large section of the city is literally overshadowed by the vast structure its inhabitants are maniacally intent on creating.

In Bruegel's second, smaller Babel painting, the tower's growth seems infinite, beyond the scope of human imagination (illus. 32). It has become an impersonal, isolated entity, occupying even more of the picture's surface than the 1563 version, its upper tiers extending far past the clouds to graze the upper limits of the picture's surface. Lacking even a surrounding city, it is oddly divorced from all human scale or sense of habitation, its builders meaningless dots on its surface. This second tower is darker, more self-enclosed and forbidding. Jonghelinck's first version, though, is still what we might now term relatable. The story's key human figure, King Nimrod, appears in the left foreground, positioned by Bruegel in a place, and in a manner, that seems to echo the mourners at the right side of Jonghelinck's *Calvary*.[39] Like them, he binds humanity to the inhuman eruption at the painting's centre. But if those holy figures had modelled a human sense of compassion for the beholder to emulate, Nimrod and his attendants model the cruelty of pride, and the human distance that it creates. Nimrod's pride signals its object, the tower, as a thing of threatening awesomeness, not of promise. In other artists' images of the construction of Babel, Nimrod consults with his architects; here, he simply lords it over his masons, who grovel on the earth before him. The legendary Nimrod was often described as a giant, and Bruegel makes him just slightly larger than his companions, but we sense that this Nimrod thinks of himself as a giant among men, that his vainglory is encouraged by his courtiers, and that he rehearses his own self-ascribed greatness when he gestures his puny underlings to the ground.

The real star of the production of Jonghelinck's *Babel*, of course, is not Nimrod: the king, like his city, is dwarfed by the tower that rises in the centre of the picture, spreading itself across our viewing horizon. Yet, in spite of its gigantic scale, the tower is also alive with humanity. At every level, in every part of the structure, people are at work – chopping and hauling, climbing and carrying, cutting and cooking and occasionally resting – so that the tower fascinates the closely engaged beholder in the same way that an anthill does: hundreds of tiny creatures all madly engaged in tasks whose purpose seems, in the end, obscure to us. For the tower is also a wonderfully senseless creation, both in the story as we know it and in the building as we see it. Bruegel's constructive imagination has created a monument so impossibly contradictory that it consumes itself in the very process of being built.[40]

For is the tower being built at all? Perhaps it is being carved. What seemed at first a man-made monstrosity is, we gradually realize, also a mountain, an impossibly singular natural outcropping alongside the river, whose great rocky crags are serving as the quarry for materials employed in building the other sections. Humanity is not merely building, but is working a strange metamorphosis upon an object in nature. In some places the transformation is complete: in the more finished portion at the left, for instance, the tower seems to have been turned into an apartment block inhabited by whole families, with plants growing in window boxes and laundry hanging out to dry. At the right, where men are still doing a kind of battle with the natural materials, Bruegel gives us a full inventory of every type of equipment and expertise known in his day for cutting and heavy lifting, including a harbour crane being used to hoist blocks of stone from one level of the tower to the next (illus. 33). While the cladding

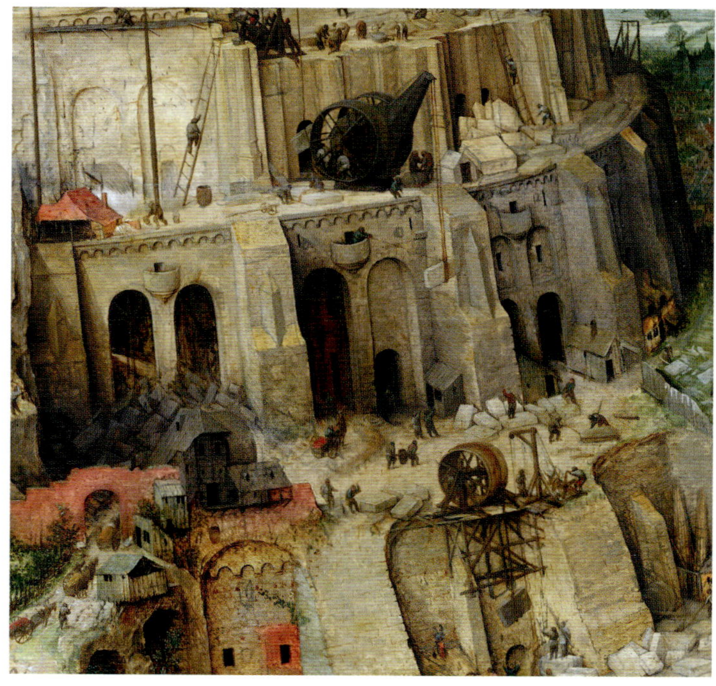

of the structure is of this quarried and cut stone, its interior
is made of bricks, piles of which have been unloaded around
the quayside.[41] We understand the complexities of how building materials are used here because Bruegel manages to show
the tower inside and out, its elevation but also its mad, maze-
like interior plan, which seems to extend ever further inward
even as the building climbs ever upward.

It had always been challenging for artists to imagine an
architectural design that could produce a tower far higher
than anything in their own world. Illuminators had tended
to think in terms of spiralled or ziggurat-like structures.
Bruegel, though, took as his model a real building that was

33 Construction work: detail from *The Tower of Babel*, shown in illus. 31.

not in fact impossibly high but which had a particular meaning to his culture: the Colosseum. He would have seen that famous monument himself during his stay in Rome, but, equally importantly, Jonghelinck and his guests would also have known the Colosseum's appearance from several series of prints, produced by Bruegel's own publisher Hieronymus Cock in the decade before this painting, which illustrated the ruins of ancient Rome.[42] Rome had been a great city that had risen too high and had fallen to ruin, the Colosseum an especially proud monument of that culture's glory that was now abandoned and disintegrating. Cock's prints had emphasized the Colosseum's current fragmentation, the way that nature was overtaking culture as plants flourished in ragged stone- and brickwork.

Bruegel's tower is, paradoxically, the Colosseum both before and after its perfect glory, for even as its upper levels are being raised higher and higher, its foundation is crumbling. On the left side, the base sinks into the swampy ground. New supports are being devised, but they will be useless, for time and hubris are dooming this construct, its growing weight gradually pushing it back into the earth from which it was created. The Tower of Babel is on its way to becoming a monumental ruin, for the products of vainglory, which foolishly challenge the God-given order of things, have no real foundation. Searching for fame and grandeur – to make a name for themselves – the Babylonians have only written the script for their own destruction.

CODA: PROUD SAUL

Your first step towards the way of life as a Christian soldier, Erasmus told readers of his *Enchiridion*, was to 'cast away the armour of proud Saul'.[43] Another Saul, though: not the one who would become Paul, but an Old Testament hero, the chosen one, anointed by Samuel to be prince of God's people in Israel (Samuel 9:16–10:24). Saul was tall and handsome and enjoyed God's favour, but he also had immense pride, and in his pride he disobeyed the Lord: a terrible error. He regretted it and obeyed God again; he even, paradoxically, erected a monument to himself as the Lord's most obedient servant; but all in vain. Disobedience to God's will is the ultimate form of pride, the one shared by Lucifer and Adam and now by Saul who, like them, will be crushed for thinking that he had the right to a will of his own.[44]

And so, in Bruegel's *Suicide of Saul* (illus. 34) we are in another mountain pass, with another army – this one not marching through but engaged in battle. Saul and his old enemy the Philistines have been locked into a great contest for the Israelites' territory, fought on Mount Gilboa. Men by their hundreds, anonymous in their armour, are tightly packed into the small space between steep hills. Some have broken ranks and are fleeing the scene, for the battle is basically over and the Philistines have won. Among the casualties have been Saul's three sons. But everything takes place far below our viewpoint, so that we are like the philosopher who, as Seneca put it, looks down upon the narrow world and says to himself, 'is this the plot that so many tribes portion out by fire and sword? How ludicrous are their frontiers!'[45] In 1589 Bruegel's friend Ortelius would use this passage as an inscription on

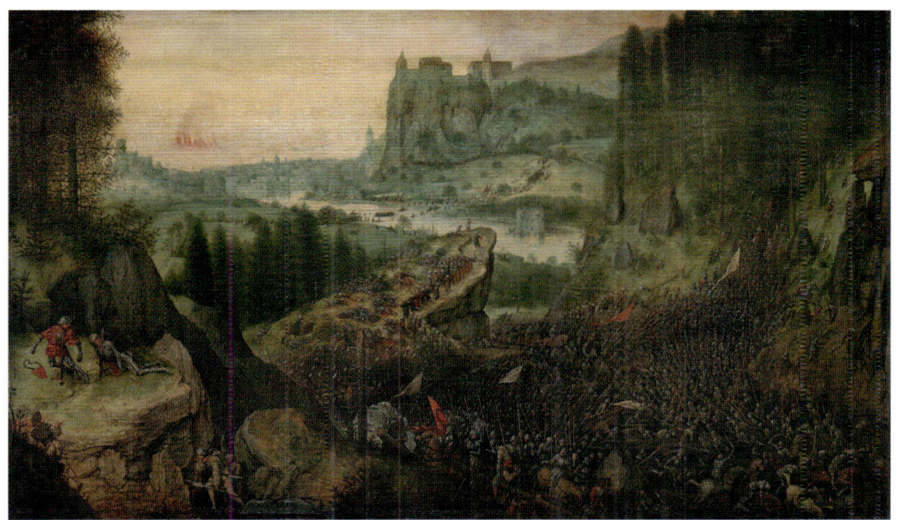

a map of the world; here, decades earlier, Bruegel paints a
world landscape that thematizes the vanity of doing battle
for territory, and how it is the downfall of proud Saul.[46]

But where is Saul, once the chosen one? Nimrod-like, he
is isolated and near to us at the left, apart from the furious
activity at the painting's centre. Saul's time as the one who
commands action is at an end. Fearful, in defeat, that his
enemies will 'make sport of' him, he – along with his armour-
bearer – falls upon his sword. This final fall is still guided by
his pride. There is no heroism to it, only the cursed outcome
of a life driven away from God by the besetting human
failing.

34 Pieter Bruegel, *Suicide of Saul*, 1562, oil on panel.

FOUR

Triumph of War: Humanity in a World of Chaos

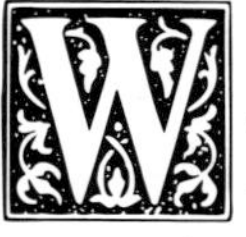HEN SAUL'S ARMY meets the Philistines, their deadly encounter takes place within a natural world carefully characterized by Bruegel in his *Suicide of Saul* as lush, verdant and peaceable (illus. 34). Humanity creates a pocket of chaos within an orderly cosmos. As the two sides clash, one armoured man against another, it is impossible to distinguish with any certainty who belongs to which army or, at a more personal level, which individual is attacking whom. Although we know the story, and thus the basic identity of these groups, we cannot narrate the individual events of battle based on what Bruegel shows us. The conflict is simply a sea of undifferentiated madness.

This is, however, not true at all of Bruegel's greatest battle scene, the painting known as the *Triumph of Death* (illus. 35), in which a vast army of human skeletons has come to earth to obliterate humanity. The clang of heavy bells above a ruined church at the upper left heralds their coming, and a white-shrouded company on the church porch blow trumpets in a cruel parody of the angelic trumpets that herald the Day of Judgement, the Christian end of time. For there is no judgement here, no joyous salvation for some group of the righteous.[1] There is a 'hell' of sorts – the central black box with its mouth-like gateway and round staring eyes, spitting fire and hosting demons; but it is merely a wheeled pageantry car, rolling along with the advancing skeletal regiment.[2] As a theatrical prop, its job is to represent the terror of a death that offers no actual afterlife, for Bruegel's end-times are resolutely worldly and allow for no hope. The troops of death are taking on every type of living person in every way that a modern, disciplined army might do, each encounter brutally distinguished and each victim clearly marked by their executioner. Figures of death behead people and hang them, pull them into the water and push them off cliffs and hunt them with dogs. In the foreground, skeletons slit throats and attack with scythes and hatchets and spears; they capture one group of people in a net and herd the main throng of the living into a great box at the right with an opened wall, resembling a mousetrap. On its roof, a lone skeleton beats out the marching rhythm on a set of drums, keeping in order the troops of death amassed behind their coffin-lid shields on either side of the fatal trap.

In the bottom right corner, news of the invasion has just begun to penetrate the group gathered to finish their dessert, which they had planned to eat on square trenchers of the type Bruegel once painted as roundels (illus. 36). One skeleton came to the banquet wearing the face mask of a living man, but he is only there to destroy the pleasures of the table, watched in horror by a fool who scrambles to hide under the table. The fool is the only one who, we think, might survive the carnage. Nearby, the musical couple so happily absorbed in one another are accompanied by a skeleton playing the tunes of their demise.

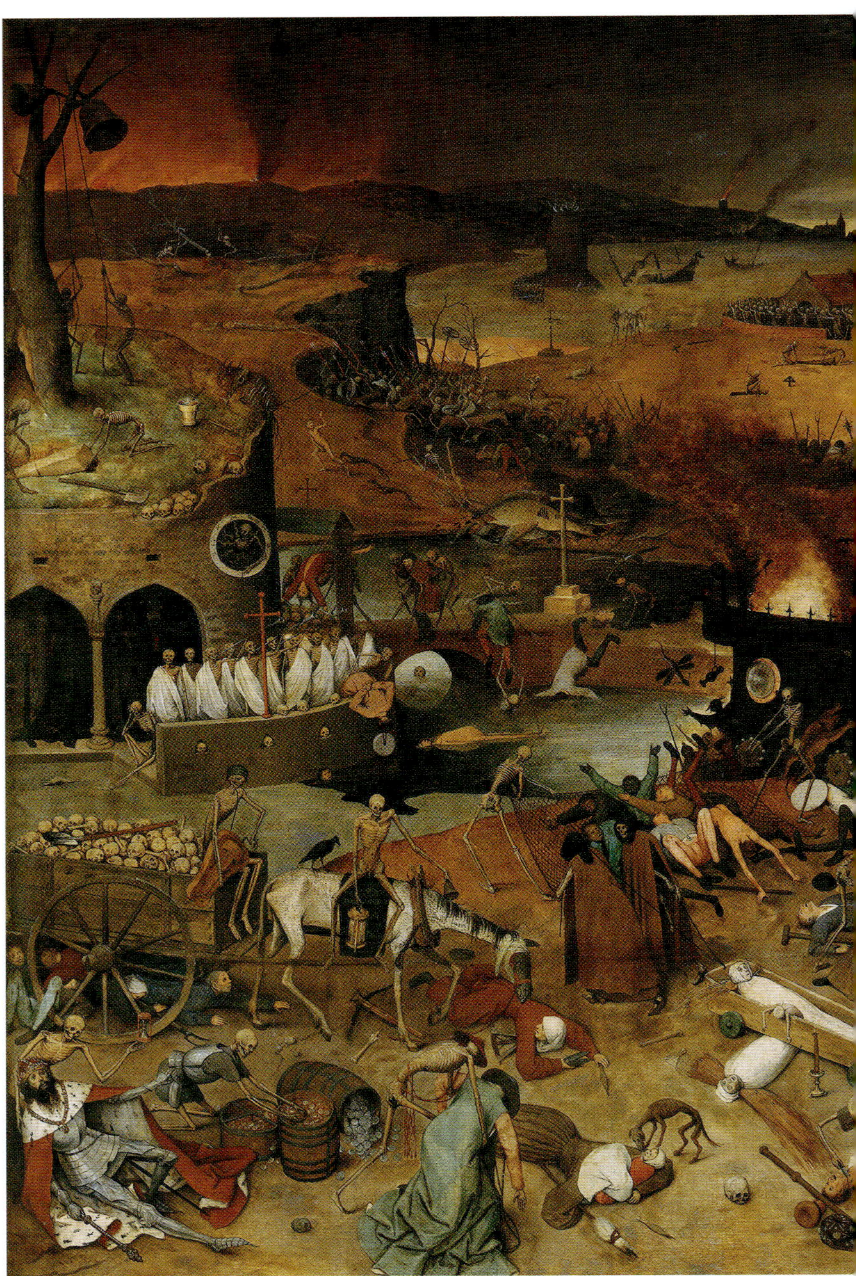

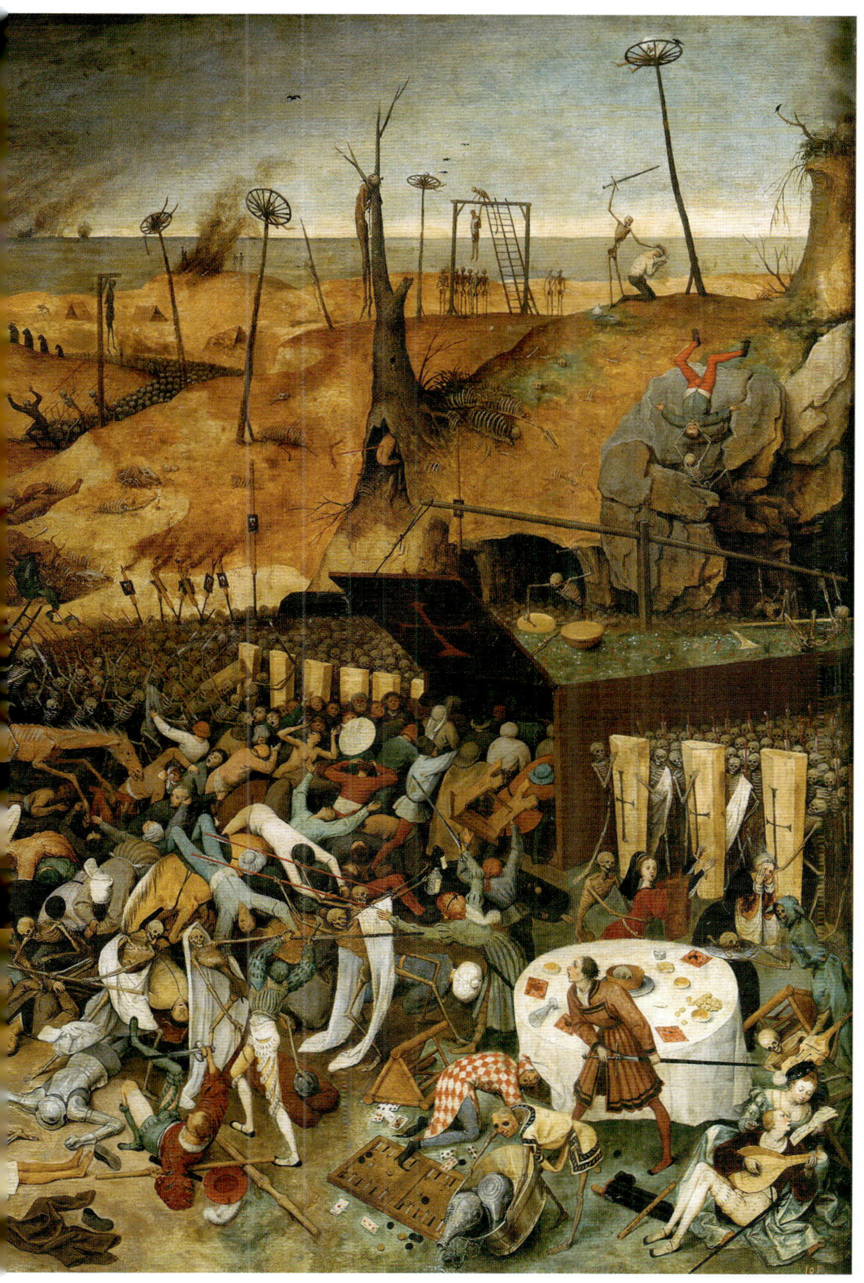
35 Pieter Bruegel, *Triumph of Death*, oil on panel.

Bruegel has been at pains to make the company of the dying as inclusive as possible, taking in men and women, old and young, social types from emperor to lame beggar, occupations from churchman to soldier, and all the peoples of the known world. Beside the central wheeled hellmouth, two skeletons with a net have scooped up three Africans along with three Europeans. Directly adjacent to the hellmouth's studded wheel, the flat white hat on a dead woman signals that she is a Roma; another hatted Roma is among the group fleeing into the giant trap at the right, as are turbaned Turks. Few of the living fight back, for even among the armed soldiers it is clear that resistance is futile: as one mercenary in elegantly slashed clothing raises his sword to smite a skeleton, that deathly figure has hooked around his leg a trip-cord that will

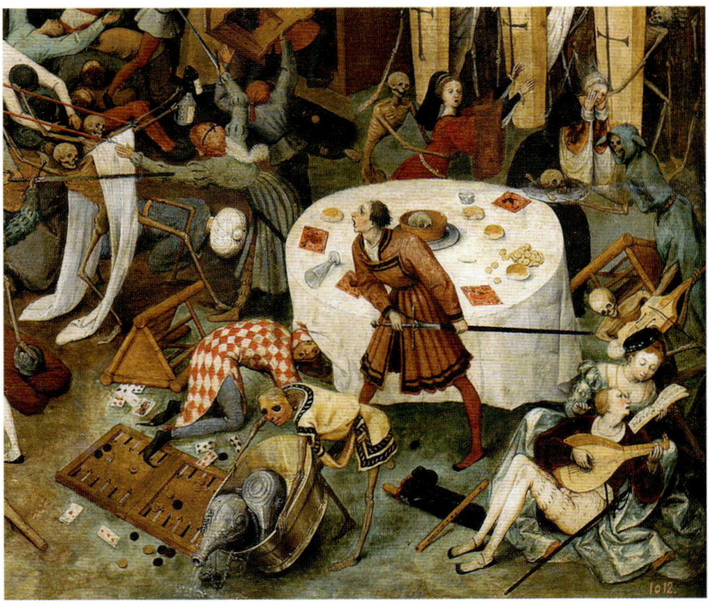

36 Interrupted banquet: detail from *Triumph of Death*.

bring him down. Death is ubiquitous, pitiless and often brutal. Death is, moreover, human: many of the skeletons still bear a fair amount of their flesh, marking them as not just signifiers of death but also as fighting dead men, men come from death to gather the rest of their human fellows into their own ranks.

In this painting Bruegel gives us not the scene of a single battle, but rather a war that has consumed the world, near and far, known and unknown. The browned landscape beyond the foreground skirmishes is utterly barren, the earth naked, the few skeletal trees so blasted that they seem never to have lived at all. The waters are nothing but aquatic graveyards. Further regiments of skeletons move through the mid-ground terrain, engaging with small doomed bands of the living. Over the edge of the distant hills at the left rises the ominous glow of fires consuming whatever it was that lay beyond them, while where ocean meets sky at the centre, smoke billows from burning ships. There is nowhere for humanity to escape to. In a war between life and death, death's victory is absolute.

Encounters between the dead and the living were a common subject in visual art in the generations before Bruegel produced this painting, but there is nothing approaching the ferocity or the utter devastation depicted here. Death normally comes for individuals one at a time, interrupting them in the midst of life with a light tap on the shoulder, the wave of a skull or an hourglass. In the famous Dance of Death series of woodcuts by Hans Holbein, which Bruegel knew, figures of death momentarily join in their victims' occupation, or wittily mimic the poses, clothing and even expressions of those whose lives they are taking. No such levity interrupts Bruegel's terrifying vision. Even when a skeleton dons a cardinal's hat and mimics the pose of his victim in the left foreground of the scene, it is unfunny: the skeleton's pose also is the careful mirror of a ravenous dog nearby that is about to eat a dead infant. Nobody is laughing at this.

In fact, Bruegel seems to have taken his primary inspiration in this painting not from the iconography of death but from that of warfare. Most easily available were German prints recording famous battles, but closer to hand and more dramatic was the great tapestry series of the Conquest of Tunis that Pieter Coecke van Aelst had been working on in 1548–50, when Bruegel was probably in his workshop, and that had been on display in Antwerp's cathedral in 1555.[3] These monumental works typically combined more detailed depictions of conflict in the foreground with an expansive mid-ground where further movements and positioning of troops could be laid out, and a view to the sea in the distance (illus. 37). The tapestries' intent, of course, was to glorify the combats they depicted and to celebrate the deeds of the great leader, Charles V, who commissioned them. Bruegel's *Triumph of Death* completely reverses the rhetoric of its source, turning 'triumph' into nightmare, and in so doing, connecting warfare not with glory but with annihilation.

In prints, textiles and also paintings, artists everywhere on the continent had responded to the wars that raged nearly constantly in sixteenth-century Europe. While art historians have wrestled with the problem of whether Pieter Bruegel's images of a war-torn world, including the *Triumph of Death*, could refer directly to the years leading up to the Revolt of the Netherlands, including the Duke of Alba's atrocities, that connection is not necessary.[4] Bruegel's travels to Italy via

France had brought him into contact with many people and places grievously affected by war, directly or indirectly. Most obviously, he was in Rome just a quarter of a century after the sack of that city (1527) had left perhaps 20 per cent of its population dead, piles of bodies rotting on streets and in churches, and he would have heard about those terrible events from his colleague Giulio Clovio and others.[5] This sack of Rome, while extreme, was not atypical of sixteenth-century warfare, for it involved the siege of a major city, was initiated by a very large army (that of Charles V) whose troops had not been paid or provisioned, and resulted in huge loss of civilian life and destruction of property. Describing Italy in these years, Francesco Guicciardini wrote that 'one saw nothing but scenes of infinite slaughter, plunder and destruction of multitudes of towns and cities, attended with the licentiousness of soldiers no less destructive to friends than foes.'[6] That sense of soldiers rampaging against an entire population, limitless violence, and the lack of any meaningful division between friend and enemy, is part of what Bruegel's painting captures.

Bruegel's visual discourse on war also joins that of writers of his period, who approached the topic from the angles of politics, theology, morality and legality.[7] What, they asked, drove human beings to make war? Was warfare a part of our very nature, or was it in some sense unnatural; in either case, was it inevitable? Erasmus, like many Humanists, detested all forms of war and repeatedly argued that it was fundamentally against both human nature and the naturally orderly cosmos. In his commentary on the adage 'War is sweet to those who have not tried it', expanded into a lengthy essay in 1515 and

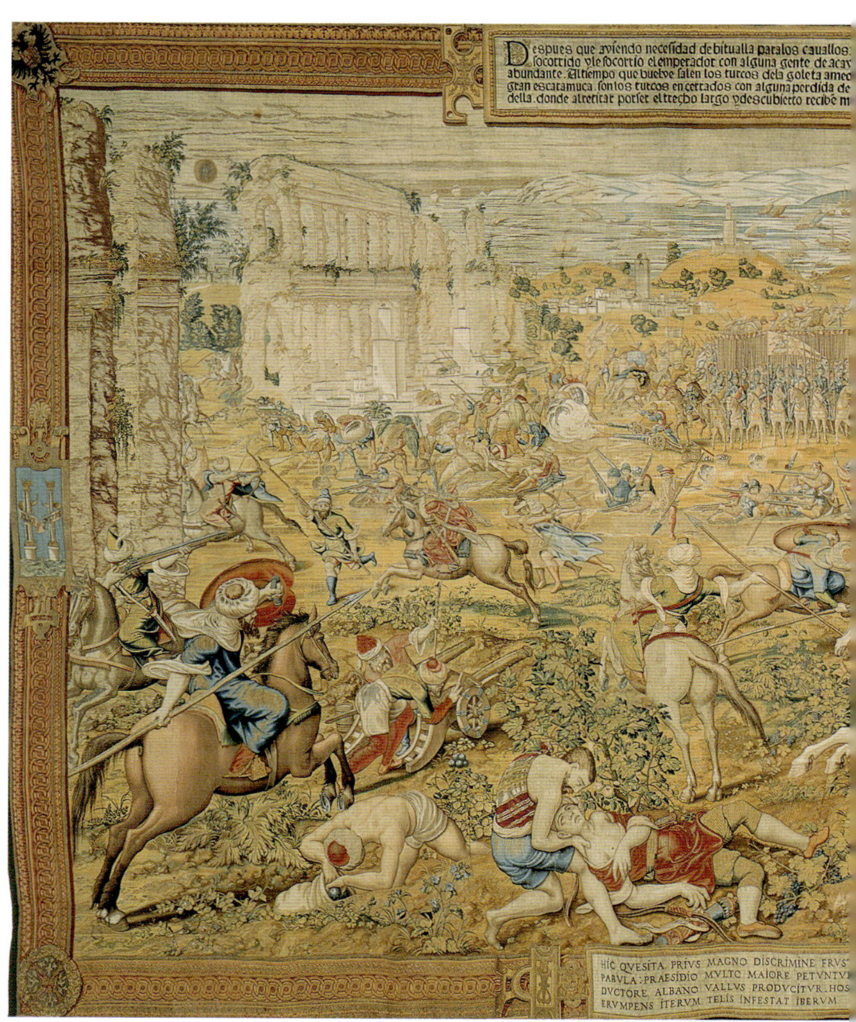

Despues que aviendo necesidad de bitualla paralos cauallos
socorrido yle socorrio el emperador con alguna gente de aca
abundante. Al tiempo que buelve salen los turcos dela goleta ame
gran escaramuca. son los turcos encerrados con alguna perdida de
della. donde alretitar porser eltrecho largo ydescubierto recibe m

HIC QVESITA PRIVS MAGNO DISCRIMINE FRVST
PABVLA: PRAESIDIO MVLTO MAIORE PETVNTVR
DVCTORE ALBANO VALLVS PRODVCITVR. HOS
ERVMPENS ITERVM TELIS INFESTAT IBERVM

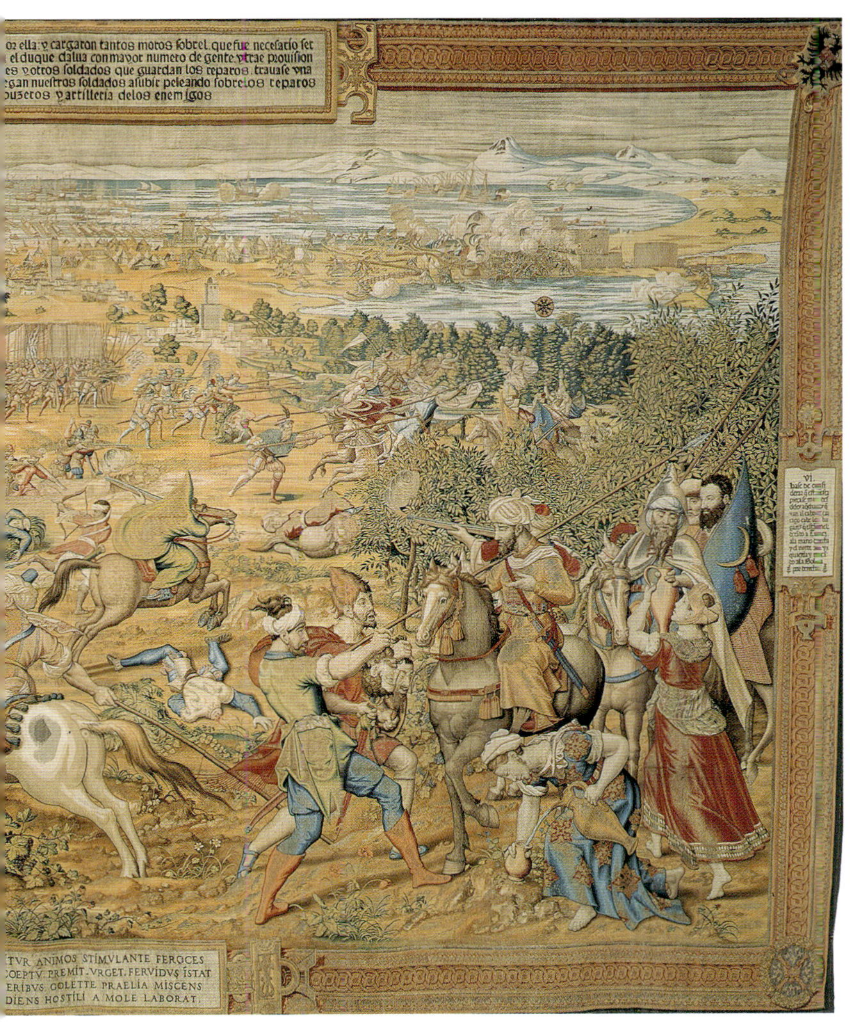

37 Pieter Coecke van Aelst, woven in workshop of Willem de Pannemaker,
The Quest for Fodder, c. 1546–54, from the Conquest of Tunis series, tapestry:
wool, silk, and gold- and silver-wrapped threads.

republished many times as a separate booklet in various languages, he claimed that human beings are made by nature to exist in harmony with one another: we have reason, we have speech, we are mutually dependent and we moreover have no natural means of attack or defence but must invent such things. All of these parts of our innate character should encourage us to friendship, not enmity.[8] Erasmus was taking his terms here from the work of Seneca, one of his favourite ancient writers, who in his essay 'On Anger' similarly argued that human beings are made for friendship and mutual help.[9] But anger, along with ambition, pride and folly, makes us go against our true natures and turn to violence against one another.

War has, moreover, a generally corrupting influence on those who engage in it. Because it is so deeply inimical to human nature, Erasmus believes, it actually changes individuals and also societies. It ruins moral standards. Humanists accepted that some individuals might have a nature that was overly aggressive, often due to the unfortunate fact of planetary influence: being born under Mars just affects people that way. However, their modified astrology held that, thanks to free will, a person could and should overcome the destiny to which they were born, as part of a general upward striving towards perfection.[10] The alternative, as always, was descent into the impulsive, bodily, corrupted side of human nature. In the Utopia envisioned by Erasmus' friend Thomas More, the perfect people of the perfect society loathe war 'as an activity fit only for beasts yet practiced by no kind of beast so constantly as man'.[11] When war is unavoidable, the Utopians hire mercenary soldiers from a neighbouring country whose inhabitants are little better than savages, who value money over human life and who have no respect for kinship or friendship. The fine citizens of Utopia consider these men to be 'abominable and impious people' and do not care if they die.[12] This is one of the more disturbing passages of More's book, laying bare an unsettling ease of dehumanizing those who fight, particularly those who, like the mercenary soldiers in More's and Bruegel's Europe, fight for payment. Those who do not value human life, we learn, forfeit their own lives' value.

In one of his later works, written in 1530, Erasmus took on the issue of how it may happen that people who ought to be good Christians come to justify the killing of others. At stake at this moment was, in particular, war against the Turks. Turks, Erasmus states bluntly, are indeed human beings; yet some people claim 'that anyone is allowed to kill a Turk, as one would a mad dog, for no better reason than that he is a Turk'.[13] The logical extension of this, Erasmus warns, would be to claim that anybody may kill a Jew. This would clearly be wrong, Erasmus is certain, yet once we begin viewing the lives of one group as worthless because of who they are, we can extend that to other groups. And the next thing you know, Christians are committing atrocities against other Christians, the Pope himself is urging warfare and we are claiming that this too is right.[14] All of these things Erasmus saw as occurring in his own day.

In Bruegel's painting, the terribly human skeletons are disposed about their boundless battlefield in units, like the modern armies of Bruegel's time, marching and searching and taking prisoners and executing them, attacking but never retreating. Those of the still-living who have been variously labelled as less than human and whose deaths this society might not have mourned – the Turks, the Africans, the cripple, even the mercenary soldiers – perish alongside the young mother and her baby, the humble pilgrim and the loving couple. All are equal before death's regiments when the world is consumed by the insanity of war. Christian religion offers no respite, as the Church itself has been co-opted by the implacable forces of destruction. At the upper right corner, a blindfolded man meets his death under the sword of a single skeleton while clutching a crucifix, praying for the promise of an afterlife. But those promises seem to have been fully obliterated in Bruegel's secular apocalypse.[15] The way the world truly ends, as Bruegel tells it, is when the nature of humanity is so corrupted and consumed by war's violence that all life gives way before death.

FIRE AND ICE

Greed, envy, pride and ambition all play their parts in causing wars, but the real evil at the root of violence is anger. So when Bruegel came to invent an allegory of that sin in 1557, to be published as an engraving in the following year as part of his Seven Deadly Sins series, his imagination turned to combat (illus. 38). Striding forward from a field-tent, the personification of Anger is a fully armed woman, bearing a sword in one hand and a burning torch in the other. Beside her, two heavily armoured figures wield a giant knife with which they are slicing through a crowd of mostly naked figures. The rest of Anger's infantry, armed with hooks and pikes and a drinking jug, advance behind a large wheeled shield. One bird-faced soldier reaches out from behind the shield to attack an armed,

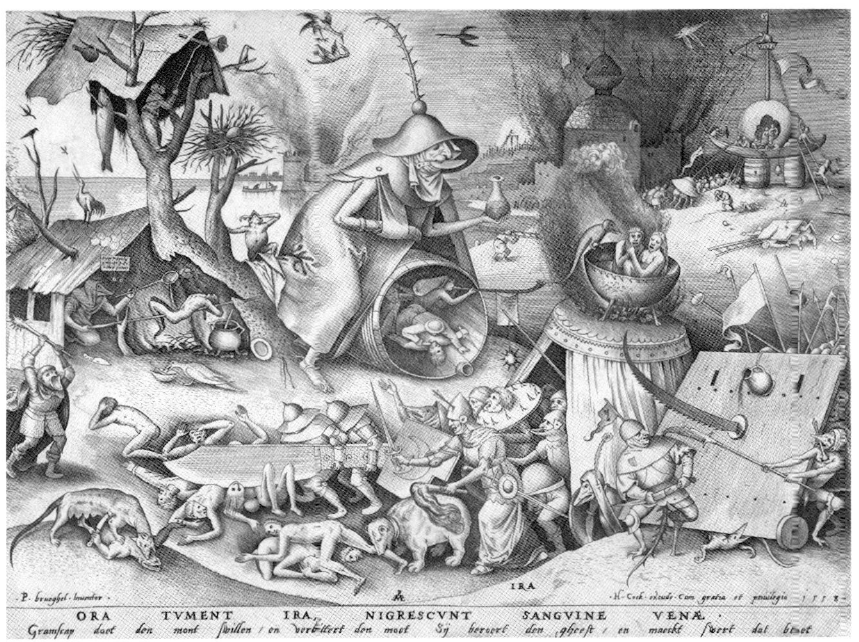

and maimed, demon standing before them. On a hill behind this unit, another group of soldiers seems to be moving to do battle with a bizarre ship settled atop two barrels, its cargo a broken egg. Nearby, and continuing along the coastline, towers and fortresses go up in flames; but elsewhere in the scene, fires are being used to cook human beings, whom demons roast on a spit or boil in a cauldron. For here, unlike in the *Triumph of Death*, we are in a truly Boschian universe where that which is serious – anger – is treated with humour and mockery rather than terror. Grim tasks are performed by ludicrous beings who may carry meanings that, while germane to the subjects of war and anger, are also presented in a way that showcases Bruegel's wit.[16] For instance, the giant in the middle of the composition,

38 Pieter van der Heyden after Bruegel, *Anger*, 1558, engraving from the Seven Deadly Sins series.

straddling a barrel and carrying a knife in his mouth, is 'armed to the teeth' – a proverb Bruegel would visualize again in his *Netherlandish Proverbs* (see illus. 6). And yet within the barrel, one armed and angry man is slitting the throat of another, and this is not funny. All of the prints in the Seven Deadly Sins series have this ludic element overlaying the performances of their central vice, but only in Anger is the comedy uncomfortably linked to battle and bloodshed.

Anger is a basic, almost physiological, aspect of human nature, easy to succumb to when an injury to self-respect or self-interest is perceived, difficult to fully guard against.[17] This is why the concluding section of Erasmus' *Enchiridion* concerns the vital struggle to control this emotion. 'Do not trust yourself in anything when you are agitated,' Erasmus warns his reader. 'Remember that there is no more difference between a madman and one who is in a fit of anger than there is between chronic and momentary madness.'[18] For anger, to Erasmus and many other thinkers, is not just another human failing. It is the one that plays on the border between reason and unreason, edging the mind from the former towards the latter, and thence to a crazed violence. 'The most hideous and frenzied of all the emotions', Seneca had called anger, 'all excitement and impulse. Raving with a desire that is utterly inhuman for instruments of pain and reparations in blood . . .'.[19] Thus are violence, anger and madness intertwined in ancient thought and the Humanist discourses that drew from them.

To link anger and actual madness was not such a great leap in the early modern concept of human psychology. Mental disturbance was understood not simply as a divergence from some norm, or as an opposite to that norm, but rather as an *excess* of otherwise normal inclinations.[20] Distraction, lunacy, melancholy, frenzy and madness were all terms conceived of as describing various states that were, hopefully, temporary, some relatively benign and others more dangerous. Madness could also be linked to the idea of folly, but only in particular ways. The 'natural fool' was a person who was, in some sense, mentally deficient. He might be quiet and passive, in which case he was an 'innocent', or he could be loud and disruptive and even angry, a 'frantic'.[21] He was most definitely not the same as the Fool beloved of courtly environments and Humanist texts, who from a perspective of assumed innocence could speak simple truths that would be unacceptable if voiced by 'normal' persons. This is folly as rhetorical ruse. The Humanist fool was a guise, a figure with little or no real psychological debility, whereas the natural fool was simply a nuisance: Thomas More himself had a madman publicly beaten for causing disturbance near his home.[22]

More's friend Erasmus lays out a neat distinction in his *Praise of Folly*, as voiced by Dame Folly herself: 'The nature of insanity,' she says, 'is surely twofold. One kind is sent from hell by the vengeful furies whenever they let loose their snakes and assail the hearts of men with lust for war, insatiable thirst for gold . . . or some other sort of evil . . . The other is quite different, desirable above everything, and is known to come from me.'[23] The folly that drives humanity to wage war is a kind of madness, driven by an angry violence that is often propelled by avarice. And this seems to be very much akin to what Pieter Bruegel depicts in his famous *Dulle Griet* (Mad Meg) of 1561 (illus. 39). Bruegel need not have read Erasmus'

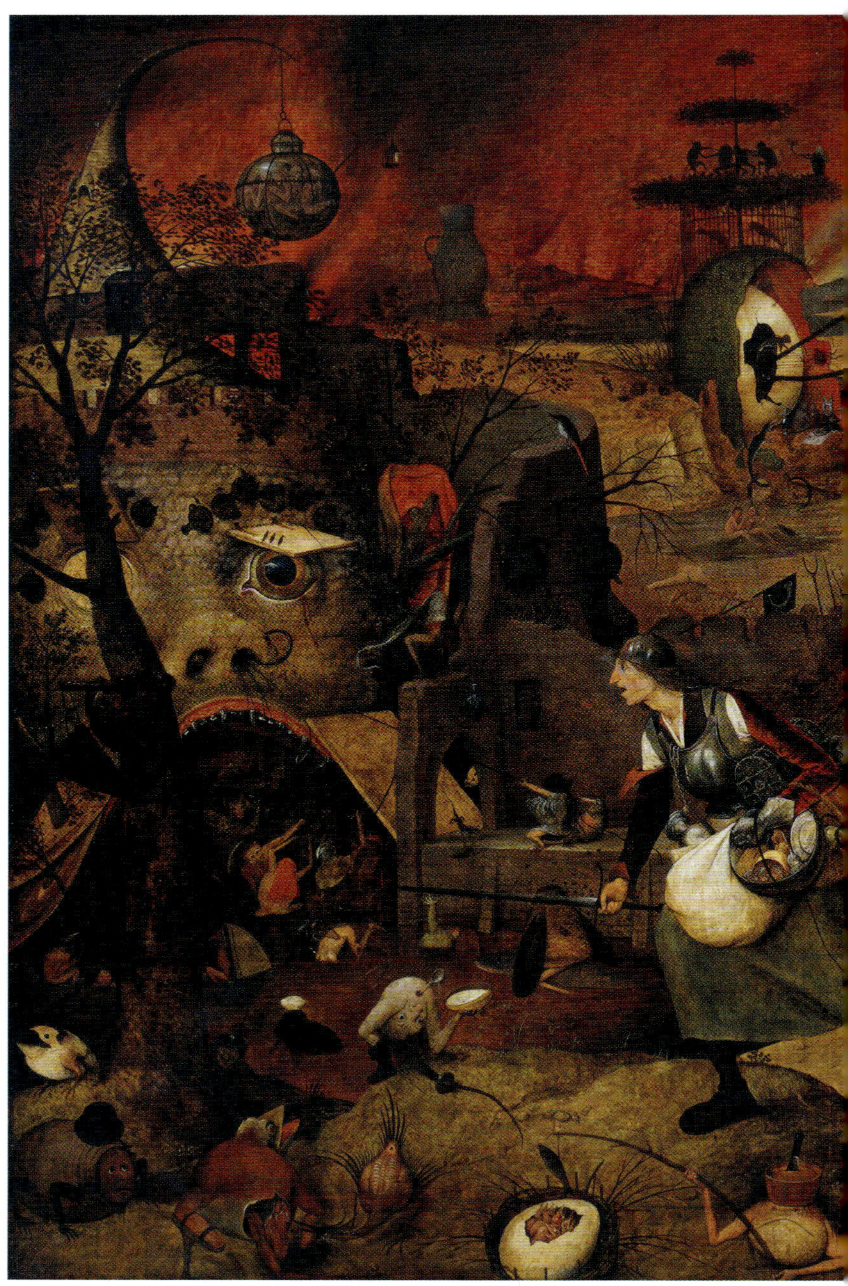

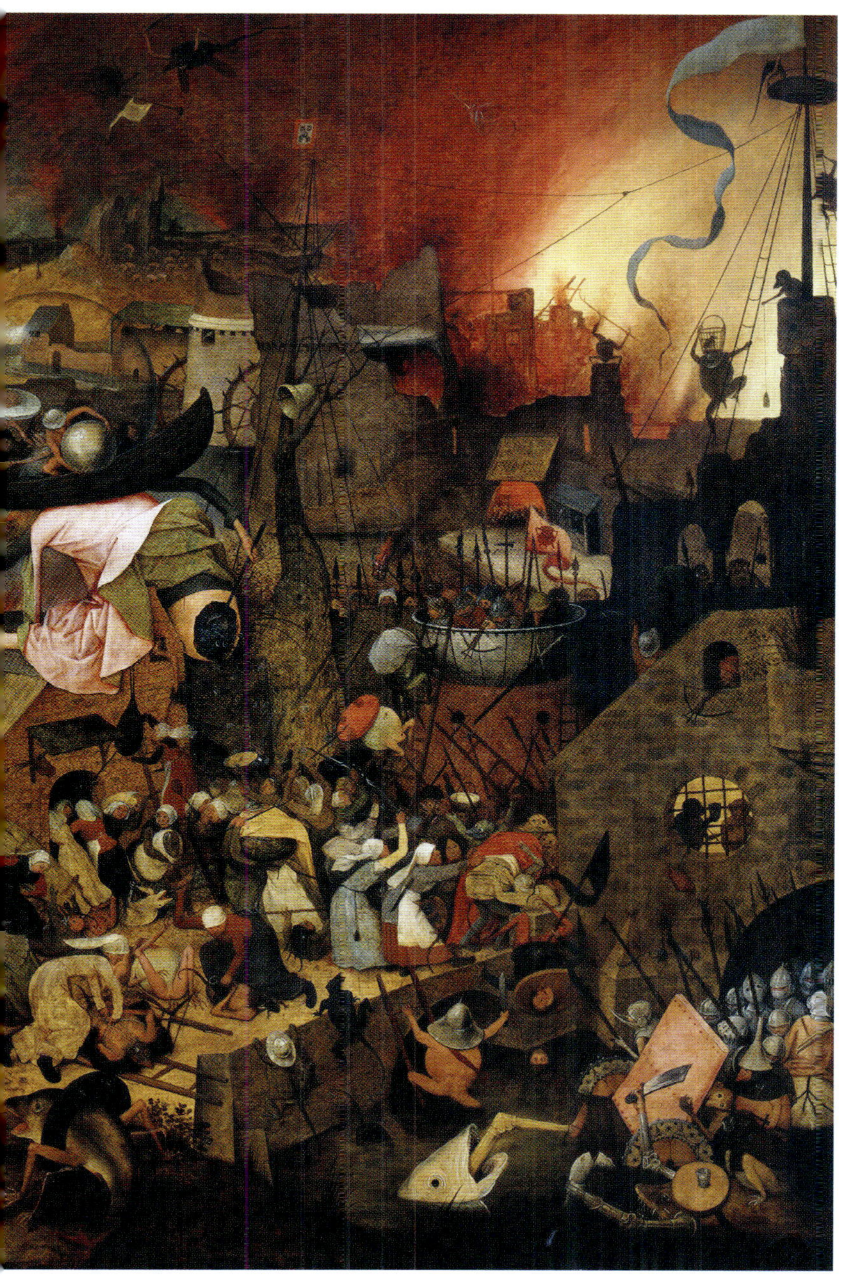

39 Pieter Bruegel, *Dulle Griet* (Mad Meg), 1561, oil on panel.

text, though, for his painting responds to a quite common way of conceptualizing violence and its relation to human nature.

The armed woman who strides across the foreground of Bruegel's scene is, then, more than an overgrown version of the figure Bruegel had invented three years earlier to allegorize the sin of anger. Her face and demeanour are marked by the unmistakable signs of raving madness: threatening look, eyes ablaze and popping out, cheeks flushed, moving at a rapid pace.[24] She is a figure of madness as it presides over a world utterly overwhelmed by fiery devastation. Her all-consuming fury is apparently motivated by greed, or avarice, for she has been filling her apron and her market-basket and even her kettle with booty as she moves forward, voraciously, towards the very mouth of hell.[25] This is how Karel van Mander understood her in 1604: 'Dulle Griet, plundering at the gate of Hell, looking quite mad'.[26] She is accompanied by a legion of assistants, who are not soldiers – indeed, the soldiers in this scene cower in their caves and cups, their units infiltrated by demons. Griet's fierce fighters are all women, not armed and distorted by rage like her, but perfectly ordinary people. Their apparel identifies them as hailing from different walks of life, but all are given the power to fight by their own angry yet methodical avarice. Some scramble to catch the coins that a giant man, seated on a brick house, is scooping out of his rear, while others do battle with the Boschian devils who populate this terrifying hellscape (illus. 40).

One woman near the centre of the painting's foreground acts out a saying Bruegel had visualized in his *Netherlandish Proverbs*, 'tying the Devil to a cushion' – a feat made possible because of the immense combative strength that an angry woman has (see illus. 7).[27] This alerts us to the fact, if we have not understood it already, that women winning the fight against demons is not necessarily a good thing. True, women engage in battle against allegorical characters in Bruegel's world, and may do so out of virtue: in his print of *Fortitude*, half of the foreground combat had been carried out by female figures, suggesting that women's struggle against internal vices was important in this society (see illus. 5). But Griet's followers are not defeating their inner weaknesses; on the contrary, they are giving rein to them. And that moral weakness that gives them physical strength, women's anger, was seen as particularly subversive.[28] Women made powerful through anger represented a force completely against the order of the early modern world, which held men – the more rational sex – to be the natural rulers and irrational women to be naturally obedient to them. Powerful women undid this bedrock tenet of social order.

Griet and her minions, with their strength through anger, have therefore done more than make war. They have unleashed upon the world forces that cannot be contained simply by binding one devil to a cushion. The mouth of Hell has opened wide, not to allow Griet to enter but to allow chaos to pour out and envelop the earth. Bruegel's painting is in fact a particularly potent image of chaos in its strange juxtapositions of scale its spatial incoherence, its lack of a sense of cause and consequence and its remarkable impression of an overwhelming confusion that confutes the efforts of beholders to impose sense upon it.[29] It shows a place that has become no-place, without passages or locations, without

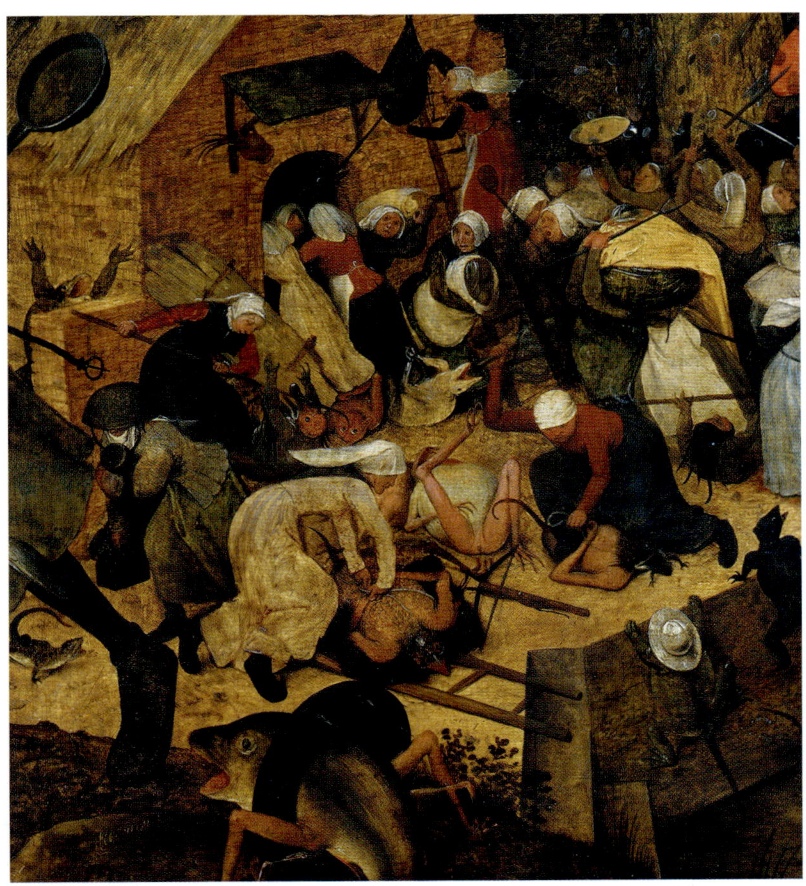

norms, without figures we can relate to or even comprehend, where the irrational is everywhere and significance is most often absent. It is an uninhabitable world of nightmare.

But what if we have to live the nightmare? What then?

Being caught up within the chaos of war, not by choice as a combatant but by chance as a civilian, was a very real prospect for people all over sixteenth-century Europe. Bruegel's

40 Griet's army fights demons: detail from *Dulle Griet*.

print of *Fortitude* is comprehensible as an allegory of internal struggle because it represents a psychologically plausible situation to a sixteenth-century beholder: a sea of actual military violence within which a single figure stands strong and maintains her composure. With the benefit of hindsight we know that, in the 1550s and 1560s, the worst was yet to come, but at the time it already seemed to people that violence was increasing, that war had grown more brutal, that the full-scale massacre of those perceived as opponents – especially on the basis of religion – was common, and that ordinary people were suffering everywhere.[30] Thus by the early 1580s, when Justus Lipsius published his essay *De constantia* (On Constancy), he was responding to an audience in need of advice in times of trouble. 'War, tyranny, slaughter, and death hang over your head,' he told his readers. 'You may fear, but not prevent; fly, but not avoid them. Arm yourself against them' – by which, Erasmus-like, he referred to an inward armature: constancy, an immovable strength of mind that would not be moved by either good fortune or catastrophe.[31] While ostensibly offering 'comfort' to his reader, Lipsius is actually quite opposed to actual pity, a weakness that can interfere with constancy.[32] Constancy, based in the Senecan Stoicism that had already made such an impact in Bruegel's circle, banishes pity and sorrow, hope and joy, fear and desire. An ideal that would be cultivated by some in the following generations, few ever succeeded in achieving perfect constancy. Pieter Bruegel's Flemish contemporaries generally moved through chaos, and viewed his representations of it, without such emotional control. The inner turmoil that they experienced in response to outward chaos and

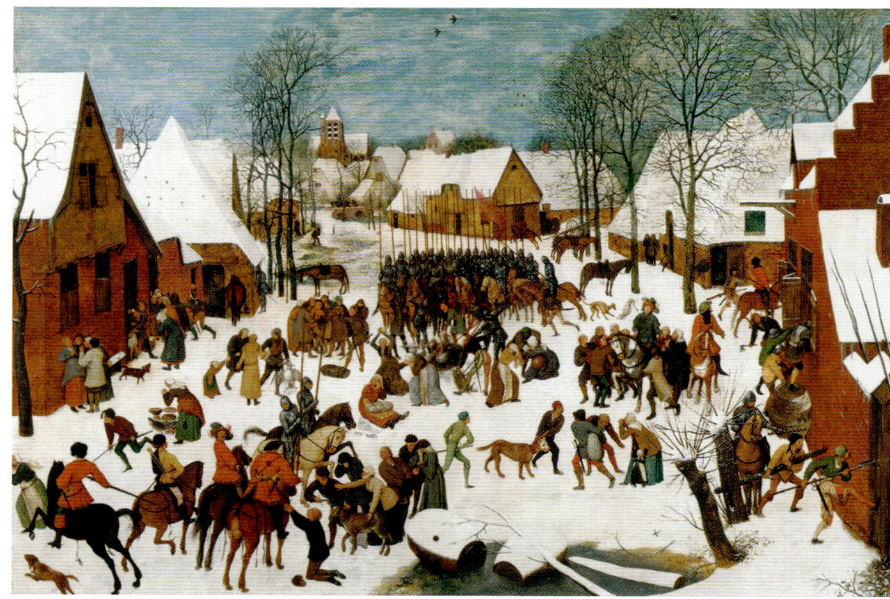

warfare is conveyed most vividly in Bruegel's famous *Massacre of the Innocents* (illus. 41).[33]

The *Massacre* exists in numerous copies made by Pieter Brueghel the Younger, and often the best of these, a painting now in Vienna, is used to illustrate the work's composition in books on our Pieter's art because the original, illustrated here, has undergone such extensive alterations.[34] Some early owner, possibly Emperor Rudolf II, found the scene of slaughtered babies either excessively distressing or insufficiently topical. The owner therefore had Bruegel's picture of a gruesome massacre repainted by an unknown hand, so that a biblical narrative became a modern genre scene. It showed, in fact, the subject to which Bruegel had originally been alluding to more metaphorically: the plunder of a contemporary village

41 Pieter Bruegel, *Massacre of the Innocents*, 1565–7, oil on panel.

by a band of marauding soldiers. A pile of infants being speared by half a dozen soldiers in the centre has here become a doomed flock of fowl; dead children are covered over with foodstuffs or bundles of goods, so that the extreme distress of the adults now seems rather overdone. But of course it is important that the picture was so easy to transform like this. Substitute a few birds for the babies, and a dreadful biblical tale becomes the traumatic story of now. Bethlehem's unbearable pain – which artists like Giotto and Raphael had striven to capture in anguishing, dramatic works of history – is, in Bruegel's hands, truly about the fury of his own time.

Civilians always suffer in wartime, but during the early modern period their suffering was particularly ubiquitous and seemingly random. On the one hand, to plunder a city after a siege, as in the sack of Rome described above, was considered a legitimate and indeed a very normal goal for a military force: it instilled fear into the enemy at all levels, motivated the fighters and provided compensation for soldiers who otherwise received little.[35] Most sixteenth-century warfare was conducted through sieges, so this was a very common situation, and while many voices lamented the suffering it caused, few actually urged, or even imagined, restraint.[36] But while sacking was a routine practice, the level and reach of carnage increased in the course of the century with the huge growth in the size of armies. No longer was the military composed of small groups of knights on horseback: now it was mostly common infantrymen, and in massive numbers. Spain's army expanded from 20,000 men in the 1470s to 150,000 in the 1550s, a degree of growth that completely overwhelmed the state's infrastructural capacity.[37] There was simply no way to feed and house this many people. Instead, soldiers lived off the land, meaning that the plundering of farms and villages for food – as shown in the revised version of Bruegel's painting – was an ongoing and even necessary aspect of troop movement. To endure this, people did not need to be near the site of a battle or siege, only along the path that the army took to get there.

The Massacre of the Innocents is an event recounted in only one Gospel, Matthew 2:16–18, where it is briefly mentioned as a pointless atrocity perpetrated by Herod. He already knows that the newborn King of the Jews has fled from his grasp, but orders the slaughter of Bethlehem's male children anyway. Thus what we have in Bruegel's original painting are soldiers perpetrating terrible cruelty not in the chaos of war, not for personal gain and glory, but under a meaninglessly brutal official command. We see an open place at the centre of a Flemish village, surrounded by ordinary houses and, to one side, an inn. It is the dead of winter, the harsh cruelty of nature echoing that of humanity. Snow lies thick on the ground and on roofs, and icicles hang from the eaves. The centre of the scene is occupied by a group of armed men, pike-bearers, surrounding their commander. They are there to represent officialdom, but the acts of violence are carried out by a motley collection of foot soldiers, some in partial armour and some not, some in the garb of Swiss mercenaries, others ordinary fighters.

The soldiers and villagers move this way and that, with the kind of low-key pictorial crowd control at which Bruegel was so expert. There is a sense of chaos and disorder in this composition. Our eye is not given one obvious path to follow, or a clear hierarchy of what is most important, for the tight cluster representing officialdom is mute and inert compared to the scattered, vivid vignettes around it, none of which claims any special primacy over the rest. But as we draw close to examine individuals and groups, we do find that every action has a motivation, every emotion a discernible cause. No single occurrence is in any sense random. Groups of villagers plead with soldiers to spare their children's lives, while others grieve their loss, or comfort others. The tiny faces repay our close engagement, for they are highly individualized and convey intense, personal experiences of misery and desperation, quite unlike the generic figures in many of Bruegel's pictures. Gestures and bodily postures act along with those facial expressions to convey each person's own internal tumult. The woman near the painting's centre who wrings her headscarf, her face contorted in grief, staggering away from the horror of the children's slaughter yet unable to turn her gaze away, is a remarkable visual formulation of extreme anguish (illus. 42). The soldiers are less dramatic. Other illustrators of this subject showed both sides of the encounter as equally directed by feeling, the wretchedness of Bethlehem's parents balanced by the ferocity of Herod's attackers. But Bruegel's soldiers go about their terrible work methodically and sometimes, perhaps, even regretfully. It is just a job.

Karel van Mander noticed this aspect of the picture too. The work made quite an impression on him, for he describes it twice: once in his biography of Bruegel, and again in his didactic poem on the art of painting, where it is used as an outstanding example of the depiction of the emotions, an

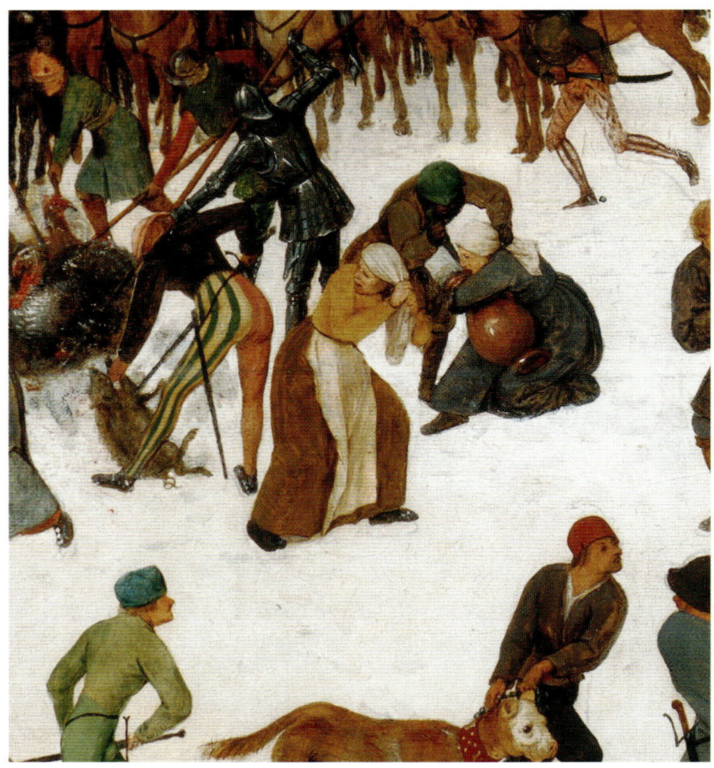

area in which Bruegel is described as 'faultless and penetrating'. In both texts Van Mander notes how well the artist represents the grief of a family begging for their child's life, and in the poem he goes on to single out the herald at the right of the scene, 'in whom quite enough compassion may be perceived, but he shows with sorry feeling the king's proclamation that one must be merciful toward none' (illus. 43).[38] Van Mander misremembers the proclamation, which is not physically in the herald's hand, but he recalls completely how he could read, from the man's face and hand gestures, his

42 Grieving woman: detail of *Massacre of the Innocents*.

compassion for the miserable peasants and his inability to disobey the orders he has been given.

Modern art historians rarely single out Pieter Bruegel as a master in the rendition of human feeling, for in his most famous works he mutes and generalizes the figures who labour in landscapes or enjoy festive occasions. Even the warrior women in Dulle Griet's train, apart from their leader herself, perform their angry tasks without actual evidence of anger. But in this painting of a village torn apart by violence, Bruegel's sensitivity to the specificity of internal experience is remarkable.[39] Figure after figure feels complex and individual, deeply

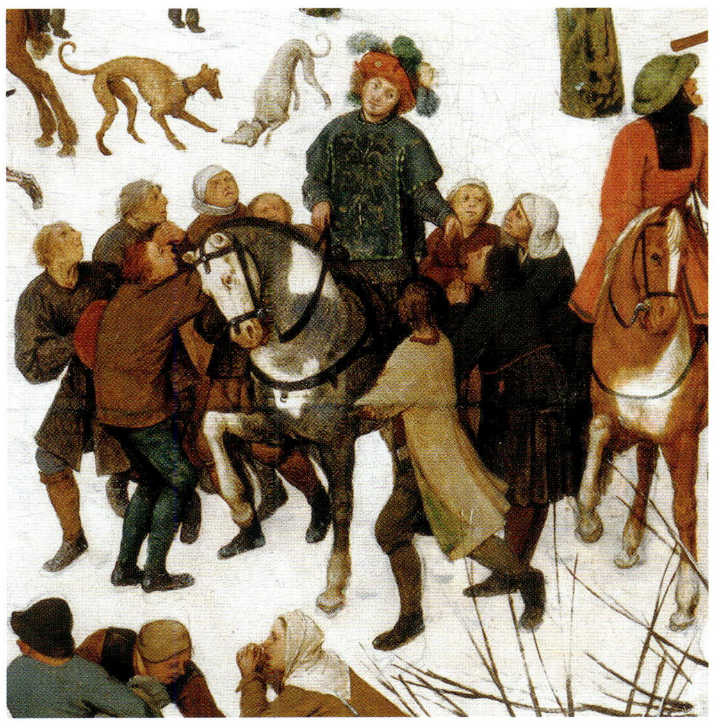

43 Herald with orders: detail of *Massacre of the Innocents*.

motivated by inner sentiment, and not drawn from any artistic repertoire of heroic visual formulae for the representation of feeling. These are peasants, not heroes. There are no heroes in the *Massacre of the Innocents* any more than there are in the warfare of Bruegel's time. There are only those who suffer, and those who cause suffering.

FIVE

Inside and Out: Natural Languages of Human Nature

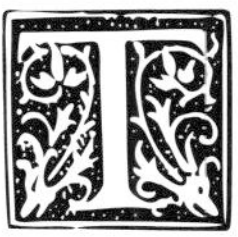WIN SONS OF A PRINCESS and a king, separated at birth.[1] One, his identity unknown, is taken in by Princess Clarina at the court of his own uncle, King Peppin. Clarina discovers a birthmark on the baby's back, in the shape of a cross, which convinces her that he is of noble blood. This child, given the name Valentin, grows up into a powerful and rather fierce young man (he murders several courtiers who displease him) before proving his valour alongside King Peppin at war against the Saracens. Meanwhile, the other twin has been raised by a beast in the forest. He too is unusually strong but, like an animal, he is covered in hair and has no language. Encountering this mute 'wild man' in the woods, Valentin conquers him, brings him to court, cleans him up and discovers that they share a birthmark. The reunited brothers set out to rescue their long-lost mother, although Clarina tries to dissuade them by proposing marriage to Valentin.

The story is far longer and more complicated than this summary, and, as a folk tale, it existed in many variants and in many languages. A group of mid-sixteenth-century Flemish players would probably have followed no text at all, simply performing the highlights of a well-known fable, and this is what Pieter Bruegel represents in his only woodblock print (illus. 44). Peppin is there, crown perched on top of an ordinary hat, a huge false beard concealing most of his face; next to him stands valiant Valentin with his sword and crossbow. The wild-man brother, sometimes styled Orson and sometimes just Nameless, swaggers towards them, a hairy creature garlanded with vines. Finally there is Princess Clarina, wearing a cloth mask and holding up the tempting wedding ring. The fact that we are not seeing an identifiable moment in the story, but something like a display of characters, or a cast line-up, emphasizes that we are looking not at Valentin and his hairy brother, but at players who have assumed their roles. The actors are not professionals of the sort who travelled from fair to fair, setting up a stage on barrels and performing comedies, but ordinary persons who belong to the same social milieu as the men in the inn who peer out of windows, or lean to put money into the heart-shaped charity jars that two women are holding up to them. Three of their friends are playing courtiers. The one in the middle, singled out by composition, texture and posture, is playing a wild man. But they know he is really a prince. But they know he is really their friend. He is all of these things together.

The mythical wild man was a favourite figure in both courtly and urban lore, representing everything that those who played him, and those who watched the performance, were not.[2] He represented the bodily, passion-driven side of human nature that civilized persons hid, denied and subjugated through reason. Normally, humans may choose between the paths of reason and impulse: the infant twins

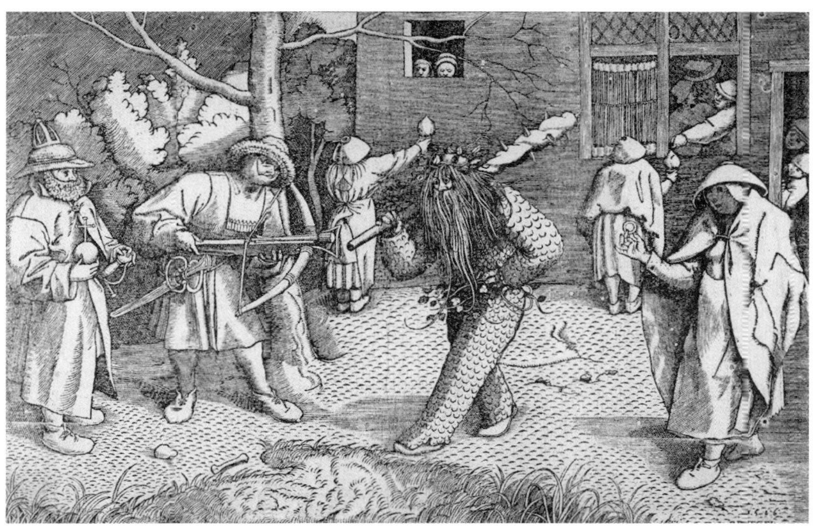

make no choices, but represent roads that can be taken and parts that can be assumed. Secretly marked by their birth as equals, Valentin and Nameless/Orson are two sides of the same being. Bruegel's villagers put on costumes – swords and doublets, vines and rough coverings – to doubly mask the truth about their selves, and to both perform and hide that which we all, in fact, contain within our own natures.

LAYERS: READING PHYSICAL SIGNS OF CHARACTER

Masking and performance, discernment and discovery, are essential parts of human social existence. For it was, in the eyes of early modern observers, a part of human nature to be forever performing and indeed to experience selfhood in what, in Chapter One, I described as layers – some presented to public view, others usually hidden. The visible self

44 Anonymous artist after Pieter Bruegel, *Masquerade of Valentin and Orson*, 1566, woodcut.

could be elaborately performative, or might conform rather comfortably to group norms, or could represent a sincere sense of the inner self (or all of these, at different moments), while another layer might be cautious, watchful and reserved, especially in an era of religious tensions.[3] 'Each of us', writes Pierre Charron, 'plays two roles and consists of two persons, one of which is external and the other essential.'[4] To Montaigne this attitude was simple hypocrisy, and he regrets that there are people who actually take pride in being always different outside and inside.[5] How can we know, and judge, people who present us constantly with a mask? Is the face performing a role, or registering the self?

To read the inner self of another on the basis of external, visible traits is a struggle, but Bruegel's contemporaries were pretty sure that this must be possible. The soul, after all, animates the body, and so the physical must always somehow register the internal, revealing to us momentary emotions but also the essential character of the person. We need only know how to read the signs of this 'natural language', as one sixteenth-century textbook called it.[6] Physiognomics, the science of discerning the truth of a person's character based on their appearance, was taken very seriously in Bruegel's time by a broad public. As Erasmus pointed out, a bit sceptically, it had a pedigree that reached back to antiquity, guaranteeing that it would be studied by the most erudite Humanists: Ficino himself claimed that in his youth he had composed a book, now lost, on the subject.[7] Inquisitors were provided with a manual guiding them on the delicate use of external signs as evidence of internal states of mind, up to and including heretical thoughts – how not to allow the mask to hide the true self.[8] People sought in the faces of others a register of virtue that could be codified as legible signs, so that the beholder (or inquisitor) would not be led astray by physical beauty but would see through to the vices beneath the skin. Hence popular books on physiognomy, of which there were many, did tend to dwell upon the negative characteristics that physical traits would necessarily reveal.

All parts of the head, from its size and shape to details of the forehead, nose, jaw, neck, cheeks, lips and teeth, were readable as character indicators: for instance, 'a person with great eyes is slothful, unshameful, inobedient, and weeneth to know more than he doth,' or 'a head fashioned like a Sugar lofe, declareth the man to be past shame, a devourer, bold and rashe.'[9] The reading of the sugarloaf head goes on to explain that physical symptoms and character traits are linked by the fact that the person's brain is dry, for physiognomics often relied upon medical/astrological theories of the humours, a balance of heat and moisture that would fundamentally determine a person's character. The degree and even direction of determination was always an issue in reading interior truths from external signs: did physical factors cause bad character, or did inherent internal evil manifest itself through face and body? And how strong was the causal relation in either direction? It was, as we have seen before, possible for a person to fight against their natural character, in which case to read character through external manifestations would be at once true and a disservice to an individual who had successfully subdued their own unruly nature.[10] Even the authors of popular texts warn that visible signs can lie, and that one should take what we might call a holistic view of the

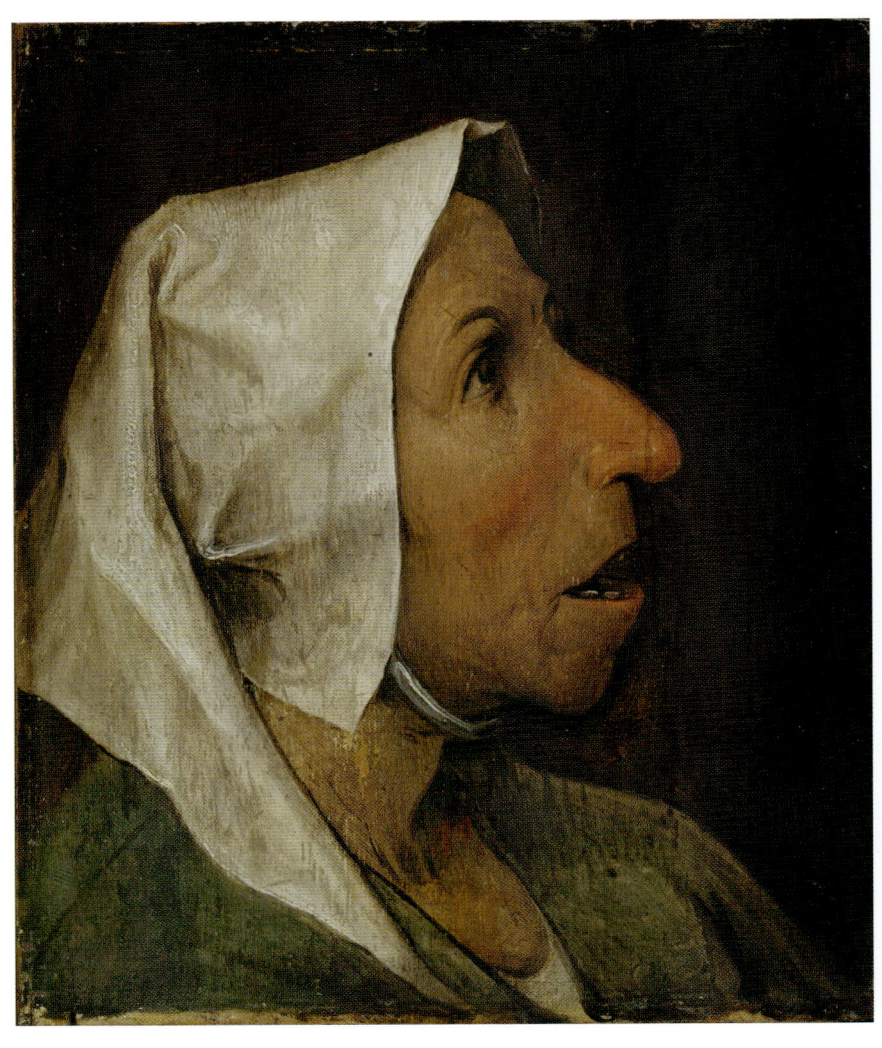

45 Pieter Bruegel, *Head of a Peasant Woman*, oil on panel.

individual, rather than passing judgement on the basis of a flat nose or a scrawny neck.[11]

Pieter Bruegel was painting for an audience trained in thinking carefully about the significance of physical traits, and to this audience he was as much esteemed as an expert in the study and depiction of character through its visible signs as he was valued for expressing human emotions through bodily forms.[12] His only surviving head study depicts an old woman in profile, her thin-lipped mouth hanging open, her eyes staring upward as if intently watching something and her nose large and slightly hooked – all features open to negative readings (illus. 45). Unrelated to any figure in a painting, and more a type than any individual, this woman exists solely to evoke a sense of character – coarse, peasantish, and for that very reason considered (by Bruegel's audience) less likely to present herself as a mask and more likely to permit her nature to be visibly manifest. Many more character heads must once have existed, for even during Bruegel's lifetime, and certainly shortly thereafter, collectors were buying such works attributed to him – Rubens owned no fewer than four – and his publisher was producing copious engravings claiming to be after others.[13] But we do not need to imagine what these lost works might have looked like, for Bruegel's paintings are filled with typecast figures whose internal traits are intriguingly manifested by their corporeal beings.

Bruegel's characters rarely give a sense that they are posing or self-consciously manifesting a particular side of themselves for public consumption. The most vividly characterized people are often those who themselves are intently watching or listening to someone or something else, as if being caught in a moment of attention leaves them particularly open to our own interpretive gaze. The *Sermon of John the Baptist* of 1566, famous for the great wall of backs that make up the crowd nearest to us, actually includes many tiny yet strongly characterized faces among those deeper within the gathering. *Christ Carrying the Cross* is likewise filled with carefully described onlookers (illus. 19–22). From the same year as *Christ*, 1564, Bruegel's *Adoration of the Kings* is a veritable study in physiognomies, distinctive types encircling the calm, idealized centre of Mary and her child (illus. 46). The kneeling king at the left has a wrinkled forehead, downturned mouth and flushed cheeks, while the tall, elegant African king on the opposite side peers with wide-eyed interest at his fellows. Behind him, contrasting with his respectable visage, are a pair of ordinary visitors, one bespectacled and with a jutting lower lip, the other with bulging eyes, a fleshy nose and thick lips, all legible facial traits indicative of inward character.

I do not want to imply that Bruegel illustrated features that his viewers would have read as if from a physiognomy text, but rather that his faces would have intrigued and delighted viewers attuned to speculating from outer signs about what sort of person they were dealing with. A prince or a wild man? A person pretending to know more than he does, a person who is shameless, lazy, malicious? Reading the signs, from those that registered true social position to those that revealed hidden vices, was a particularly important exercise in the ever-expanding early modern city. In this urban environment, people were being faced with a rather new challenge: increasing numbers of people whom they did not know well but with whom they had to interact.

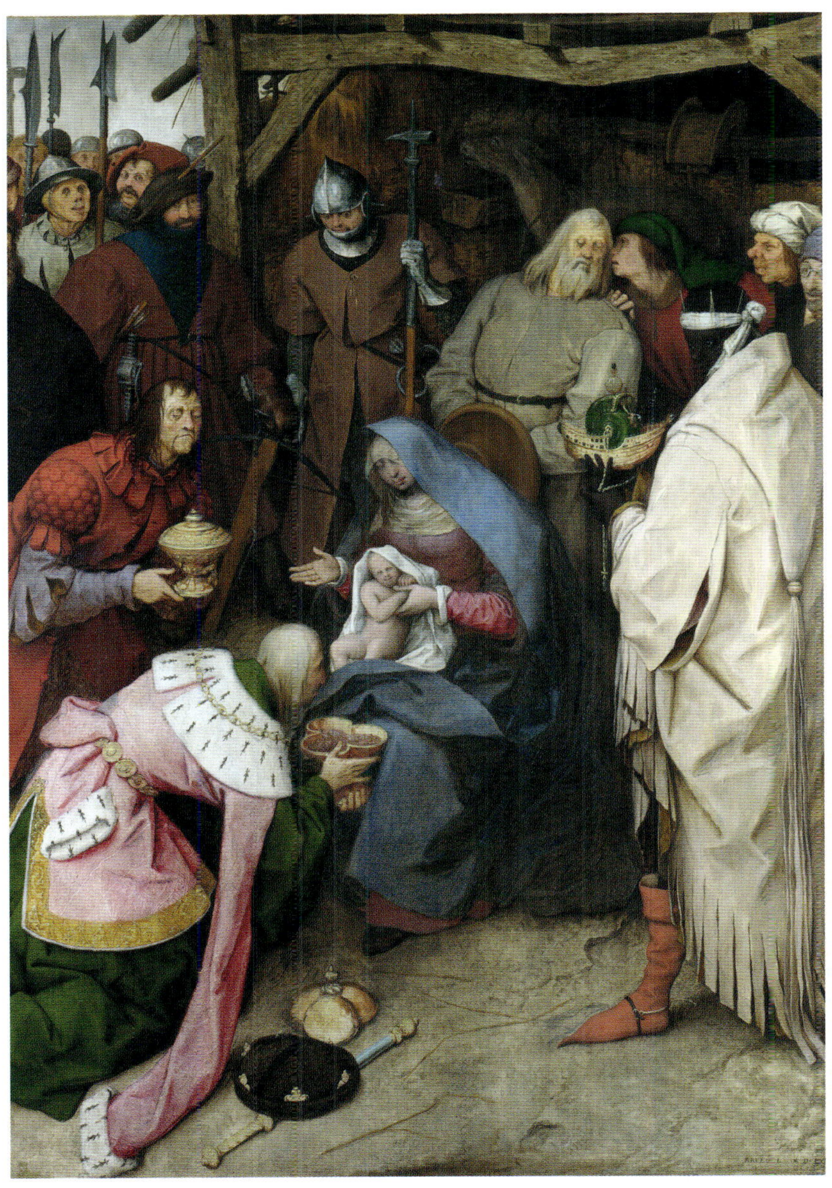

46 Pieter Bruegel, *Adoration of the Kings*, 1564, oil on panel.

Bruegel's art offered his patrons, in Antwerp and Brussels, many opportunities to practise their face-reading skills, and to ponder the actual utility that those skills offered in a world of masks.

CARNIVAL AND LENT: PERFORMING SIGNS IN THE CITY

'A red face and short signifieth a person full of riot . . . A fat visage full of rude flesh signifieth gluttony, negligence, rudeness of wit and understanding,' while a long, lean face signals one who is 'hot, disloyal, spiteful, cruel'.[14] Vice parades itself openly and even joyously on the left-hand side of Pieter Bruegel's *Battle between Carnival and Lent*, but what do we really know about the performance of virtue that opposes it in Lent (illus. 47)?

Bruegel's painting of Carnival and Lent extends, through a whole society and through time, the human duality dramatized by *Valentin and Orson*, the tale of the princeling and wild man with which this chapter began. At the painting's centre, the untrammelled expression of base instinct does battle with the forces of civil restraint. The scene also poses more elaborate questions about the ways in which we know, understand and judge human nature from its outward signs. Bruegel offers us an amazingly thorough census of the population of a Flemish town, or perhaps the corner of a large city. The figures encompass a remarkable range of age, social status and trades, but also of attitudes, habits and behaviours: it is an ethnographer's view of the urban community, made strange for the gazes of those to whom it is, in some sense, entirely familiar. Nothing is actually normal and ordinary. The everyday of life is banished from the stage of the town square, and infinite performances take its place, so that truths about humanity are elaborately enacted by actors who sometimes, paradoxically, represent themselves, and sometimes don masks and costumes to play symbolic roles.

Although the painting feels chaotic, it would have been less so to Bruegel's original audience, attuned as they were to the seasonal customs and performances of this world. The scene is composed on a kind of horseshoe layout, from back to front and left to right, along which are positioned activities related to the first three months of the calendar year. The horseshoe is rooted first at the far end of the street that enters the square just left of centre, where New Year's bonfires cleanse the city of all the leftovers from the previous twelve months.[15] From there we follow the procession of lepers, which occurs on the first Monday after the feast of the Three Kings (6 January), down the street and into the town's main square. Various amateur fund-raising performances, played outside two inns, are associated with the parade; the last of them, the play of the 'Dirty Bride' at the left, is the pivot point that curves us around to the main conflict playing across the painting's foreground. There, costumed townsmen representing Carnival on the left, and the season of Lent on the right, along with their retinues, stage a mock battle. Next we move back into the picture's space at the right side, from the festive season ruled by Carnival into the long, sombre days of Lent. This trajectory is defined by the structure of a church and, in the distance, its cloister. Human movement on this side proceeds outward from that building. A group

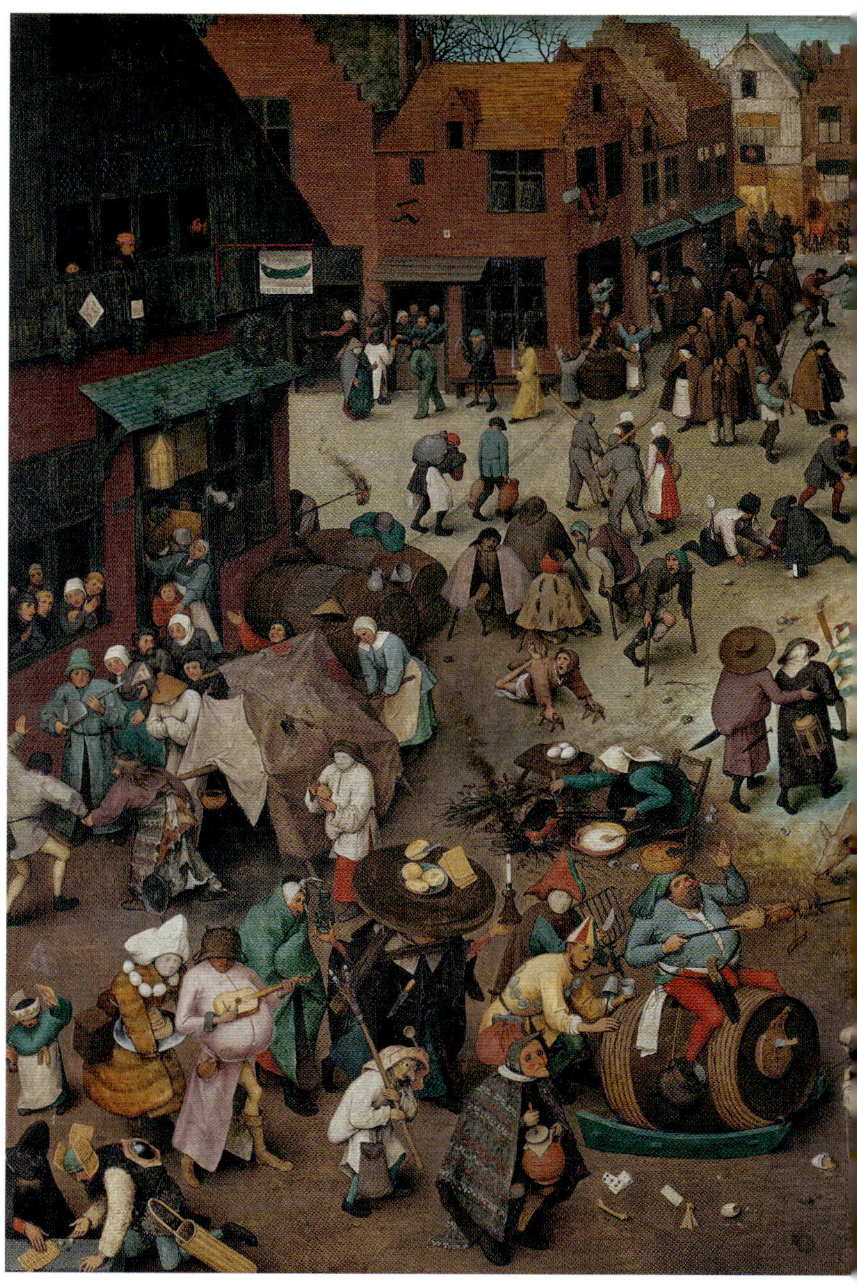

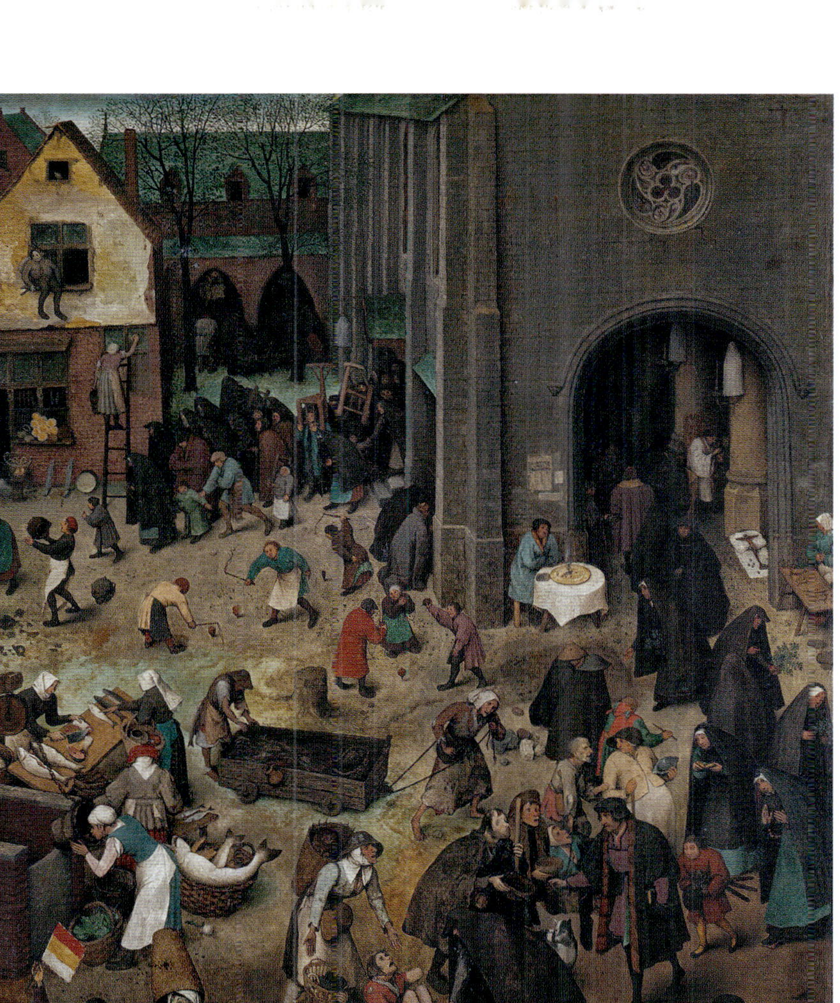

47 Pieter Bruegel, *Battle between Carnival and Lent*, 1559, oil on panel.

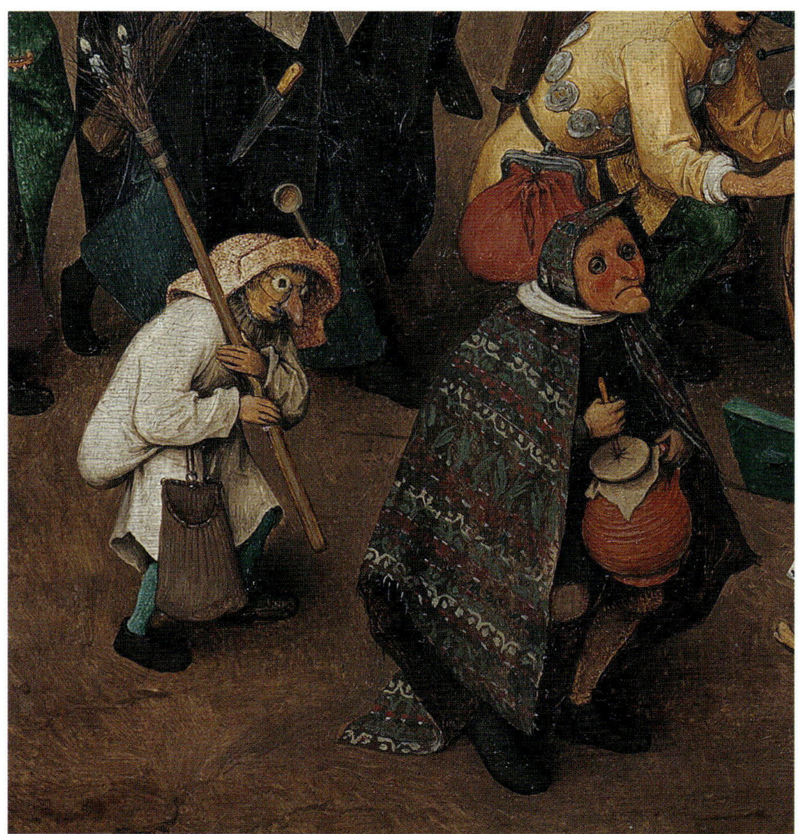

near to us at the far right encounters a line-up of beggars as they leave the church service, while a second group of church-goers exiting from the building's side door carry the chairs and stools they have been sitting on during Mass. In the cloister behind them, the trees show new leaves: it is spring. The procession of people has just reached a bakery where spring cleaning is in progress, so that the cycle closes, as it began, with a ritual of cleansing. Meanwhile, in the centre of

48 Masked players: detail of *Battle between Carnival and Lent*.

the square, games are played, additional seasonal rites are performed and appropriate foods – waffles for Carnival, fish for Lent – are prepared and sold.

While the full painting encompasses an arc of considerable time, the focus in the foreground is on the single moment of conflict that gives the work its traditional title: Carnival versus Lent, festive play and consumption play versus abstemious piety. Carnival is the quintessential figure of gluttonous stupidity as described in the physiognomy books: no mask needed here, for this townsman himself perfectly embodies the concept he performs. Riding astride a barrel, he is armed with a roasting-spit and reaches up, nervously, to steady the bird pie balanced atop his head. But while Carnival can play his role naturally, his companions have donned elaborate disguises to perform their parts. Two wear the simplest kind of facial covering: a filmy white cloth that largely conceals their own features without substituting another set. We are simply left with no way to read these people feature by feature: they have rendered themselves visually meaningless, so that only their place in a context, that of the procession tells the beholder – or the bystander – who or what they are. The woman playing Clarina in Bruegel's *Valentin and Orson* print had worn such a cloth, as does the alms-collector for the play being performed behind Carnival's crew. Two others in Carnival's train, both evidently children, wear proper face masks: the foremost a full covering with a hooked nose, turned-down mouth and jutting chin, and the smaller child what seems to be a partial mask with bulging eyes, perhaps indicating spectacles, and a very large nose (illus. 48).[16]

Both children have also extended their disguises beyond the face. The first has draped himself in a kind of blanket that is often, in paintings of this period, associated with Gypsies: he is a local, urban boy feigning wildness and outsiderness. The noise he makes with his *rommelpot*, a homemade instrument particularly associated with carnival celebrations, joins the cacophony being produced by the other marchers using their own makeshift noise-makers – a grill and knife for a loud portable harp, two metal cups for cymbals. The twin of that grill appears again far back in the painting in its normal place, at the bakery, for like the humans in this painting, objects too can assume new roles completely divorced from their everyday function.[17] Repurposing objects estranges them, making us see them as something new before we register their actual familiarity. The second child plays at this too: he carries a twig broom, so useful in activities of cleaning, that he has transformed into a torch. Hanging from a belt at his waist, a great purse claims for this child the status of an adult, and he has further attempted to stuff his tunic to mimic a hunchback. Bodily mis-making is the order of carnival time, as the real adult strutting behind this child has grotesquely padded his stomach, turning himself into a parody of his leader Mr Carnival. This man's face is almost concealed by a cooking pot, housewares becoming a device of masking or reforming identity. At the very end of Carnival's train, a tiny child wears a printed crown left over from January's Three Kings celebration, playfully claiming an elevated status although he is the last and lowliest member of the procession.

On Lent's side of things, there is far less masking. Indeed, it is difficult to decide who is and is not out of their own character. Figures tell us about themselves, even as they play roles: they are doubly self-revealing. Lent herself, armed with the baker's peel, seems to be a man clothed as a nun: his slightly unshaven cheeks reveal the truth of his gender. But the tonsure of the monk pulling Lent's cart suggests that his role is the same in life as in the pageant, although his averted face prevents us from knowing any more about him. And nobody among Lent's followers has any 'role' at all. In fact they are all children, humans untutored in the feints and pretences of adulthood, simply enjoying their part in the festivities. On Lent's side of the picture, we think that we can believe what we see.

The battle between Carnival and Lent, a traditional performance staged at the end of carnival season in Netherlandish towns, signifies a fundamental duality in human nature, riotous appetite pitted against restrained sobriety.[18] It is also, in Bruegel's town, played out in terms of how human nature is *known*. Carnival's licence allows its followers to blur the usual lines of connection between the internal self and external signs. But in the process of assuming alternative identities, these townspeople perform a fundamental truth about human nature: that we all have a side that is normally masked by our social self-performance as serious and pious people. Restraint itself is an act, a disguise, covering over a part of the self that we know exists but prefer to keep unseen. Who then really wins this battle? The scope of the year tells us that Lent is always the victor, that restraint will reimpose its mask over riot. But through the past performances of carnival, we remain aware even through Lent that the riotous underside of human nature exists.[19] The couple who wander through the scene at

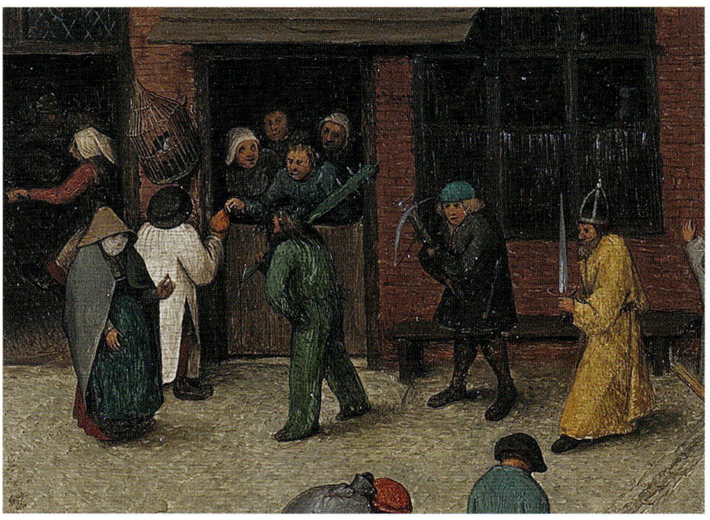

its geometric centre – always a key spot for Bruegel – thus face a very real choice of which way to turn. Will they follow the fool with his torch, who marches resolutely back towards true feints of licence, or will they continue their forward path to the time when constraint's lying mask proclaims its own truth?

In this staged battle, every person plays a part but nobody except the two main combatants is a specific character: they are all ciphers of a way of being, not full individuals who happen to behave this way. Even Mr Carnival and Sister Lent are performing allegories, and in that sense have no 'real', internal character that their external signs mask or reveal. That is not true, however, in the secondary performances that occur under the aegis of festivity on the left-hand side of the picture. Closest to us, a group is enacting the play of the 'Dirty Bride', a burlesque that involves urban people

49 Valentin and Orson: detail of *Battle between Carnival and Lent*.

performing the parts of peasants, whose raucous festive customs will be the subject of the next chapter. The two leads do not seem to wear masks at all; their audience knows exactly who they 'really' are, even as they make themselves comic for the show's duration. It is their gestures and costumes that inform the audience of their assumed characters. Only their money-collector, paradoxically, hides his face under a cloth mask. Before the inn back near the lepers' procession, a more familiar scene is enacted: Valentin and Orson, with King Peppin and even Clarina with her ring (illus. 49). Only she is masked, once again. The courtiers have minimal disguise, only attributes. But Orson is a hairy monster, altered from head to toe by his wild, uncivilized upbringing. He exemplifies how not only the human face but also the body can be a sign, available to be read carefully by those attuned to the multiplicity of truths it holds, and its potential to lie. Bodies will join faces as another major aspect of legible, meaningful display and problematic deception in the urban world of *Carnival and Lent*.

MIS(IN)FORMATION: BODIES, TRUTHS AND THE CHARITABLE IMPULSE

Carnival's mummers are not the only figures in this urban square whose bodies are misshapen. Each major trajectory, that of Lent and that of Carnival, contains an extensive collection of figures who are, to varying degrees and from varying causes, deformed. Today we would call them impaired, and speak of disability; in Bruegel's time, many of them would have come under the harsher rubric of 'crippled', while others are blind or simply bent.[20] On both sides of the picture, these malformed people are associated with local support for the impoverished, ill and disabled. Well-to-do townsfolk leaving the church just behind Lent's procession are accosted on all sides by disabled beggars and respond by giving alms, while on Carnival's side of the scene the festive trajectory begins with a procession of lepers, some still whole, others horribly disfigured by disease. The lepers too are here to ask for charity, and the plays of the dirty bride and of Valentin and Orson are performed for their benefit. In staging charity around the bodily misshapen, Bruegel poses questions about how non-normative physical bodies can tell us about themselves at moments of social pressure, when regular members of the social body make decisions about how they will share with those in need. Juan Luis Vives claimed that 'there is a desire marvellously built into the human heart that generous spirits wish to do good and to help as many as possible.'[21] That part of our nature is tested in Bruegel's painting by what he presents as the need to discern, from outer signs, whose demands upon our generosity are worthy, and whose are not.

It was Vives himself who spurred a debate about the proper organization of charity and the judgement of the physical bodies of its recipients that has continued, in various permutations, until our own day. His *De subventione pauperum* (On Helping the Poor) was first published in Bruges in 1526; less than a decade later, the first Dutch translation appeared, and another edition followed at mid-century.[22] Already in 1531, Charles V had issued an edict in line with Vives's advice: to suppress begging as a primary way for the poor to support themselves and instead order towns to maintain their indigent populations through organized fund-raising and a centralized 'common purse', from which distributions would occur in an orderly fashion.[23] Vives's motives for urging this change were not kindly sympathy to the poor, though. On the contrary, he was voicing a solution to the poverty problem in line with the general antipathy to beggars of all sorts, which he shared.[24]

The years around 1500 saw a marked change in attitudes towards the poor: poverty was losing its medieval associations with unworldly virtue and becoming perceived, instead, as a register of vice: shiftlessness, laziness, deceitfulness. Vives is particularly disgusted by the sick and disfigured, who 'make their way through the densest crowd with their foul sores and give off a stench from their whole body'.[25] Lined up outside churches, they repel good people by both sight and smell. Indeed, the whole spectacle of want and necessity is, to Vives, a blot upon the urban landscape: his vivid descriptions register complete revulsion, and it therefore truly amazes him that any person, however well intentioned, gives charity at all. What then to do with the indigent? Vives, like many of his contemporaries, believes that most of the poor are just too lazy to work and must be forced to do so. 'No one is so feeble that he completely lacks the strength to perform some task,' he insists.

Beggars are also crafty liars and cunning cheats. This is the other problem with relying upon donations from the kind-hearted to aid the needy: how do you know who actually deserves charity? Therefore, at the same time that publishers were offering books about physiognomy, they also marketed texts that would inform the worried reader about bodily signs as manipulated in poverty's elaborate underworld in the cause of easy money. The earliest of these was the *Liber vagatorum* or *Book of Vagrants*, first published in around 1510 and available in Antwerp in translation by 1563; take-offs in other languages also abounded.[26] These texts unfolded a variety of reasons why disabled beggars were not to be trusted, or funded, focusing on ways in which the poor supposedly manipulated visual signs of impairment. Most notably, the books claimed that many of those pleading for alms had elaborately feigned the disfigurement of their perfectly whole bodies for the sake of easy money. 'Before' and 'after' images showed the reader how an able-bodied person could assume the disguise of a cripple, an epileptic, a blind man.[27]

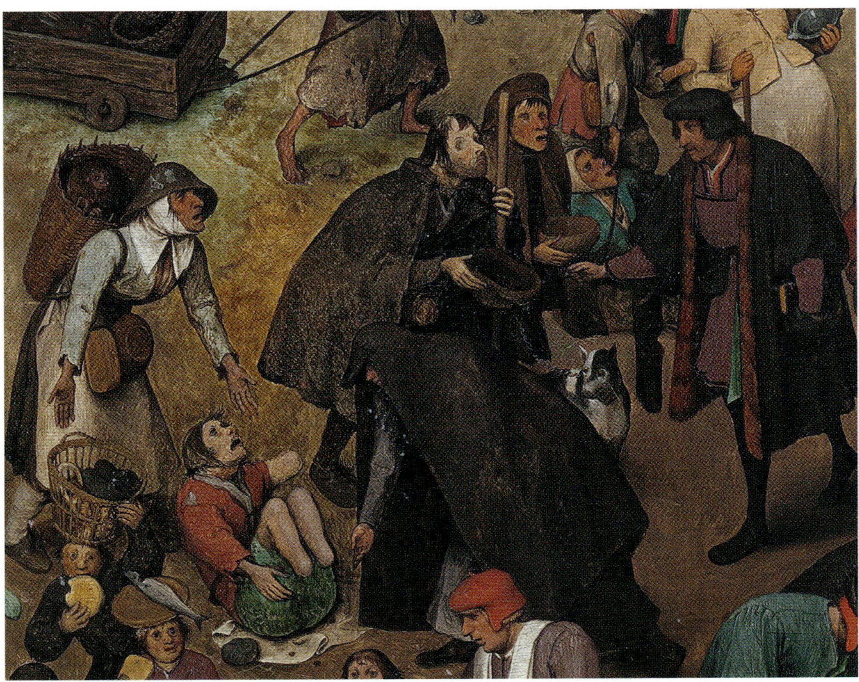

50 Beggars by the church: detail of *Battle between Carnival and Lent*.

But even the truly handicapped were not to be trusted, for bodily deformation could be a sign of internal corruption. The conviction that evil minds inhabited malformed bodies was strong in the Renaissance, informing writers from Luther to Shakespeare, although earlier generations often believed this as well.[28] As in the case of facial features, some authors questioned how this connection was formed: did the deformed body directly corrupt the mind as a *cause*, or was it simply a *sign* of the evil soul and therefore open to interpretation? But this was not to question that a connection of some sort existed.[29] The Bible, in particular the Old Testament, gave ample support for a belief that disease and disfigurement were a punishment from God for human transgression, and thus an indisputable sign, although Christ's words in the New Testament sometimes directly argued against reading impairment as the result of sin.[30] So while in theory the jury was out, in practice it is clear that even the genuinely disabled were disliked, mistrusted and often the subject of marginalizing ridicule and mockery. At the same time, those physically unable to work (*pace* Vives) needed help. If they were indeed genuine.

The citizens leaving church at Lent in Bruegel's *Carnival and Lent* painting encounter the town's most helpless and destitute residents (illus. 50). All the individuals in need of aid seem to come from within the town – there are, for instance, no Gypsies, or anybody who is obviously a wanderer; and this matters because the well-to-do donors know the people asking them for alms. They have a responsibility for these unfortunate members of their community and are less concerned about possible deceit. Bruegel tells us little about some of the needy, like the two figures in dark cloaks sitting nearest the church door, receiving alms from a woman in a black *huyck* or mantle. Other beggars we see very clearly. An aged man leans on a crutch and points downward to his companion, whose facial expression suggests mental deficiency or difference. Next are two blind men with a dog; their aid comes from perhaps the wealthiest individual in the scene, who wears a fur-lined robe. The blind are followed by a man who has undergone extensive bodily suffering and alteration, whose wife stands behind him pleading his cause. He is not a leper (we will get to them shortly), so his drastic losses probably stem from some kind of circulatory disease. Finally, in the lowermost right corner, a woman with her small child sits next to a pile of cloth; originally, a dead body was visible here, presumably that of her husband. No deformity, then, but another sort of loss which, when suffered by women with children, put them among the worthy recipients of charity.

In Lent's time of undisguise, people from the margins of local society emerge to confront those from society's centre with the truth of their needs, and the pious churchgoers respond with generosity. Only one figure signals a problematic edge to this praiseworthy scene: the fool, just behind the old man. Unlike his companion in the painting's centre, he has pulled back his cap to bare his head: he is signalling his own unmasking. In that spirit, perhaps, he seems to guide the impoverished woman staggering behind him, pulling a cart that formerly contained a dead body, now painted over. She is the most dubious figure here: not an obviously virtuous local widow like the woman in the corner, childless and alone, she comes to claim a share of charity. She is at once the most utterly destitute and the least socially located person in this company, and she will test the townspeople's ability to judge, as well as their essential generosity.

The display of disability and disease occurs quite differently on Carnival's trajectory, where the new year's bonfires are immediately followed by the annual procession of lepers, heavily covered from head to foot as was often required of lepers in public places. They carry noise-making clappers to warn of their approach, for they are a fearsome assembly and in normal times the townsfolk would flee them in fear of contagion. As the more severe forms of leprosy progress, the disease causes extreme disfigurement, from grotesque facial sores and staring, round eyes to blindness, paralysis, clawed hands and other contraction deformities, progressing to loss of digits and even limbs. It erodes the familiar outlines of the body's form. Six sufferers at this later stage of the disease cluster ahead of the walking lepers (illus. 51). They are performing a savagely unfunny dance, led by their legless red-crowned mock 'prince', his cloak bedecked with fox tails that signal deceitfulness.[31] Even though these people are truly diseased and disabled, lepers were frequently accused of being wily cheats, visible deformity reading as a marker of internal vice.[32]

Leprosy, with its attendant informative signals of deformation, was treated quite differently from other diseases and disabilities in the early modern city, and those who suffered from it were perceived in a particular way.[33] Modern medicine has discovered leprosy to be unique among communicable diseases in two ways: the incubation period between infection and symptoms is exceptionally long, often lasting several years, and 95 per cent of people are naturally immune to it.

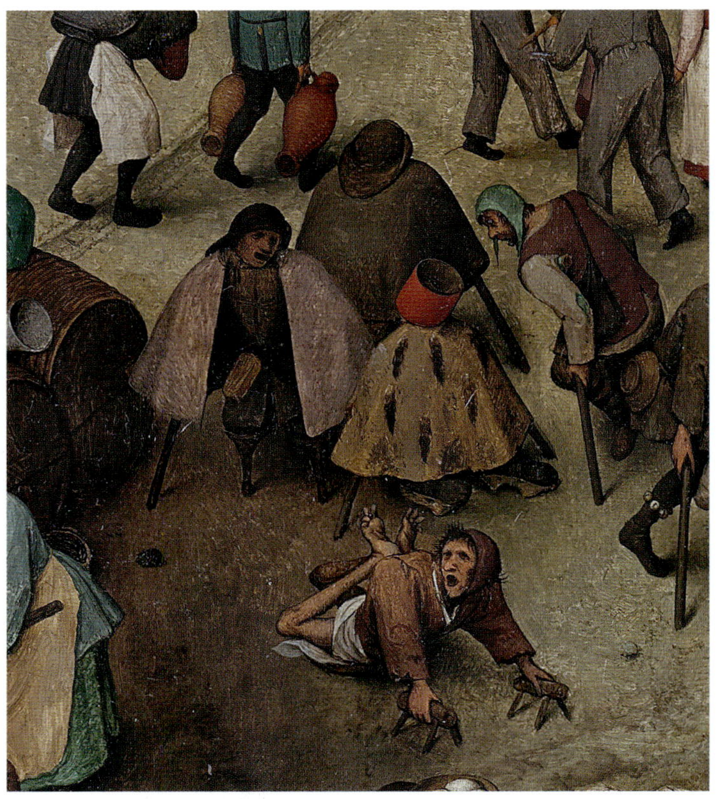

In Bruegel's time, these characteristics made leprosy appear
to single out its victims with cruelly deliberate specificity.
The only possible explanation was that God visited leprosy
upon particular individuals in punishment for their sins, first
horrifically disfiguring and then eventually killing them. The
Bible singled out lepers as unclean, and this sense of lepers
as repellent, degraded, dangerous creatures continued up
to Bruegel's time. In 1179, the third Lateran Council had
called for the segregation of lepers from society, spurring the

51 Lepers: detail of *Battle between Carnival and Lent*.

creation of leprosaria – communal dwellings for those stricken with leprosy – outside of towns.[34] But who actually went to live there? Leprosy is difficult to diagnose: many skin diseases manifest similarly to early signs of leprosy. Tribunals were established to judge, by visible signs, whether an individual would be sent into permanent exile.

However, the exiles re-entered their towns on particular occasions, when those who were otherwise considered grotesque outcasts became the kings, were feted and celebrated. They were given food and drink, as we can see around the walking lepers in Bruegel's painting, and donations to their leprosarium poured in. Indeed, at this season, being a leper suddenly became a desirable position, and now towns had to deal with people feigning the ghastly disease. Nuremberg offered a special leprosy examination before their festival to sort the true lepers from the false, and hundreds of applicants failed the test: the inspectors reported elaborate fakery of skin lesions using glue and plasters.[35] At a moment when identity as a social outcast made one, briefly, the centre of festive and charitable attention, extremes of disfigurement were being assumed as a desirable disguise.

Bruegel's parade of the afflicted, and especially the terrible dance of their most malformed companions, take their place easily among the other performances for the lepers' benefit. Everybody is at once presenting themselves as concept or character – Carnival, wild man, lying leper – and denying that role's true connection to what lies underneath. The dancing lepers are themselves performers, but the role they enact is a hyperbolic version of themselves. Normally unseen by their compatriots, on this day they play the part of leprous cripples, exposing the hidden truth of their horrible existence to the people of the city. It is interesting, then, that nobody is actually watching their theatrics. Their mouths are wide open but nobody attends to the hoarse cries produced by their afflicted throats.[36] In fact, the people nearest to the lepers have their backs turned, so that only we are witnesses to the awkward capering of these misshapen men, and we view them not as equivalent to the limbless beggar outside the church door, but as part of the festive spectacle of winter. The horrible truth of their difference only becomes clear when we pause and look very closely.

Nearly a decade later, in 1568, Bruegel returned to the dancing lepers, making them the subject of their own painting (illus. 52). Here, five lepers are performing a second annual display, this one held at Whitsun or Pentecost, eight weeks after Easter in the late spring.[37] Just behind them, again, a female companion collects alms for the severely compromised dancers, for it is the worst off who stage the show, who animate their broken bodies for public consumption. This later work is truly tiny, one of the smallest that Bruegel ever produced. In fact, the panel is even smaller than the segment of *Carnival and Lent* depicting the six lepers: illus. 51 represents an area of about 25 × 22 cm (9 × 8¾ in.), while the entire independent painting is a mere 18 × 21 cm (7 × 8¼ in.). The viewer must therefore draw extremely, uncomfortably close to see these lepers properly, engaging almost intimately with a type of body from which we would normally maintain a considerable distance. This is disarming. The grotesque is too close for comfort, pressed towards us by the brick buildings behind the men in a picture without other, more pleasant distractions.

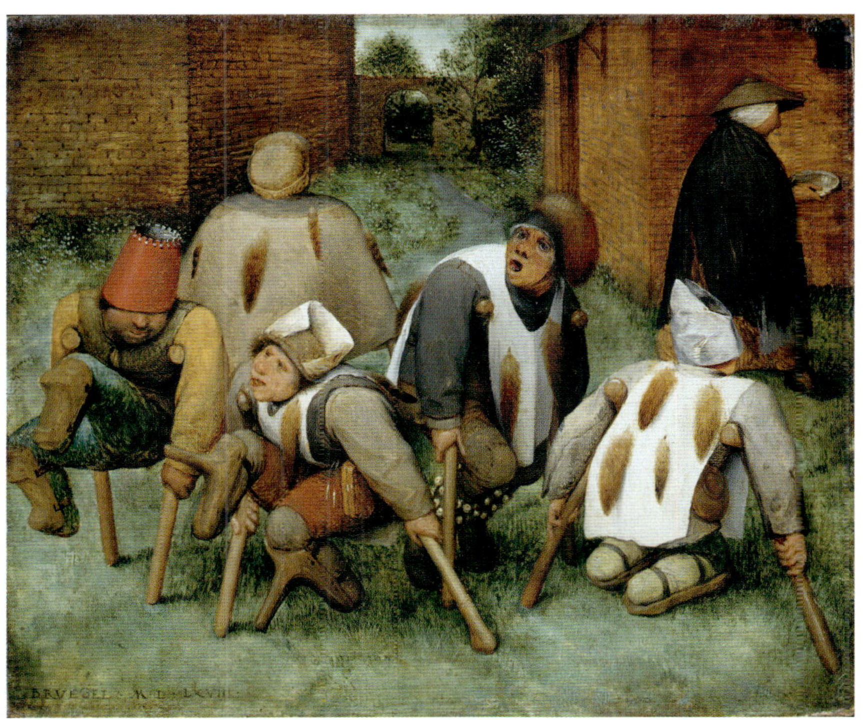

The faces of the three men we can see are roughened and blemished from disease, their noses bulbous, their mouths agape; but even without any of those signs, the horribly dismembered bodies of all five dancers announce their terrible infection. The men are also artificially marked, wearing signifiers that tell us things about them that are both true (we believe) and false. Four of the five wear the fox tails of deceit sewn to their clothing, asserting the supposed internal corruption that underlies their eroded bodies. This we believe, for we have been conditioned to expect external flaws to index internal ones. Three wear further signifying headgear: the

52 Pieter Bruegel, *The Lepers*, 1568, oil on panel.

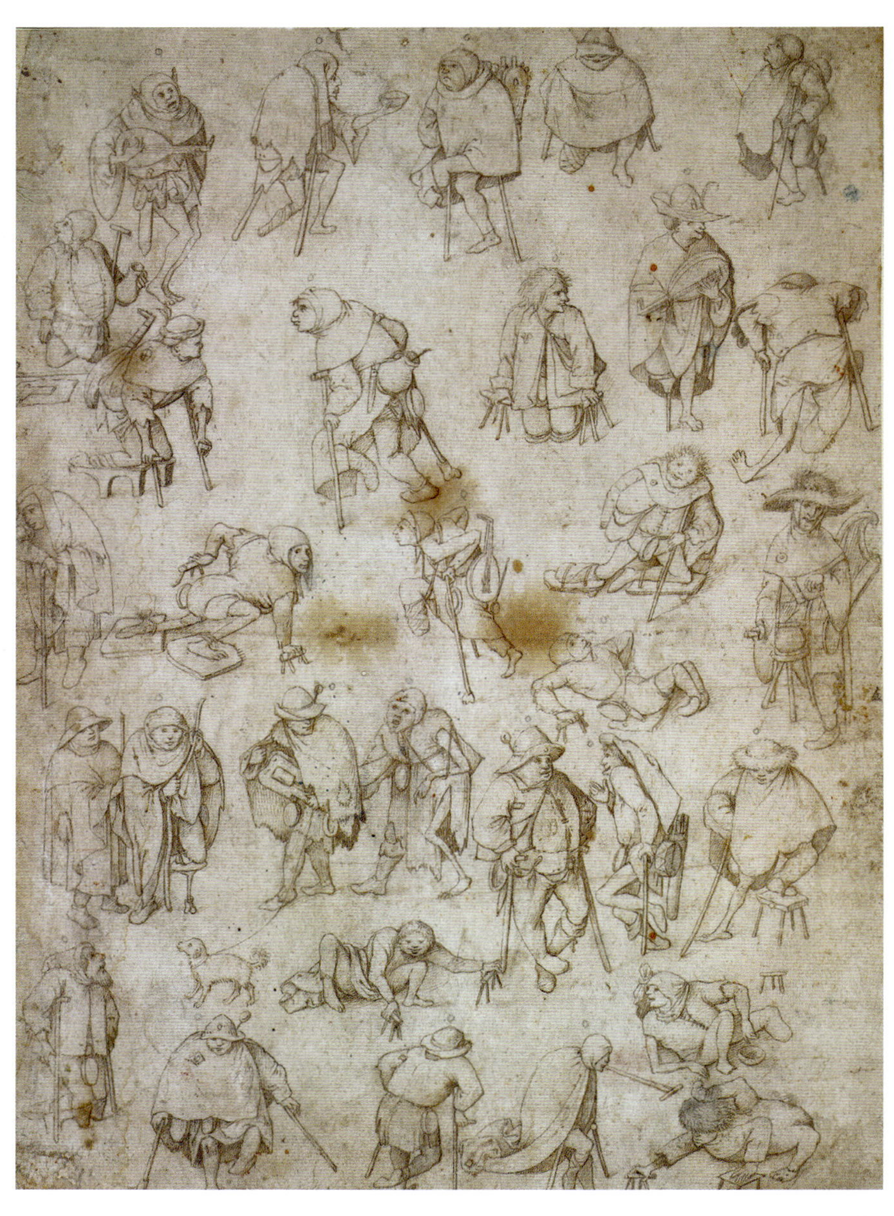

53 Manner of Hieronymus Bosch, *Beggars and Cripples*, drawing, pen and brown ink.

red king's crown familiar from *Carnival and Lent*, a printed paper half-crown and a mock bishop's mitre. This last is worn by the legendary 'Cripple Bishop', who leads his band of deformed followers in their lazy pursuit of easy money.[38] But of course the man we see is only playing the part of that infamous character, for a festive occasion when he and his fellows momentarily encounter townspeople who know the stories. He styles himself the Bishop to open himself to the disdain, and the laughter, of the townsfolk. This audience permits the costumed play of self-mockery and mock self-revelation to be performed within the city because, as a ritual, it confirms that the lepers' outsider status is something that really comes from inside of them.

Bruegel's pictured lepers were inspired in part by designs of and after Hieronymus Bosch, whose exuberantly mal-formed human beings seem to be less players in a real-world drama and more the products of Bosch's fertile imagination and artistic process (illus. 53). Rather than depicting figures that play roles, Bosch as artist plays with the human form, twisting and manipulating it even beyond what nature, through disease, can do. He slips in a fool among the warped little figures; a printmaker in Bruegel's time will add an inscription invoking the Cripple Bishop.[39] These spidery line figures are meant to amuse and to delight, eliciting at worst revulsion or at best mild disdain. Because we relate the fig-ures to one another within a spectrum of absurdity, rather than to a social situation or to normative bodies, we are not really called upon to read, understand or judge them. When Bruegel paints five performing crippled lepers, however, they push into the beholder's consciousness with all the vigour of

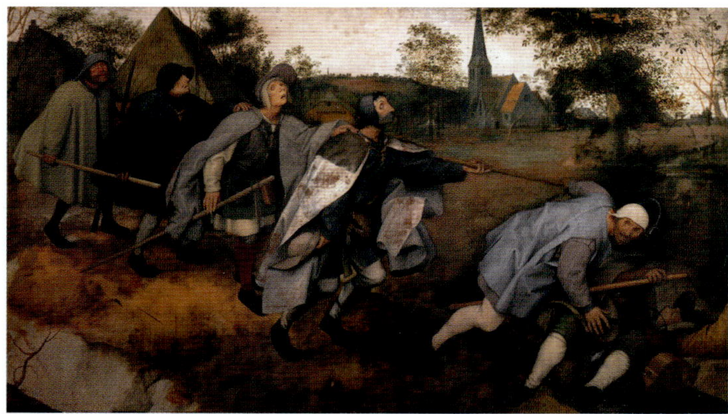

real, stigmatized social beings. It is different, and more difficult, to laugh at them. Their socialized situation and deep if
corrupted embodiedness demands an unpacking of the layers,
a reading from outside in.

Laughter at the foolish, malformed and disabled was
common among all social levels in early modern Europe – *Don
Quixote*, for instance, abounds in such mocking humour –
but there were voices of strong disapproval as well, particularly
among Humanist writers. Vives found it 'inhuman' to mock
the mentally infirm in order to exacerbate their foolish
behaviour, and in Thomas More's *Utopia*, laughter at the
disfigured is held to be disfiguring of the one who laughs.[40]
By Bruegel's time, in Antwerp, mock combats in which blind
men tried to club a pig and only ended up beating one
another no longer starred actual blind people: instead, sighted
men wore blindfolds, assuming a disability that, in its actual
form, had provided such amusement to earlier generations.[41]
The value of the impaired as spectacle was diminishing but
of course their needy presence remained, offering itself to be

54 Pieter Bruegel, *Parable of the Blind*, 1568, distemper on canvas.

read, as if a culture was gradually making a turn from Carnival to Lent.

To which of those two seasons do the men in Bruegel's *Parable of the Blind* belong (illus. 54)? The painting dates from 1568, the same year as the tiny *Lepers*, and it too is a physically exceptional work for Bruegel: it is one of his few surviving paintings done in tempera on linen, a method that is quicker and cheaper than oil on panel but more challenging in that the artist cannot correct his own errors. It is also much less stable than oil on panel, which is why this work looks so much less sharp and colourful than most Bruegels. In it, the painter returns to his interests of a decade earlier, not only in depicting the visibly impaired but in rendering them proverbial. The six men enact a common saying that stems from the Bible: if the blind lead the blind, both shall fall into the ditch (see Matthew 15:14, Luke 6:39; similarly at Romans 2:19). The saying, as used by Christ and in the early modern period too, actually pertains to spiritual blindness, a blindness that is internal, so that physical blindness is only a metaphor for this invisible trait.[42] Three blind men had meandered across the horizon in Bruegel's *Netherlandish Proverbs* of 1559 (see illus. 6), barely discernible figures reminding the beholder of the dangers of choosing the wrong path to knowledge. For the proverb is less about the blindness of the impaired man than it is about his need to choose a person of understanding and virtue to guide him. In Netherlandish art, the blind man generally has a guide, on whose shoulder he leans – it is how we can recognize him as blind.[43] The analogy that Christ intends is that all mankind is internally blind, in need of finding a trustworthy guide on whom we can lean.

Bruegel's six men have no guide but one another, and there is no doubt about their disability. The eye sockets of the first who still stands seem entirely empty, the eyes of the second roll upward so that only the whites are visible, the eyes of the third are sunk deeply into his head, and the last man's eyes are narrowed to empty slits. So vivid are these descriptions that modern diagnosticians have speculated as to the particular cause of each man's blindness: Pieter Bruegel must have carefully looked into the faces of real blind people to so perfectly register their sightlessness.[44] The eyes of the fallen man, and the man in the dark hat and cloak, are concealed from us. But to read the inner state of the blind, it does not matter whether or not we can see their eyes. The aspect of blindness that makes it so unsettling to sighted people is that the eyes, 'windows of the soul', are failing in that function: not of seeing outward, but of allowing others to see inward. Books on physiognomy devoted disproportionate space to reading eyes, but those eyes were assumed to be functional, and directed, so that the manner in which they took in the world also registered the person's inward self: as Guy Marchant says, when in doubt about reading an individual, focus on the eyes, 'for they be most true and provable'.[45] Living eyes peering from behind a mask are one way of estranging legible exterior from true interior, but the blind person naturally bears the reverse of this, a living face without real eyes, an invisible mask that causes fear and aversion.[46] The literary and folkloric character of the deceitful blind man, the trickster, is an accusation against his illegibility: we can never read who he is.

The heightened visual attention Bruegel pays to his characters' blindness plays up their lack of vision and our lack of knowledge; but ultimately it means their lack of knowledge as well. Clutching one another's sticks or touching their fellow's shoulders, they move inexorably onward towards the ditch that has already consumed their leader. They are trusting, in the way that the blind must be, that the person they know, touch, feel, is a worthy guide. For they cannot see the warning marks in other people. Visible signs that speak to the rest of us are mute to them. Those who cannot be read also cannot read.

SIX

Laughing Man

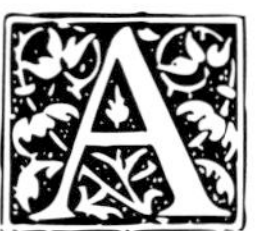CCORDING TO HIS first biographer, Pieter Bruegel's greatest talent lay in his ability to make people laugh. 'One sees few pictures by him', Karel van Mander assures us, 'which a spectator can contemplate seriously and without laughing, and however straight-faced and stately he may be, he has at least to twitch his mouth and smile.'[1] But at what, in the sixteenth century, were Bruegel's beholders laughing so uncontrollably? The question is not entirely easy to answer. While tragedy's great themes are universal and easily recognized across times and cultures, comedy is more contingent.[2] Much of it depends on social attitudes, behavioural conventions, and political and philosophical beliefs. Humour based on verbal plays is relatively straightforward, and something that Humanists would have praised as 'wit' is readily apparent in Bruegel's clever transformations of proverbs into literally enacted form: the guests at the dinner party described in Chapter One, who flipped over their plates to discover a painted proverb, surely laughed at what Bruegel had done, and we can laugh with them. But that is not the main kind of Bruegelian humour that Van Mander refers to. He points to the comedy we see in the gestures and postures

of Bruegel's figures, specifying details of characters within paintings even as generally serious as the *Christ Carrying the Cross*.[3] And he tells us that Bruegel also enjoyed observing, and painting, the amusements of the peasants. All these forms of comedy are more difficult to pin down from our very different historical moment, and yet they are essential for understanding the artist's view of human nature. For it is human nature to laugh.

Of all the creatures of the world, humans alone laugh: *homo risibilis*, we are uniquely gifted with laughter. So said Aristotle, and any early modern thinker who considered the subject of laughter – as many did – reached back first to this touchstone of philosophy as part of their argument.[4] Laughter was a serious business to Renaissance Humanists in several ways. On the one hand, as a rhetorical device, laughter could be weaponized in moral or political debate: rouse your audience to laugh with scorn and contempt at the other side, and you have won the argument. This was the laughter approved of by Aristotle, as the Renaissance understood him. Another form of laughter was said to arise from simple pleasure or happiness: we laugh with joy to encounter an old friend, or to watch our children.[5] Such laughter is universal, and does not divide superior from inferior, or normative from marginal.[6] This second kind of laughter is serious because of its very ability to cross those social boundaries and address fundamental elements of human nature. Laughter, whether joyous or critical, is good, natural and expected, although it can be excessive: in his treatise on civility, Erasmus counsels that to laugh at everything is the sign of a fool, although to laugh at nothing is the sign of a blockhead. Laughter, he goes on, should not be too loud, nor should it shake the body. Only fools use expressions like 'I am bursting with laughter' or 'I am dying with laughter', but should you be uncontrollably convulsed with mirth, at least cover your mouth with your hand.[7]

That Erasmus needs to counsel against great, bodily laughter, a laughter that is instinctive and beyond the control of reason, suggests that such laughter occurred even in his own highly educated circles. In contemporary Italy, Castiglione's *Book of the Courtier* describes members of the assembled elegant company who 'burst out laughing' when some remark sets them off. On one occasion this leads the group to a long, more theoretical discussion on the important topic of what kind of humour is appropriate to the ideal courtier. After a nod to Aristotle, one speaker argues at more length for the naturalness of laughter, a sign of the 'hilarity of the spirit' which is fundamentally attracted to pleasure and desirous of rest and recreation.[8] Humanity has therefore, he says, devised many ways of provoking laughter, both techniques that are individual and private, but especially social, public occasions like 'festivals and various kinds of spectacle'. A historian though would point out that even the laughter of spectacle has two possible natures: it can be controlled and official amusement, used to emphasize social hierarchy and division, or it can be a folk humour, unofficial, inclusive and perhaps more ambiguous.[9] In this second kind of humour, those who laugh may also be those who are laughed at, so that separation and contiguity are interwoven in a kind of loose festive fabric. It is that communal, festive form of laughter that Pieter Bruegel took on, first in prints and later in paintings, in works that at

once explored occasions of comedy and provided beholders
with the opportunity to express their own humanity by laughing with, and at, those who participate in those occasions:
villagers, farmers and peasants.

HOLIDAY: PRINTED PLEASURES

In or around 1559, the year he painted the seasonal rituals of
Carnival and Lent discussed in the last chapter, Pieter Bruegel
designed two large prints depicting a different annual holiday:
the *kermis*. Kermis had originated as a religious holiday, *kerk-mis*
or church mass, most often marking the anniversary of the
dedication of a church or celebrating the feast day of its patron
saint: thus any place with a church, be it a village or an urban
parish, should have at least one kermis.[10] Villagers were encouraged to attend kermis in other nearby towns, and the Catholic
Church even offered indulgences for such visits. The holiday's
key element was a religious procession followed by a special
Mass, after which general celebrations ensued: these included
games, competitions, dancing and feasting, as well as an open
market in foods, toys and minor luxury goods. Piety was thus
combined with harmless fun and special retail activities.

Kermis as a folk holiday meant in practice a universal loos-
ening of social norms and an embrace of the impulsive and
natural side of human behaviour. But in sixteenth-century
German print culture, the holiday had become associated
with the peasantry, whose wild and rude kermis behaviour
was depicted in such a way as to provoke Aristotelian scornful
humour rather than joyful hilarity. By linking kermis riot-
ousness to a specific class, printmakers in Germany created

a suggestion that both that class and that behaviour were unworthy of civilized regard. Spreading from Germany to the Netherlands, peasant kermis imagery showed an unfortunate side of human nature that culture, particularly urban culture, needed to override. When Pieter Bruegel took up the subject of the village kermis, he dealt directly with that pictorial topos. But he shifted its brand of caustic, class-based humour to one that allowed him to explore a less hierarchical, more expansive, sense of humanity's shared comic experience.

The experience of kermis was one that was indeed widely shared, by burghers and peasants alike. Flemish people routinely journeyed for considerable distances to visit another town's kermis, and such travel was considered an essential aspect of local character.[11] When Antwerp residents wanted to join in some happy festivity that would take them outside of the normal strictures of urban life, the place they most often went was the nearby village of Hoboken. Situated only 6 km (3¾ mi.) outside of Antwerp, it was an easy day trip. The lands of Hoboken were owned by a leading Antwerp family, who invited large groups of friends to attend village festivities and, in the early 1560s, adjusted the local beer tax to attract more day-trippers from the city.[12] Hoboken held a kermis no fewer than three times each year – twice in the spring and once in the autumn – and Bruegel's first ever kermis image showed the May festivity which celebrated not the church's dedication but the feast day of the patron saint of the archers' company (illus. 54).[13]

Like *Carnival and Lent*, the *Kermis at Hoboken* advances chronologically from background to foreground, moving from

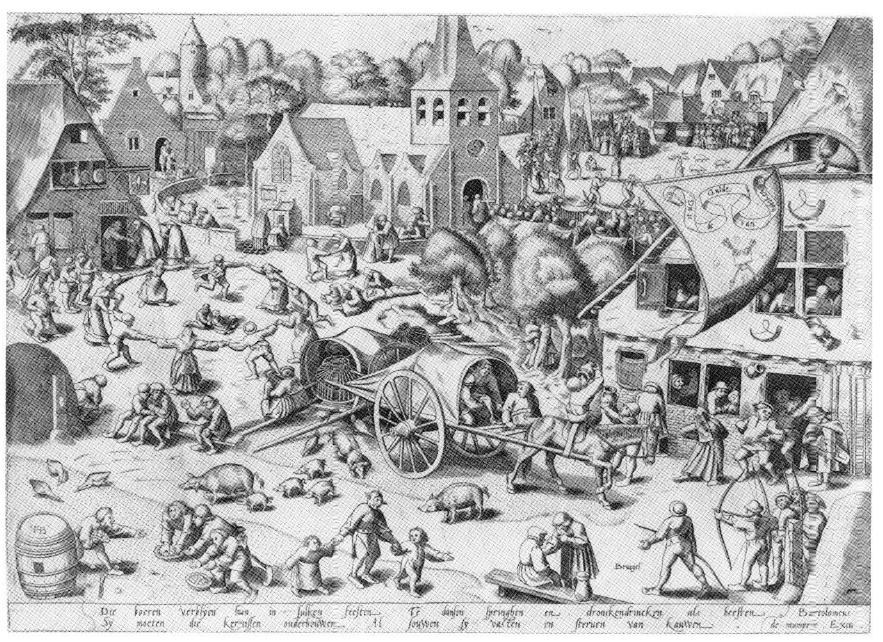

religious ritual to carefree festival. But Bruegel's division is more subtle than that. The area in the distance, where the procession of banners and images passes, is a place of performance. Players have erected a theatre atop barrels and put on their comedy before a crowd; a pair on another platform sing and sell broadside ballads to their audience; and while some villagers participate in the religious procession, one man drops to his knees as it goes by. This is an area in which people are divided between those who act and those who react. Completely the opposite is true of the rest of the image, where everybody is to some extent involved and nobody is merely a spectator. Kermis's true nature, as depicted by Bruegel, is participatory and inclusive, its laughter universal and levelling:

55 Frans Hogenberg after Pieter Bruegel, *Kermis at Hoboken, c.* 1559, etching with engraving.

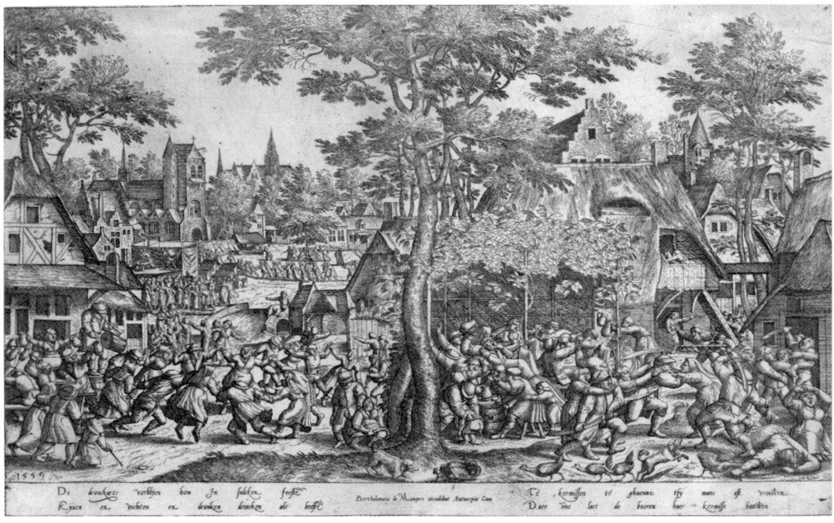

Hoboken villagers and their visitors are all simply having fun. A large crowd has gathered at the foreground inn, which displays the archers' banner, and a few are spilling out of the door, ready to start dancing. Perhaps they will make their way to the ring dance behind the visitors' wagons, where ten adults caper around two children to the music of bagpipes; several other couples seem ready to move in and join the circle. Other couples are embracing under a tree, or by the churchyard wall, while in the churchyard itself a man relieves himself against the building, as does another at the left foreground near the archers' target. Men also urinate against the walls of both inns, the raucous one in the foreground but also the one nearer the church, where two pilgrims are being greeted by the inn-keeper. In the lower left corner of the scene, a group of youths are playing a game with stones or marbles, while behind them, two children lead a fool towards a bench where a pair of elderly

56 Pieter van der Borcht, *Peasant Kermis*, 1559, engraving.

men, who have brought their tankard of ale out of the tavern, are engaged in conversation.

It is not easy to describe everything that happens in this busy scene, and it is even harder to gauge what Bruegel meant us to make of the joys of the fair as he describes them. Certainly we register a lowering of inhibitions, so that the participants in this festival behave according to their nature. But for better or for worse? Bruegel's publisher for this print, Bartholomeus de Mompere, pushed the beholder in one direction by adding an inscription beneath the scene which refers to peasants as jumping about and drinking to excess, insistent on the pleasures of the moment although later they will starve and die of cold. This cynical view of festive human nature positions those who indulge it, peasants, as the opposite of the prudent townsfolk in Bruegel's Seven Virtues series, also from 1559, who had remained constantly vigilant in their preparation for future trials (see illus. 9). In his *Praise of Folly*, Erasmus' Dame Folly claims the anti-Prudence position for fools, who are, she says, always happy precisely because they never think of the future.[14] If this is the spirit in which the fool inhabits Bruegel's kermis, then perhaps immersion in the fair represents an impulsive, unthinking side of human nature that ought to be suppressed by reason.

But the story is not so straightforward. The publisher's caption is adapted from another kermis print that he produced in the same year, designed not by Bruegel but by Pieter van der Borcht (illus. 56). This print is closer to earlier German kermis images, a more conservative or old-fashioned work which Bruegel clearly adapted and diverged from in his view of Hoboken. And Van der Borcht's view of the kermis really does reflect what the caption describes. Reading from left to right, peasants dance wildly, jumping into the air; next they feast and drink to excess and relieve themselves with a notable immodesty far more extreme than Bruegel's Hobokeners. Quarrels begun while drinking spin out of control and culminate in a brawl at the right-hand side of the scene, where swords have been drawn. Finally, one man lies dead on the ground, mourned by his wife. A left-to-right chain of action and consequence leads clearly across the foreground, from extreme dancing to wild drinking to violence and death, as if the classic sins of lust, gluttony and anger have been laid out as the narrative of peasant pleasure. The conclusion of this trajectory is not, in fact, particularly funny, even in a scornful way.

Bruegel took many elements directly from Van der Borcht's print: in fact, the two scenes almost seem to take place on the same stage set, although Bruegel elevated our viewpoint and made the church a more central part of the scene.[15] That refocusing on the church plays into other changes of his which all vastly alter our sense of festive behaviour: the dance is calmer and centres on children, there is little obvious drinking, people play games and flirt instead of quarrelling and fighting, and the wagons suggest that people have travelled to be in Hoboken today. In all these ways, the festivity associated with a religious holiday feels benign and enjoyable instead of threatening. Much the same is true of Bruegel's second kermis print, the *Kermis of St George*, probably produced in around the same year by his regular publisher, Hieronymus Cock (illus. 57). A very large print, complex in composition and more densely populated than that of Hoboken, it must have been a

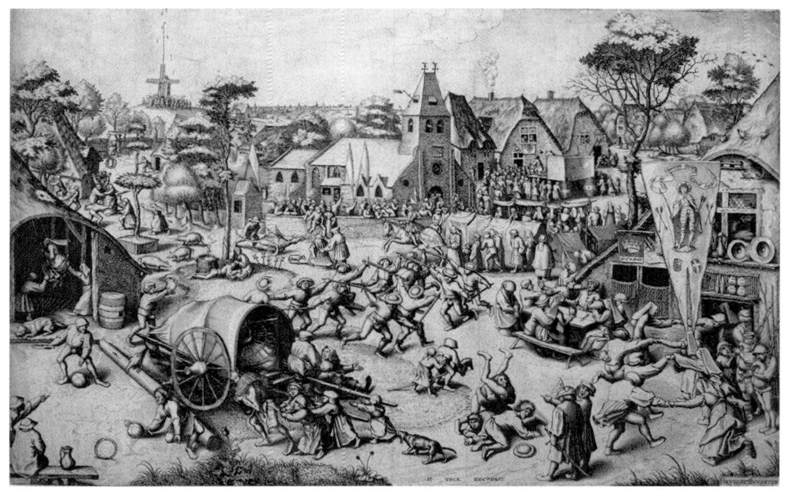

rather expensive piece. The scene is now set in an anonymous village near a large city and shows an archery guild's St George kermis; the saint's banner hangs on the inn, and a shooting competition occurs around a windmill in the distance. Toy windmills have been a big souvenir item at the fair, and a cluster of them are planted under a tree in the centre of the scene, near where a group of villagers are staging a play in which St George (armed) attacks a dragon (wheeled) to save a tiny princess, played by a child whose parent accompanies her (illus. 58). Other children ride a hobby horse and do gymnastic tricks in the foreground, while four more trail about after a fool who is now the leader of their procession. Near them men are playing a game with balls and a hoop, and in the shed at the left edge of the picture, women are playing on a swing; near the inn on the other side of the foreground, couples are line-dancing to bagpipe music, their performance mirroring the sword dance at the centre of the scene.

57 Joannes and Lucas van Doetecum after Pieter Bruegel, *Kermis of St George*, *c.* 1559, etching with engraving.

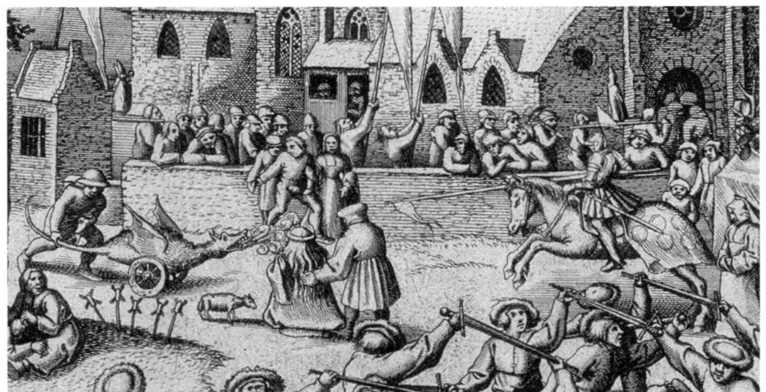

Play, dance, swing, tumble, ride: nearly everybody in this scene is intensely, kinetically engaged. Here and there people pause to talk – a couple by the visitors' wagon, two men near the tumblers, some villagers drinking by the inn – but the overwhelming sense in both kermis images is of bodies in fun, festive motion. That sense of bodily turbulence almost completely precludes any sort of grace or physical composure, for these are figures meant for action, not for posing. Certainly some, in the procession and around the market, move with more careful deliberation than others, but in neither kermis scene do we find persons whose way of moving, or of standing or sitting, would clearly identify them as civilized in the terms of Bruegel's time; this, as we will see, is precisely what makes them peasants. But in the two prints it seems to make them something else as well: it makes them children.

It is not always easy, in Bruegel's printed kermises, to decide who is a child and who is an adult. What of the youths playing marbles in Hoboken, or the tumblers of St George's Day? Who swings on the swing, or pushes the fiery dragon? Very young children we can gauge by their proportions, larger heads

58 Play of St George and the Dragon: detail of *Kermis of St George.*

to shorter bodies, but the activities the people engage in, as well as the movements of their bodies at play, deliberately confuse our sense of adult propriety. In fact, the work by Bruegel that relates most closely to the kermis scenes is not *Carnival and Lent*, but *Children's Games*, painted in 1560 (illus. 59). It is at the intersection between the child and the peasant that we can locate Bruegel's early understanding of what festive, or playful, comedy means.

CHILD'S PLAY

Children's Games is a remarkable work. It is not just a catalogue of games, although it is that – over ninety of them have been identified by scholars.[16] It is also an entire coherent city environment, complete with a town-hall-like building at its centre that has been taken over by children. They are of differing stages of childhood as those were defined in Bruegel's time, some squat little mites like the definite children in the kermis scenes, but others closer to adolescence or what we would call early teens, with bodies proportioned like the people we often thought were adults in Hoboken.[17] Some of the games they play are identical to those shown in the kermis prints: a girl on a swing, a group of boys playing a game with stones or marbles, a little boy with his hobby horse, a mock tournament using play windmills, tumbling and climbing upon one another. Notably absent are structured competitions like those of the archers in both kermis scenes: competition here is more low-key and haphazard. The children also play at mimicking acts and rituals of adult life. A pretend baptismal procession wends its way across the left foreground, while at the very centre of

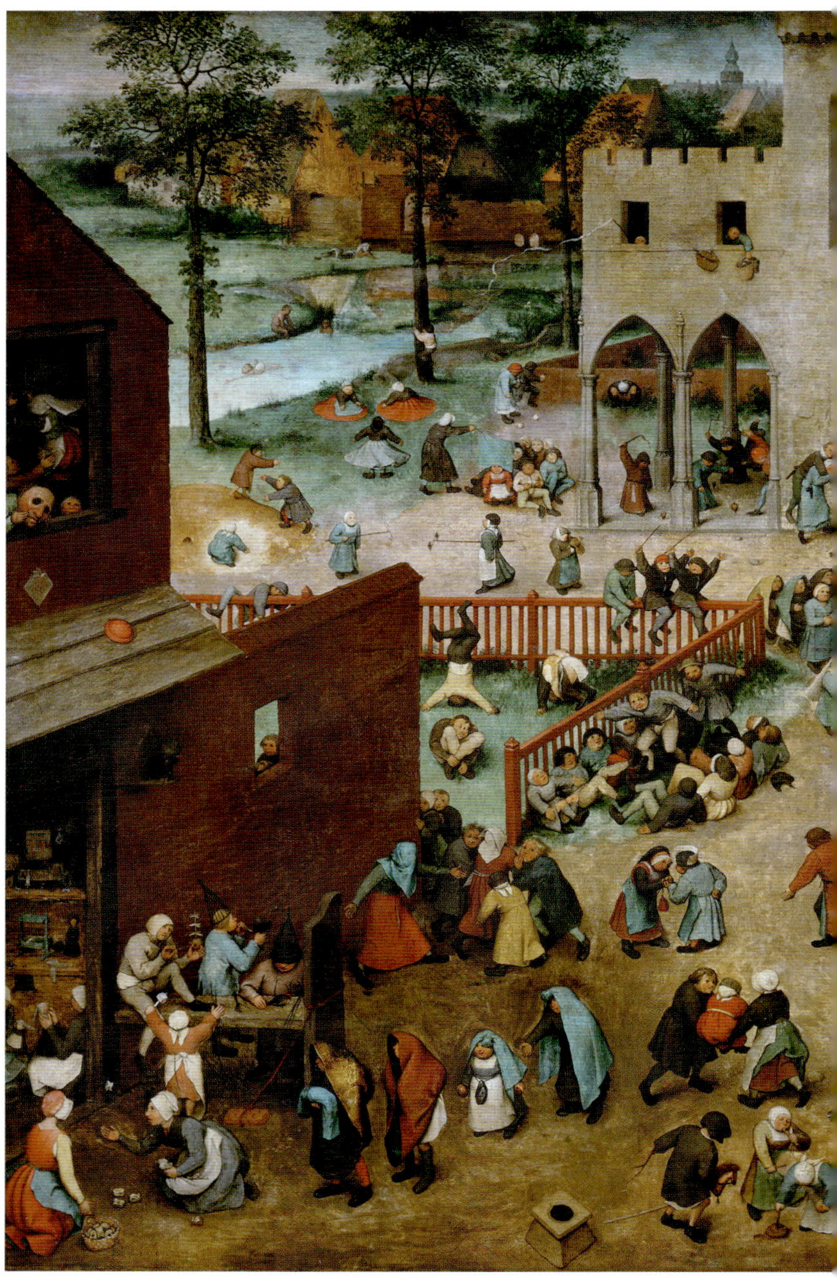

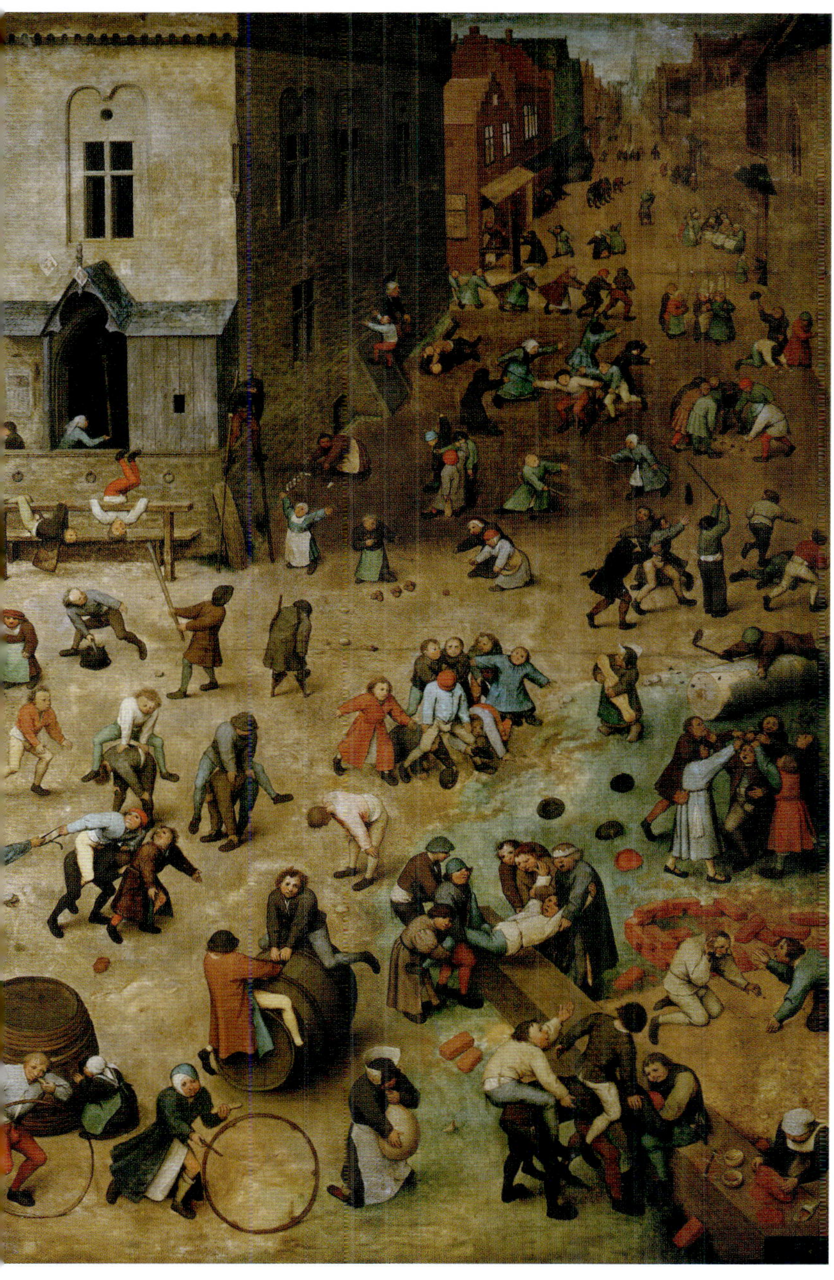

59 Pieter Bruegel, *Children's Games*, 1560, oil on panel.

the panel, a little girl similar to St George's princess at the kermis is acting the part of the bride in a mock wedding ceremony, accompanied by even younger children and overseen by an older one (illus. 60).

Childhood is humanity's playtime, and people in the Renaissance, as today, accepted this as a fact. Not that the nature of that play was unimportant. Erasmus devoted one of his colloquies to a conversation between a group of boys about sport (they debate the merits of handball, sending a ball through an iron ring, jumping and leapfrog), and the penultimate chapter of his hugely popular *De civilitate morum puerilium* (On Good Manners for Boys), a short book devoted to teaching children good manners, concerns behaviour at play.[18] A child's character, he writes, is 'nowhere more readily apparent than in a game', for negative instincts like deceit, anger, arrogance, dishonesty and even violence will all emerge in that context. The play approved of by Erasmus is something children engage in not in pursuit of winning or reward but simply for fun and 'the spirit of the thing'. That is just the way Bruegel's children tend to play, often without evident goals but with a sense of pure kinetic enjoyment: running uphill and down, shinning up a tree trunk, spinning until they fall, floating down the stream (illus. 61), leapfrogging across the centre of the square. Even the nearby tug-of-war teams struggle in a non-combative way. In the absence of adults to impose order, play proceeds with a kind of joyous and endless absorption in the fun of it. There is also a degree of childish intensity to some players, like the girl at the lower right who is grinding up bricks to make red pigment, ready to play salesperson to potential play painters.[19] But most players lack her make-believe foresight and simply embrace the immediacy of the moment.

Festive pleasures and childish games manifest the same side of human nature in Bruegel's rhetoric: a joyful and deeply embodied side of nature. A negative side of humanness that either kermis or play could allow, one that slipped easily into greed and violence, is deliberately excluded from his picture. Contemporary reformed writers portrayed children as entirely tainted by original sin, a view going back to St Augustine's pessimistic view of sin as the dominant feature of the human soul; but this was a view that Erasmus, and many other Humanist writers, strongly disagreed with.[20] After all, Christ himself offered the little child as a model for his followers (Matthew 18:3). And for somebody like Erasmus, and I believe Bruegel, who saw human nature as good (although corruptible), children allow us always to witness human goodness. Even though we strive to advance beyond childhood simplicity to a higher level of rational goodness and belief, it is in the guileless child, incapable of masking its true nature, that we see a positive mirror of our inner selves.[21] This is part of why we joyfully laugh as we watch children. In *Children's Games* their unfeigned hilarity exists in a complete game-world, as if the self-absorbed, special world that play normally creates as apart from dreary reality has turned the tables and enveloped reality in its own ludic mode.

So too the kermis, a specific time in a specific place, cut off from all that is ordinary life in that city that punctuates the horizon in the *Kermis of St George*. But the very separateness that allows for a childlike hilarity at the kermis raises the question of how participation in it can be valued. After all,

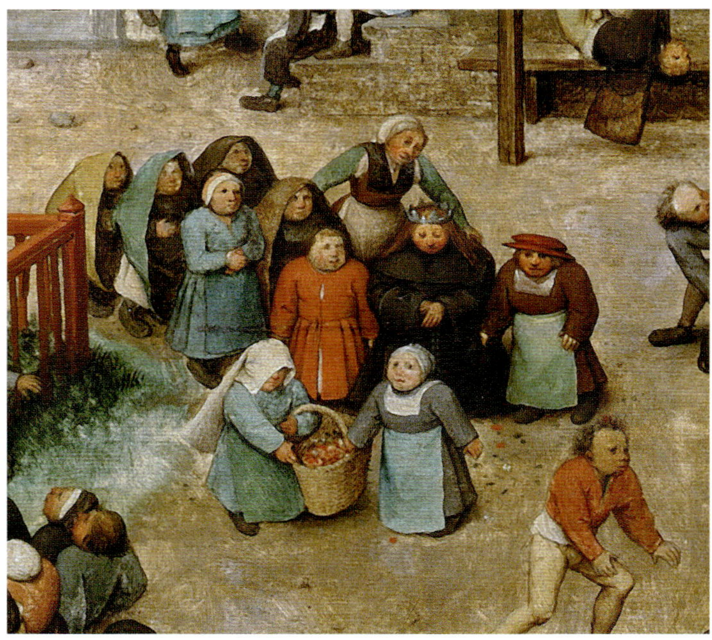

we do not imagine ourselves returning to the city of children
and joining in its fun: it makes us laugh, but we are always
distant from it, and hopefully better in our more advanced
rationality. The kermis offered real opportunities for participation, not just by villagers but by visiting city folk too, and
many people who bought Bruegel's prints had probably taken
advantage of those opportunities. There were mixed feelings
in the sixteenth century about the propriety of joining in
popular festivities like this. Castiglione's Italian courtiers have
a spirited debate about whether the ideal courtier should
participate in the games at 'some country show, where the
spectators and participants [are] common people'; Signor
Pallavicino points out that in some places, 'young gentlemen

60 Play wedding: detail of *Children's Games*.

are to be found, on holidays, dancing all day in the open air with the peasants, and taking part with them in sports', and he sees this as completely appropriate, although some of his friends disagree. In his pictures of countryside leisure and festivity, Bruegel's colleague Pieter Aertsen frequently included very well-dressed city visitors participating in the fun. They have taken advantage of geographical distance and holiday relaxation to indulge their own festive natures.[22] Bruegel, though, is not so clear about this. Some have suggested, for instance, that the two men in the foreground of the *Kermis of St George* are visiting townsmen, since they seem to be spectators more than participants, and to be well dressed. But what of the man dancing right behind them, or the man seated

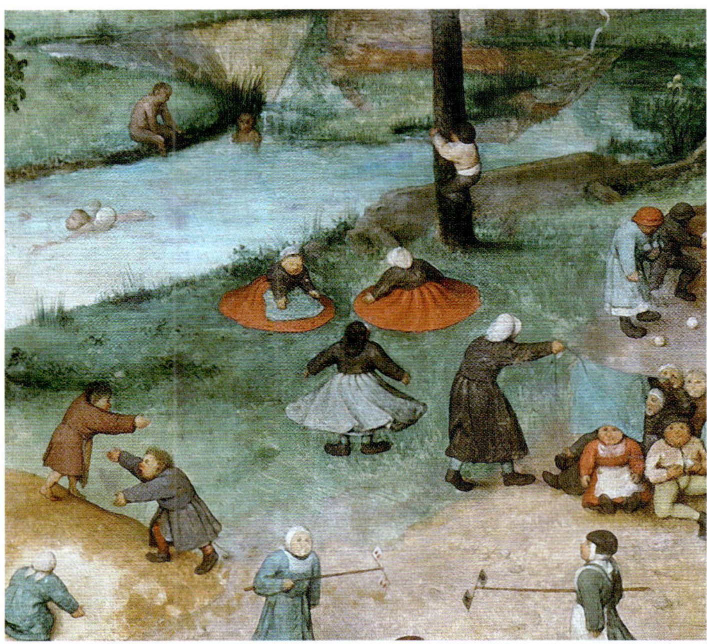

61 Twirlers and swimmers: detail of *Children's Games*.

on the shaft of his wagon, or many of the people attending the free market by the church? As Bruegel uses bodily form and actions to make adult/child divisions indistinct, he also blurs us/them social distinctions. Other artists used clear markers such as clothing, movement or posture to let contemporary beholders divide the natives of kermis-land from those who were just passing through. In Bruegel's kermis, though, everybody is a peasant, a child, a human being.

The one inhabitant of both of Bruegel's printed kermises who is clearly not just another villager is the fool, who walks through the centre foreground of each scene accompanied by small children. He is the character who interprets for us what it would mean to be as a child, or as a peasant – which part of our nature is promised indulgence at the fair. Children and fools were regularly compared to one another in the copious popular literature of Renaissance folly, from Sebastian Brant's late fifteenth-century *Ship of Fools* to Erasmus' *Praise of Folly* two decades later.[23] We love children from newborns to adolescents, says Erasmus' Dame Folly, precisely because of the 'charm of folly' they possess, which gives us pleasure.[24] The fool and the child both appeal to our sense of their innocence, their lack of guile and corruption.

We should tread carefully here, of course. As we saw in Chapter Four it was the 'natural' fool who was a perpetual child, who was sometimes referred to for that reason as an 'innocent', who was unable to form judgements like a rational, adult human being, who had no care for the future and lived for the moment.[25] Guided by instinct and appetite, such fools were figures of fascination but also deep aversion, the mirror reverse of rational humanity.[26] Erasmus' Folly, like the court jester, is an artificial fool, putting on a childish guise in order to speak truth to power in ways that are witty and provoke laughter.[27] Such folly is a rhetorical device, but it speaks of something true about human nature: that we are all fools at heart. Erasmus' Folly insists upon that. 'A foolish man', she says, 'is not unfortunate, because this is in keeping with his nature,' and the happiest men are those who follow nature as their only guide.[28] Lest you think for a moment that you should take this seriously (although it is true), Erasmus then lets Folly move on to celebrate the happiness of animals because they operate only by instinct. Peasant–Child–Fool–Animal. When do we stop joining the fun and laughing with pleasure, and begin distancing ourselves as more rational and respectable beings? What are the lines between these types of laughter, as we experience them at Bruegel's printed kermises?

Bruegel gives us little guidance in answering that question. It is the very difficulty of making judgements about our own inclination to laughter and to pleasure that makes his two prints so intriguing. They do not offer stereotypical peasantishness in the way Van der Borcht's print had, which made scorn such an obvious reaction. Bruegel's benign re-staging of that kermis allows us to think about festive humour as part of human nature, the inclination that every human being had as a child and could potentially still retrieve and indulge as a visitor to a time and place of festive comedy. That is the side of human nature that peasants continually embody, for they (Bruegel implies) are people who have not outgrown impulsivity in favour of rational self-control. At the kermis, and only then, we might allow ourselves to join

them. Bruegel keeps the peasants' instinctive folly bound to
innocent childishness, making our distancing difficult and
our laughter easy. In both of his kermis scenes, but especially
in *Hoboken*, our viewpoint is raised above the goings-on so
that we may survey them with a somewhat withdrawn perspective and may weigh our own reaction to the invitation
to laugh along with the dancers and the players. We laugh
because we recognize commonality, and it's a funny thing.

WHEN PEASANTS DANCE

Pieter Bruegel was not just the ultimate painter of laughter,
according to Van Mander, but also the ultimate painter of
peasants. In fact, we are told, his origins lay in the very world
he would depict, for he hailed from 'an obscure village amidst
peasants'.[29] Having moved to the city and become a successful,
well-connected craftsman, he maintained a fascination with
peasants but from that different, distanced perspective: no
peasants themselves, he and the merchant Hans Franckert, his
patron and friend, 'often went out of town among the peasants . . . to kermises and weddings, dressed in peasant clothing,
and gave presents like the other guests, pretending to be family
or friends of the bride or bridegroom.' While at the festivities,
Bruegel 'enjoyed observing the nature [*wesen*] of the peasants
in eating, drinking, dancing, leaping, lovemaking and other
entertainments, which he then most amusingly and subtly
imitated with paint, in watercolour as well as oil paint'. Since
burghers from the city regularly attended kermis in nearby
villages, it is interesting that Van Mander insists that Bruegel
went in disguise, mingling with peasants as if he were one of

them. It draws Bruegel as an observer closer to his subjects, while also emphasizing that he is an interloper into their world, somebody who does not really belong. He is there to study.

We might doubt Van Mander's account – too good to be true, perhaps – if Bruegel's paintings themselves did not attest to his exceptionally careful observation of peasant life. They are filled with details that modern scholars have confirmed to be authentic folk practices, from aspects of clothing and ornamentation to types of kermis play and wedding customs.[30] But clothing and game choice are not what matters to Van Mander when he describes Bruegel's interests as watcher and recorder. To him, what makes Bruegel's peasant paintings fascinating to their beholders is the way they register acts and activities – things that involve bodily movement. Of course the careful details of costume matter as verifiable guarantors of personal study. But if Bruegel was a proto-ethnographer of sorts, he was principally concerned with peasant bodies in motion, and what he was observing at festive occasions were the habits of movement that made those bodies distinctive and different from the bodies of his friends and patrons in the city.

Bruegel often painted precisely the two kinds of peasant festivity mentioned by Van Mander. Only three of these works survive, two set at weddings and one at a kermis, all created in the last years of his life. From documents, we also know of others, often recorded as having been painted on cloth so that they were perhaps less expensive and certainly less durable. At least three Bruegel paintings of peasant festivity were owned by a single patron: Jan Noirot, master of the Antwerp mint.[31] He also owned paintings of festive peasants by other artists (including Hieronymus Bosch), as did his colleague at the mint, Joris Veselaer. These men were associates of Niclaes Jonghelinck, so Bruegel's kermis and wedding paintings were viewed within the same social circle as his paintings of peasant labour. Those images had included references to leisure among the imagery of work, suggesting that the former was an expected reward for the latter, from the skaters of winter to the distant village shooting competition in the hay harvest (see illus. 14, 17). But festivity is different from leisure. It is a time apart from normal life, a celebration that marks some point in an annual cycle (kermis) or moment of life change (wedding).[32] Bruegel's late monumental peasant paintings explored bodily habits in these conditions of exceptionality, displaying what it was to inhabit a natural, untutored human body at a particularly uninhibited moment.

Bruegel's *Wedding Dance* (illus. 62) of 1566 is probably the earliest of his painted peasant festivities. It would have been more unusual in its own time than we feel it to be now, with centuries of familiarity and derivative works, for it is a cross between the already popular 'peasant wedding' genre that focused on the bride seated at her table, and the 'peasant dance' genre where individual couples, often outside of any context, cavorted in lumpen, comic awkwardness.[33] Bruegel's dance is an occasion, one aspect of a ritual and festive moment. All the adults in the village seem to have turned out for this event. We can map out the scores of people, and their distances from us, by the measure of the women's clean white linen kerchiefs. The dancing women have turned up the long ends of their kerchiefs that still trail down the backs of women further behind, marking the foreground as a space

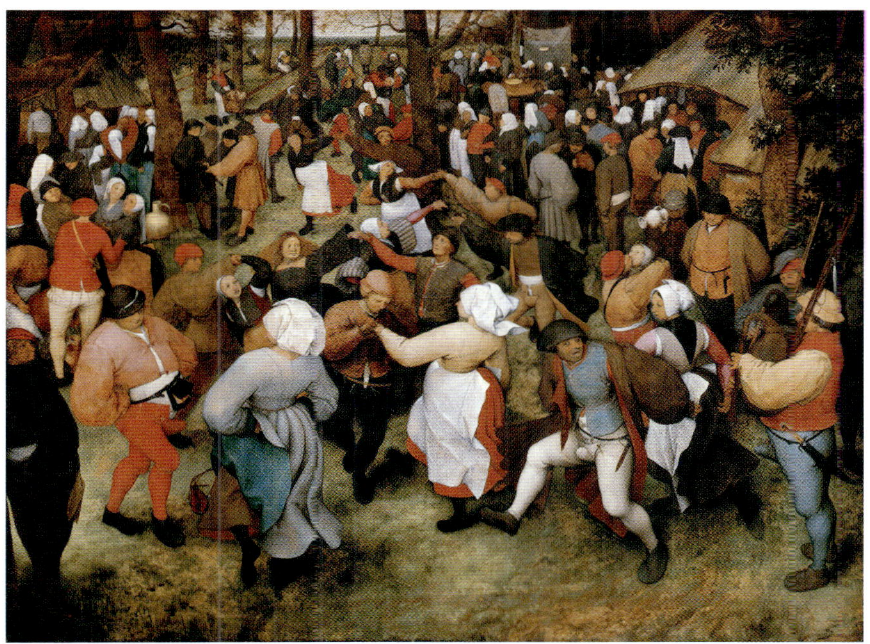

of motion and the distance as a place of more sedate behaviour.
At the furthest distance just right of the centre, two white
kerchiefed women sit chatting before a green cloth over
which hangs the bridal crown; but missing, in between them,
is the bride herself. She is a merry participant in the foreground dance, the lone woman with no kerchief, her long,
thick hair flowing loose.

There are actually only eight couples in motion here, two
sets of four couples, a triangle of energy moving to the tune
of a pair of bagpipers, but their dynamism so dominates the
scene that it is easy almost to ignore the other, less energized
guests — except, perhaps, the couple at the right near the bagpipers, locked in an enthusiastic kiss. The four more distant

62 Pieter Bruegel, *Wedding Dance*, 1566, oil on panel.

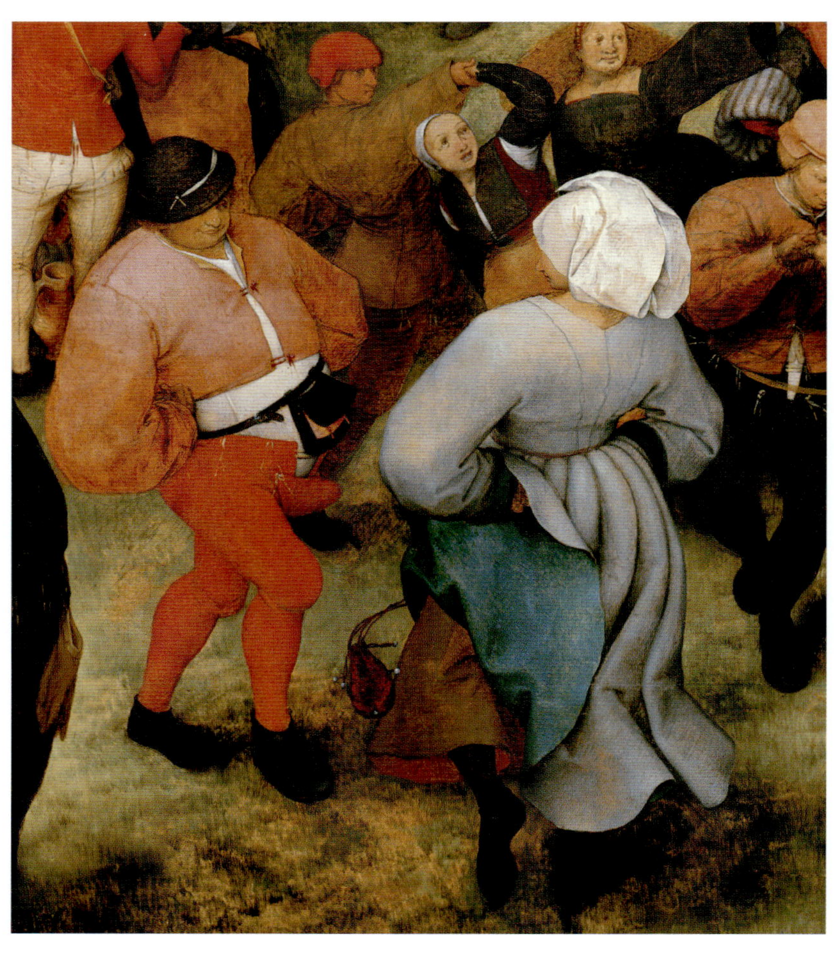

63 Detail of *Wedding Dance*.

dancing couples, beginning with the one just by the central tree and culminating with the bride and her partner, are all doing a dance that involves making a gateway, with the bride appropriately at the head of the set.[34] Each person here has their outside hand on their hip and clasps their partner's hand with the other; but not entirely, for one woman has forgotten to make the hand-on-hip gesture, while the couple behind the bride have lost hold of one another's hands – the woman has, perhaps, turned too soon. Faces look surprised, amused, confused; bodies strain, stamp and skip.

But the awkward missteps of these dancers, and their failure to cohere as participants in a set dance, are as nothing compared to the four couples who occupy the foreground. In this set, no pair's movements exactly repeat another's, as if they are each at a slightly different moment of the same dance. The couple at the left, facing off with hands on hips, do not touch one another, but the man's flirtatious smile, tipped hat and protruding red codpiece suggest his pleasure in partnering with a woman whose bejewelled red purse swings so freely as she flips up her overskirt to kick with gusto (illus. 63). The central couple are likewise doing a balance step, but they seem more restrained: the man with his eyes lowered, the woman with her skirts down, holding hands and matching one another's movements. The man in the couple nearest the bagpipers is the most exuberant of all the dancers, lifting his leg high and panting with effort. Perhaps he has had too much to drink; certainly he is fumbling his moves. He should be twirling his partner, like the pair at the left, but he is confused: which way to twirl, which hand to hold? His smiling partner has to run to keep up with him, and we smile with her. This is folk dance as comedy for participants as well as for beholders. Everybody laughs together.

The peasants' movement is fast yet heavy. Bruegel gives men and women alike rather large feet in dark shoes, so that we feel their steps as solid upon the ground, an almost audible thumping rhythm that tells us visually about the nature of the bagpipers' tune. Although they are performing a specific dance, the peasants' movements are extremely individual, keeping to the music but often missing the pattern set by the dance itself. Bodies do not fully follow the set actions of the performance because Bruegel the 'ethnographer' is not actually there to record for us the specifics of that peasant custom. What he has closely observed, and wants to register in this painting, is how human bodies move when they are not simply obeying social rules but are caught up by the energy of the occasion and the rhythms of the music.

Unlike the bodies of Bruegel's beggars, those of his peasants are never in any way malformed, and yet they are still telling us things about these people, the ways in which they are both utterly human yet not like us. The peasant bodies are lumpen, their movements jerky and rough. The non-dancers in the scene, as we scan into those background groups, often do not stand fully upright, nor are they gracefully balanced. They tilt or push their heads forward, or slouch a bit, or curve their spine to push out their stomach. It is thus not merely that the foreground group of peasants are forgetting themselves at a moment of dance; it is the moment of dance that allows Bruegel to best display what bodies do when they have not internalized the proper habits of comportment. Peasants let go more fully than city dwellers would because they lack that underlying development that keeps the burgher composed and upright.

The Renaissance developed a distinctive vision of the elite human body, and a discourse around that body, that separated it from the bodies of those outside the elite. The way a person carried themself was enormously important, from the first impression their body made when they entered a room or were introduced to a new acquaintance, to the body's appearance in action when at play, or hunting, or dancing. Castiglione's ideal courtier has a very specific bodily type: not too tall and not too short, strong and supple, and above all graceful at all times: 'let him laugh, jest, banter, romp and dance', says Count Lodovico, but 'let him say and do everything with grace.'[35] The courtly body, and those of the generations of non-courtly people all over Europe who read Castiglione's best-seller, was intended to be beheld, judged and admired, for it would be constantly revealing a person's civility. To declare to others your standing in the world, it was necessary to possess such a body[36]

Civility and grace were things to be cultivated. Castiglione tries to have it both ways – grace is purely natural, but grace can be acquired by the naturally graceless. Erasmus is concerned with manners and decorum rather than 'grace', but he too can sound curiously ambivalent about the relationship between that which is acquired and that which is innate, counselling the young reader of his *De civilitate* that while 'external decorum of the body proceeds from a well-ordered mind', they must also train their bodies to reveal their natural goodness.[37] Therefore he devotes the first and longest section of his popular treatise to matters of physical bodily performance.

For the schoolboys who were his intended audience, he covers all sorts of bodily situations, positions and exigencies. He gives advice on how to sit, stand and walk; on how to compose your facial expression pleasantly, how to wipe your nose when necessary, when and how to relieve yourself or even vomit (they are natural things, but please not in public). At the heart of this discussion is standing posture, which should be 'gently erect . . . the shoulders should be evenly balanced', the head neither drooping forward nor tossed back.[38] Do not sit or stand with your legs too wide apart, do not cross your legs, do not scratch your head. This sort of advice, explicitly addressed to any young reader and not just to princelings, is supposed to be of universal application, for all children are naturally good, and all can express that by cultivating civility through the body.

When Erasmus warns against bad habits, his negative comparisons are to idiots and fools and buffoons, implying people who are socially like us but who are failing to behave correctly. Very rarely does he call a form of behaviour peasantish, and then it is not about posture or movement, but ill-mannered gestures like dipping half-eaten bread into the soup.[39] But in the visual arts of his time, social distinctions were organized precisely around basic bodily manifestations. Early in the century, Albrecht Dürer had developed a stereotypical form of the comic 'sturdy peasant', very squat and awkward, which had permeated the broader print culture: Pieter van der Borcht's peasants are its descendants.[40] Bruegel's peasant bodies are not usually like this: their proportions are more normative. It is their subtle habits of movement that mark their less cultivated, more natural way of inhabiting the world, and that can make us laugh with rather than at them. This kind of differentiation can be clearly seen in Bruegel's *Proverbs* (see illus. 6), where the figure of the prince in the right foreground stands upright, his legs gently extended, his gestures graceful; beside him, the man pulling with all his might on a pretzel, or the man nearby filling the ditch after the calf has drowned, are by their very poses absolutely peasants. Effort, whether that of work or of play, distorts the body, while a well-trained body avoids being distorted.[41] No figure in Bruegel's peasant scenes ever looks like the proverbial prince, for even when still, they lack his easy, self-conscious grace. Peasants do not behave in order to be seen. They are natural.

The peasants cavorting merrily at Bruegel's wedding are natural in this way, but they are not caricatural. Even the codpieces, which can seem comically over-sexualized to us, are just the peasant equivalent of equally extreme ones worn by the elite men of Renaissance Europe in their portraits.[42] Some of the peasant bodies are a bit stocky, or are made so by thick, heavy clothing that sways and flips with the exuberance of their movement, as they kick and hop. Generally, it's all about effort. Even the bagpipers who provide the music show effort, filling their lungs and puffing their cheeks: part of why the bagpipe was considered a lower-class instrument was its visibly distorting effect on the body of the player.[43] There are beholders of the dance within the scene – the man leaning against a tree at the left corner, and two men near the bagpipers – but the only dancers who seem cognizant of a gaze are the pair at the left who face off against one another, bodies and eyes matched in confrontation. Otherwise the scene, and especially the dance, comprises people whose bodies are untrained and uncomposed, so that, thanks to the careful observations of a disguised observer who has gone among them like another peasant, we can see not exactly human nature, but natural humanity.

FEASTING

The other extensive section of Erasmus' *De civilitate* treats behaviour at a banquet, because this is a social situation of great complexity, at which a person may encounter all sorts of behavioural challenges and will be observed by all those in attendance. No fidgeting, elbowing or kicking your neighbour, warns Erasmus, and don't drink too much or be greedy. Sit up straight! Be cheerful, laugh moderately at the wittiness of others, but do not laugh at any social errors they may fall into.[44] So what did the well-trained, civil beholder make of Bruegel's peasants at their banquet (illus. 64)? The painting, or one like it, hung in the dining room of mintmaster Jan Noirot's Antwerp home, where (one presumes) proper banqueting etiquette was observed or at least expected.[45] It is thus a work more difficult to imagine enjoying with detachment than the *Wedding Dance* had been, because it was meant to be observed from a situation comparable to that which it represents. And while the *Dance* was viewed from a somewhat elevated viewpoint, at the *Feast* we are pulled down close to, into, the action. The table's strong diagonal also breaks the self-enclosure of normal banqueting scenes, where the table is parallel to the picture plane: here, the depicted space and ours are drawn together. Compared to most Bruegel images, we have an unusual amount of staged physical access to this scene.

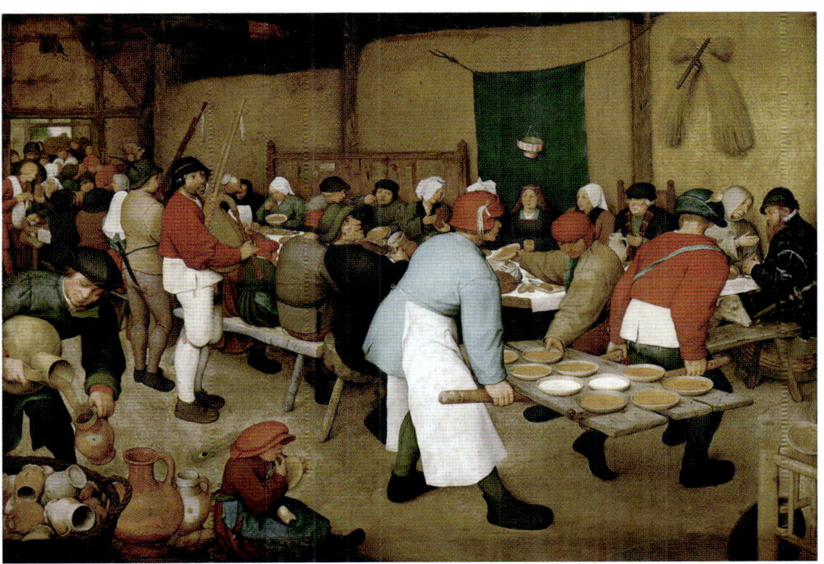

This peasant scene is particularly full of careful details,
some that are 'ethnographically' correct (the costumes are
exceptionally, complexly, accurate) and others that resonate
in a general way with peasant habit and tradition. The old
door used as a tray to bear the delicious rice pudding, and the
haphazard bits of furniture and other repurposed farm items
that have been utilized to accommodate so many guests, all
feel appropriate to these people. Specific wedding customs
– the crown poised over the placid, seated bride – meet
seasonal ones – the 'final sheaf' hanging on the wall, signalling
that this is the end of harvest season, when food is plentiful
and labour is done. It is when peasants rightfully relax and
celebrate, and weddings were often held at this time of
year. All of these things assure us that what we are looking
at is the truth of rural life, and in that sense Bruegel's work

64 Pieter Bruegel, *Peasant Wedding Feast*, 1567, oil on panel.

is entirely unlike the raucous burlesque peasant wedding scenes produced by other painters at this time, which were clearly intended to generate mocking laughter.[46] The things in Bruegel's painting that make even the most straight-faced person smile, as Van Mander claimed, are individual human moments rather than a general tone or behaviour.

The guests and the waiters, the musicians and the wedding party – everybody at Bruegel's wedding feast is intensely characterized through posture, gesture and facial expression,

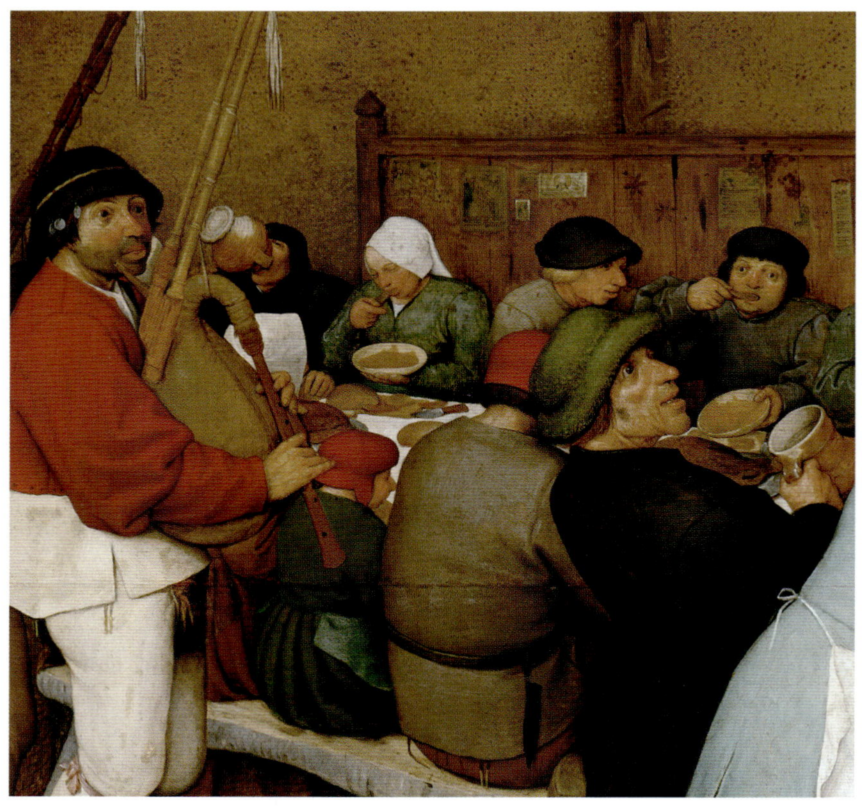

65 Detail of *Peasant Wedding Feast*.

and these characterizations are often wonderfully humorous. A wide-eyed bagpiper, in need of a shave, has paused from his playing to gaze longingly at the rice pudding, hoping that the treat won't all be gone before he gets his turn at it (illus. 65). Nearby, a man with a long, craggy face, whose jug is empty, leans back as if trying to find somebody he can signal for a refill. These men's expressions are both highly individualized and yet entirely uncomposed in the sense that sixteenth-century viewers were used to seeing individuals' features deliberately arranged for portrayal, in portraits or even history paintings. Their expressions of excitement and desire are incorrect from an Erasmian point of view, for civility counsels facial composure (calm, steady eyes, a smooth brow) in all circumstances, but their deviance as represented by a great painter registers something basically human: the instinctive feelings that learned civility forces well-trained people to suppress. Across the table from the bagpiper, some guests are mildly uncouth in their happy consumption or lively conversation, their faces amusingly animated. But nobody is actually *badly* behaved, and other guests talk and work and eat without any impropriety at all.[47] It is precisely the easy combination of the proper enjoyment of a festive occasion with individual instances of unabashed intensity of pleasure in the moment, that allows us to read humanity in the peasants.

Under the gaze of the watchful artist-visitor, peasants reveal their true nature because, as simple people, untutored by learning but also uncorrupted by city life, they haven't the guile to put on a face, a figure, that would disguise by conforming.[48] This view of uneducated, transparent country folk is exploited by Bruegel in these late monumental depictions of human festive impulse, works that are comical not because we laugh *at* them but because we recognize in them aspects of human nature that have been allowed to escape the artful confines of rationality and emerge uproariously into view. The work that most fully plays this out is the one surviving painted *Peasant Kermis*, which takes the freedom of a village holiday and makes it bold, intense and individualized (illus. 66). Again we are low, close down to the dirt road leading into the village, as if our feet could beat along that path and join the dance. The figures we see are familiar from Bruegel's previous peasant scenes: the ill-shaven bagpiper now puffs mightily, distorting his face with effort, while the craggy man rushes in from the right with his partner to join the dance. Both are coarser, but also more laughable, than they were at the banquet, as are the broadly gesticulating fellows at the table to the left, who are related to drinkers in the *Kermis of St George*. The wonderful kissing duo behind them are likewise more comical cousins of the pair in the *Wedding Dance*. Among the dancers, the couple just below the church seem to perform the same dance as the four pairs in that same picture. But the pair in the centre are just kicking up their heels to the bag-piper's tune, and the pair at the right are an entirely new invention, he proceeding at a quick jog, she running to keep up with him.

Because our viewpoint is so low, the number of characters we can see is limited and we spend more time with each of them. It is only after we have engaged with all the adults, whose faces appear in a limited band across the centre of the picture, that we discover the two figures who are actually nearest to us: a girl and a much younger child whom she is

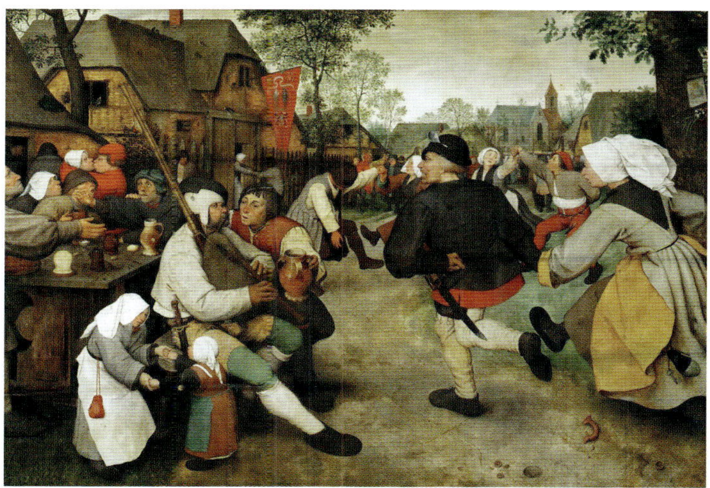

leading in a dance to the sound of the bagpiper. Children
learn by mimicking their elders, both in the civilized rituals
of adulthood that Bruegel showed in *Children's Games* but also
in habits of enjoyment and pleasure.[49] In one of Bruegel's
lovingly precise details, the smaller girl has a round bell on a
string pinned to her sleeve, so that her parents can find her as
she wanders about the village. Now, she is ringing as she dances.
But her bell is not just a random detail of folk custom, for
Bruegel is using it to link the foreground children to the other
belled figure in the scene: the fool, towards the background
but just above the arms of the central dancing couple, whose
bells hang from his fool's cap. He stands beside a dour man,
a non-participant, a watcher of the festivity, to whom he is
apparently speaking with an expansive gesture. To this straight-
faced visitor, he urges a smiling response to the festivity that
they witness. Peasant–child–fool. Those who fully inhabit
their own humanity are the happiest of us all, as Folly has

66 Pieter Bruegel, *Peasant Kermis*, oil on panel.

assured us, and while we are too wise and too civil to be so foolishly joyful, we may take pleasure in understanding the part of human nature in which children, and peasants, are absorbed.

Conclusion: Speaking Truth

THE ABILITY TO SPEAK, even more than the ability to laugh, defined what it was to be human in the Renaissance. But speech could also define what particular kind of human you were: many were the 'sins of the tongue' that would reveal a person's ethical deficits.[1] Thus Erasmus, who has words on every subject relevant to early modern humanity, includes near the beginning of his lengthy essay on the tongue, 'Lingua', a discussion of the benefits of taciturnity: 25 pages, in a modern edition, extolling the silent and decrying those whose speech is undisciplined, 'leaky' or simply excessive.[2] The loquacious philosopher moves on from there to dissect a variety of spoken evils, of which the primary one is lying (a sin particularly hated by God, who is Truth) and especially falsehood as manifested in slander and calumny, the very works of the Devil. Above all, Erasmus is agitated about slanderous tongues that defile a person's good name, a subject on which he becomes remarkably heated. 'It is a most grievous sin to defile another man's wife,' he argues at one point, 'but more grievous still to defile your neighbour's reputation.'[3] The epitome of wicked speech is calumny by innuendo, which makes the charge nearly impossible for the victim to deny: in

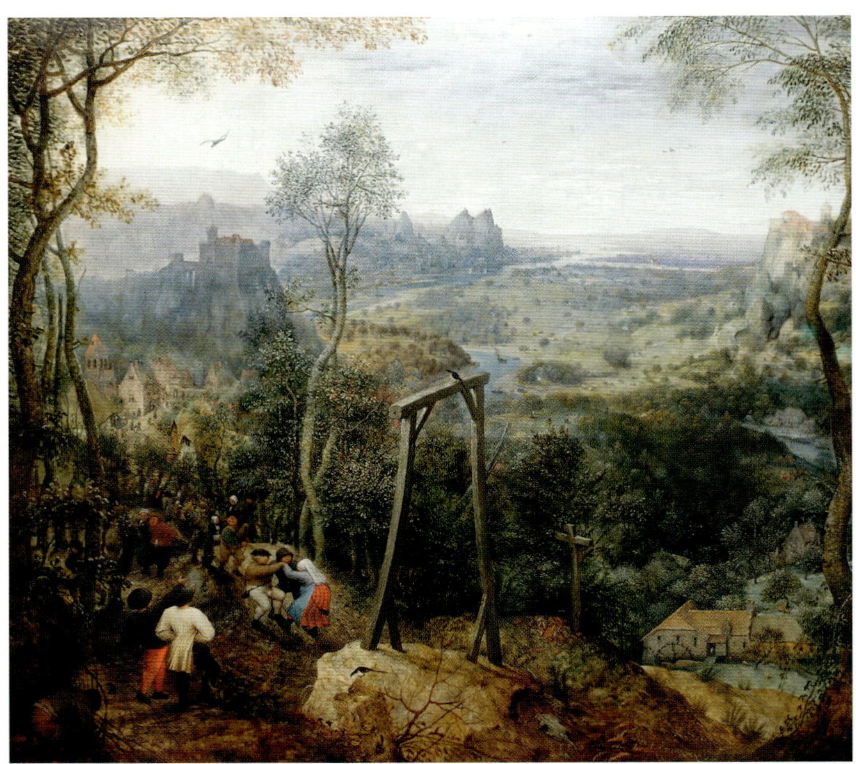

this slippery zone, the lie easily takes hold in people's minds as being the truth.[4]

Pieter Bruegel, painter of pictures of Babel and translator of the oral wisdom of proverbs into visual form, was himself a 'very quiet and moderate man, not of many words', or so we are told by Van Mander. The biographer's life of Bruegel is full of quirky personal anecdotes that probably reached him from Bruegel's cousin Gillis van Coninxloo, a Protestant refugee to Amsterdam from Catholic Spain's crackdown in the south.[5] One story that could have been passed along in

67 Pieter Bruegel, *The Magpie on the Gallows*, 1568, oil on panel.

the family concerned an old girlfriend who was an inveterate liar, to Bruegel's great annoyance. He made a deal with her: 'he would carve all her lies onto a tally stick, for which he made one that was quite long – and if in time the tally stick should be filled then marriage would be entirely off the cards' – as swiftly happened.[6] Here we have Van Mander (or the Bruegel family) setting up a picture of a man of whom Erasmus would have approved, one careful with his own words and unable to stomach a person careless with theirs. Bruegel's caution continued onward to his deathbed, when he asked his wife to burn many captioned drawings or designs for prints 'because they were too caustic or derisory' and she might, eventually, have to answer for them. He also left to her in his will one painting, his recent *Magpie on the Gallows* (illus. 67) of 1568: 'by the magpie he meant gossiping tongues, which he committed to the gallows.' Finally, Van Mander adds that Bruegel 'also made a picture of Truth Will Out – this (according to him) was the best he ever made'.[7]

Art historians are wary of unverifiable tales like these, told a generation later by a writer who perhaps knew a cousin but had no direct guarantee of the story's truth. And yet we have no better source of information. Our plight, and that of Van Mander as a biographer, is a common one that was encountered with some urgency by Pieter Bruegel's contemporaries. How to decide what is true in a time of chaos and uncertainty? Basic information about rebellion and warfare, in a time before newspapers, arrived informally and was often impossible to verify, yet might be of enormous consequence. The internecine conflicts of the sixteenth-century Netherlands were particularly fraught with rumours, tales sometimes deliberately spread by partisans of one side or the other, which could directly affect the course of events. Chronicler Godevaert van Haecht, who was extremely careful to note and weigh his sources, recorded that in July of 1567, in Antwerp, 'there was more rumour of war than I [can] write . . . One ought not to write this down before the event occurs, yet it must be recounted because of the magnitude of the rumour.'[8] And the next month, the Duke of Alba arrived with his Spanish army, determined to destroy heresy in the Netherlands. In the following years, his Council of Troubles would try 12,000 people, sentence 9,000 to death and actually execute over a thousand.[9]

Prosecution for heresy was widely resented by all sides in the Netherlands, in part because such trials were run on an inquisitional basis rather than according to the local custom of accusatory trial.[10] In a traditional accusatory trial, the credentials of witnesses were examined by the authorities before any arrest was made, thus affording greater protection to the accused; but inquisitional trials proceeded on the basis of suspicion leading directly to arrest, and might be investigated by means of torture. The inquisitional mode meant that rumour and gossip played serious and frightening roles in matters of life and death. This had been true of local heresy trials for some time, but the issue had become hugely magnified in the years just before Bruegel's death in 1569. Even in trials of important persons, testimony might be based largely on hearsay, reputation and matters said to be of 'common knowledge'.[11] Thus it mattered greatly that his wife should not have to answer for the artist's caustic ideas. Gossiping tongues were a genuine danger. Power over the gallows had slipped away from traditional local controls that safeguarded the innocent. It was never even clear whether heresy was a crime of mere thought, or of uttered (or pictured) word, or of actual deed.

So if Bruegel told his wife to burn his drawings, and left her a painting about loose talkers, what were the ideas and the gossip actually about? Better that nobody should know. While many of Bruegel's works are slippery in their meanings, easily taking on different implications according to audience or context, *Magpie on the Gallows* goes exceptionally far in the disconnect between its apparent simplicity – landscape, peasants – and the confusion produced by closer examination. The painting is relatively small among Bruegel's works and is square in format, so that instead of moving across a horizon as in his other landscapes, the eye is drawn inward. From the foreground hill we are projected into a remarkably beautiful landscape with a vivid sense of atmosphere, less crisp than the *Months* had been, more poignant. Detail is implied, but not provided.

In a typical gesture, Bruegel has positioned at almost the exact geometric centre of his panel a casual yet key element: the magpie, bird of endless chatter. But not just benign verbiage, for the magpie had a particularly bad reputation for malicious gossip, deceit and even betrayal.[12] This magpie is perched on a gallows, but that structure is as untrustworthy as the words of the magpie. While its horizontal element seems steady, forming the straight pointer that leads our gaze towards the landscape's beauties, its two vertical supports are impossibly skewed. It is hard even to make sense of how this simple construction has been built here at all, precariously perched on a rock, unanchored, its left support warped into an arc while the other remains rather straight. A tiny village like the one at the left, from which the string of peasants are making their way up the hill, would not have a permanent gallows and would rarely see an execution at all. The awkward wooden structure looms in the foreground like an interloper, a character become the star of a drama where it doesn't belong.

For wasn't this supposed to be a world of comedy? We might have been forgiven for thinking so, since nearest to the gallows, a peasant couple are doing a merry dance to the tune of a bagpiper who has walked with them up the hill from the village below. But the couple's friend in black is reaching out to each of them, pressing them to stop their mindless celebration and take heed of their surroundings. The road on which they are dancing is about to take a sharp downward slant, and they risk a tumble. The urgency of the man in black points to the instability, literal and figurative, of those who pay no heed to the chattering informants that lord it over them, the danger of falling beneath the gallows.

The road on which the couple dances forks, and forks again, as if cataloguing choices that people face as they make their way out of the village. To the left of the bagpiper, three peasants have taken a road that will avoid the gallows rock altogether. The dancers are at the next fork. They could move leftward, up a path on which two men are standing, backs to us. One of them gestures expansively outward: behold the world, in all its beauty! Like the dancers, his perspective on the world is uninterrupted by the gallows. The second branch of this road would take the dancers downward towards a watermill in the valley. On their way, they would pass a cross with a tiny image inset just beneath its horizontal bar, a simple roadside shrine. Crafted from the same wood as the gallows, it is evidently connected to that central player but stands in its shadow. It may be there to play either the role of supplement or opponent, ratifying the justice of the gallows, or countering secular judgements with a higher, divine truth. If the peasants dance between the two, what will it mean?

The obliviousness to the gallows of both watchers and dancers is a problem. Absorbed in the pleasures of visual contemplation or in full-bodied festive celebration, they have cast aside caution, or what the Renaissance would have called prudence. From our own position the gallows and its malicious, feathered visitor are unavoidable. Although perhaps uncertain as to the nature of the choices that face this place's inhabitants, the reason for their dance, the function of the cross, we nevertheless know the dangers of loose talk and caustic opinion. Perhaps, in fact, it is interpretation itself that is dangerous. Who has the right to lay claim to a particular way of understanding when the nature of fundamental truths is so hotly contested? A century earlier it had been possible (although still not unproblematic) for the Italian Humanists to argue that every philosophical or religious tradition contained some fragments of a greater truth that was not grasped by any one individual.[13] Yet already by the time of Erasmus, a theologian honestly attempting to steer a path between religious positions could, as he bitterly pointed out, be denounced as a heretic. By the 1560s, things were much worse, divisions more rigid.[14] The magpies of the sixteenth century dealt not in petty gossip but in deadly accusation. Untruths? Perhaps, but as Erasmus' Folly had pointed out, 'man's mind is so formed that it is far more susceptible to falsehood than to truth.'[15] It is human nature to embrace, and enjoy, lies and deception.

Pieter Bruegel was a man prudent with his words, careful of expressing critical truths and cautious about needing to answer for opinions. Four hundred and fifty years after his death, we still know nothing certain about his own beliefs, what he felt to be true: like the great writers of the sixteenth century, in rhetorical terms he knew how to play the fool, to speak in ways (like proverbs) that made a meaning particularly hard to pin down ('it is said . . .'), to use paradox and other feints that would render his intentions ambiguous. The missing signature on the print of *Justice*, discussed above in Chapter Three, is one of the clearest signals that the artist had an opinion on some matter – and the signal is just an absence. Working for the economic elites of Antwerp and the political elites of Brussels, powerful groups not always in

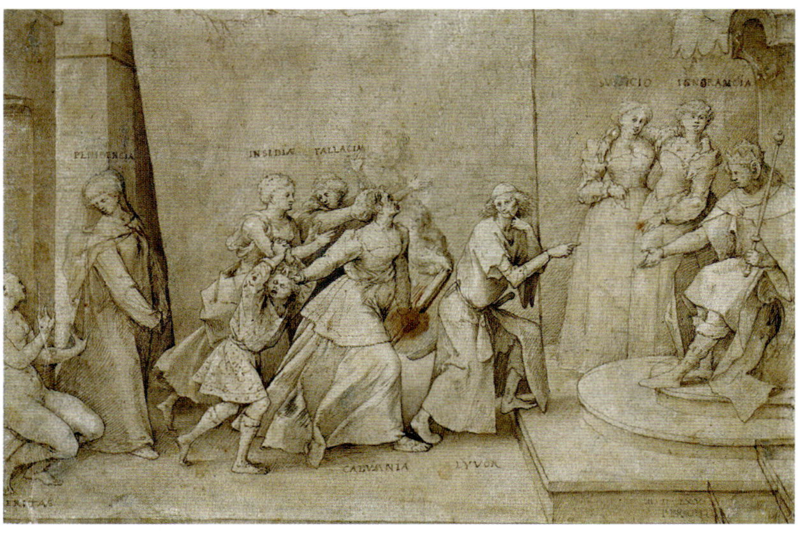

68 Pieter Bruegel, *The Calumny of Apelles*, 1565, drawing, pen and grey-brown ink, with grey and brown wash.

harmony with one another, he knew that some of his own works were too critical to be made public. So what Truth would be revealed, in the picture called *Truth Will Out* that (according to Van Mander) Bruegel called the best he ever did?

No surviving painting fits this description, but a drawing does: the *Calumny of Apelles* of 1565, made just a few years before Bruegel's death (illus. 68).[16] Different in technique from his other drawings, it was probably the study for the painting mentioned in the records of an art dealer in 1670 as 'the calumny of the Old Bruegel'.[17] And its subject is the evils of malicious rumour, false tales invented and spread to ruin the reputation of an innocent person: not just any person, either, but an artist. Bruegel's drawing recreates a painting described by the ancient Greek writer Lucian in his essay 'On Not Believing Rashly in Slander'. According to Lucian, a rival of the great artist Apelles was so jealous of his success that he spread a rumour that Apelles was plotting against the king, and the painter was condemned to death. Cleared at the last minute by counter-testimony, Apelles made a painting that would describe, in allegorical terms, the terrible experience he had undergone. Lucian's text had been mined by other writers (notably Alberti) and other artists (notably Raphael and Botticelli), and Bruegel probably drew upon several of these sources.[18]

The king, sitting at the right, has very large ears because he is so ready to listen to false rumours. He is also prepared internally to believe the lies he is told, for Ignorance and Suspicion, personified as two courtly ladies, have paved the way for his mind to embrace untruth. Calumny herself strides forward in the centre of the composition, a robust woman carrying a burning torch in one hand and, with the other, pulling her victim by the hair: Bruegel has shown him as a mere child, to emphasize his innocence. In front of Calumny shambles Envy, an awkward fellow who smiles foolishly and pulls on his lip as he looks out at us. Envy is the idiotic guide of Calumny, leading her malice to its target, but his gaze also pulls us into the situation. We see all, but can we discover the Truth?

Truth is hard to find in Bruegel's drawing. She is more or less where she belongs: at the end of Calumny's procession, behind the sad figure of Repentance – but she does not obey Lucian's description. Her nudity is not in his text, or in most artists' illustrations of it, but is a decision made by Bruegel to signal Truth's unadorned, simple purity. Truth hides nothing.[19] But Lucian does describe Truth as approaching, actively making herself known. Other artists rightly gave her a major, visible part in the scene, standing tall, walking, even flying in to save the day. Bruegel's Truth, though, is immobilized at the edge of the scene. She sits, or crouches low, as if a counterpart to the royally enthroned king at the other end of the composition. The gestures of her hands and tilt of her head suggest that she is speaking with Repentance: she is telling her own story, the true one. But if these two figures remain wrapped up in one another, what is to halt the procession of false words that is moving towards the king's ears? Bruegel slants Apelles' visualization of his own vindication towards something more pessimistic. We hope that Truth Will Out, but Bruegel seems uncertain about that. Words of malice, words that destroy reputations, that cast accusations, that pull people towards the gallows – they have strength, and the king is only human in his eagerness to take the lie for the truth. From gossip to rumour to slander, people delight in believing the worst of others.

The people who once laughingly flipped their dessert plates and discussed proverbial wisdom and human nature may wish to guard their words. But their discussion is no less important for that. Finding the truth about humanity is the most difficult task of all.

Chronology

<table>
<tr><td>1525–30</td><td>Birth of Pieter Bruegel, possibly in town of Brueghel in North Brabant or in nearby Breda</td></tr>
<tr><td>1540s</td><td>Probably moves to Antwerp; studies with and/or works for painter and tapestry designer Pieter Coecke van Aelst there and then in Brussels</td></tr>
<tr><td>1550</td><td>Death of Pieter Coecke van Aelst</td></tr>
<tr><td>1550–51</td><td>In Mechelen working for artist/dealer Claude Dorizi. Paints outer wings of an altarpiece (now lost) with grisaille figures; interior painted by Pieter Baltens</td></tr>
<tr><td>1551</td><td>Registers with painters' guild in Antwerp</td></tr>
<tr><td>1552</td><td>Travels via Lyons to Italy, going as far south as Sicily</td></tr>
<tr><td>1553</td><td>Is in Rome. Meets and collaborates with miniaturist Giulio Clovio</td></tr>
<tr><td>1554</td><td>In Antwerp working for print publisher Hieronymus Cock</td></tr>
<tr><td>1555–6</td><td>Creates designs for the Large Landscapes series of prints</td></tr>
<tr><td>1557–8</td><td>Decorates sets of wooden trenchers, his earliest surviving painted works</td></tr>
<tr><td>1558</td><td>Publication of Seven Deadly Sins series</td></tr>
<tr><td>1559</td><td>First major paintings: *Battle between Carnival and Lent* and *Netherlandish Proverbs*. Seven Virtues series published in these years</td></tr>
<tr><td>1560</td><td>Paints *Children's Games*</td></tr>
<tr><td>1561</td><td>Paints *Dulle Griet* (Mad Meg)</td></tr>
<tr><td>1562</td><td>Paints *Fall of the Rebel Angels*</td></tr>
<tr><td>1563</td><td>On 25 July: announcement of betrothal to Mayken Coecke, daughter of Pieter Coecke van Aelst, at Antwerp</td></tr>
</table>

Cathedral. August: marries her in the Kapellekerk, Brussels. Paints the large *Tower of Babel* for Niclaes Jonghelinck of Antwerp and *Flight into Egypt* owned by Cardinal Granvelle

1564   Probably in this year: his son Pieter Brueghel the Younger born in Brussels; paints *Death of the Virgin*, owned by Abraham Ortelius

1564–5   Paints *Christ Carrying the Cross* and *Months* for Niclaes Jonghelinck

1566   21 February: Niclaes Jonghelinck puts up his art collection as security; it includes sixteen works by Pieter Bruegel. Bruegel paints *Wedding Dance*. On 29 September: baptism of Bruegel's daughter Maria in the Kapellekerk, Brussels

1567   Paints *Conversion of Paul*

1568   Paints *The Lepers* and *Parable of the Blind*.
          On 20 August: baptism of Jan Brueghel, second son of Pieter Bruegel. The godfather was Thomas Broeckman, rhetorician of Brussels

1569   Dies in Brussels, possibly in September

Key events in the Netherlands

1555   25 October: Charles V abdicates, handing sovereignty of the Netherlands to his son, Philip II, whose key courtiers include the Duke of Alba and Antoine Perrenot de Granvelle

1559   Philip leaves the Netherlands for Spain. He appoints his half-sister Margaret of Parma as governor, with Granvelle to remain as her chief councillor. The considerable power that local nobility had had under Charles V is sharply curtailed

1561   Nobles begin campaign against now-cardinal Granvelle

1563   Formation of the League of the Nobles against Granvelle by major nobles: William of Orange, the Counts of Egmont and Hornes and others

1564   William of Orange gives a speech to the Council of State promoting religious tolerance and freedom of conscience.

	March: Philip removes Granvelle and reinstates the great nobles as Margaret of Parma's advisors. This does not change issues of religious policy, persecution of heretics and so on
1565	Lesser nobility forms 'Order of the Compromise' against the Inquisition and its legal procedures. Philip roundly rejects their suggestions late that year
1566	5 April: 'compromise' nobles petition Margaret of Parma to moderate Spain's religious policy in the Netherlands. Protestant 'hedge-preachers' give well-attended sermons outside the city walls. Late summer to autumn: iconoclasm in Antwerp and many other cities in the Netherlands. Margaret of Parma announces modification of persecution. Philip II sends orders to the Duke of Alba to take the Spanish army from northern Italy to the Netherlands
1567	August: the Duke of Alba arrives in Brussels at the head of 10,000 troops. His goal: to suppress heresy in the Netherlands. Margaret of Parma steps down as governor
1568	The Duke of Alba establishes the 'Council of Troubles'. Thousands are tried and over a thousand executed. Execution of the Counts of Egmont and Hornes on 5 June shocks the public

REFERENCES

1 Humanity and Self-knowledge

1 Claudia Goldstein, *Pieter Bruegel and the Culture of the Early Modern Dinner Party* (Farnham and Burlington, VT, 2013), pp. 4–5.
2 On the use of dessert trenchers see Victoria Yeoman, 'Speaking Plates: Text, Performance, and Banqueting Trenchers in Early Modern Europe', *Renaissance Studies*, XXXI/5 (2017), pp. 755–6; the source for this imagined scene is Thomas Middleton's play *No Wit Like a Woman's* (1611), in Thomas Middleton, *The Works of Thomas Middleton*, ed. Alexander Dyce (London, 1840), vol. V, pp. 40–42.
3 Manfred Sellink, *Bruegel: The Complete Paintings, Drawings and Prints* (Ghent, 2007), pp. 123–4.
4 For an example of proverb-inscribed tableware that generates conversation see Desiderius Erasmus, 'The Godly Feast', in *The Colloquies of Erasmus*, trans. Craig R. Thompson (Chicago, IL, and London, 1965), p. 62.
5 Roger van Schoute and Hélène Verougstraete, 'A Painted Wooden Roundel by Pieter Bruegel the Elder', *Burlington Magazine*, CXLII/1165 (2000), pp. 140–46.
6 On Coecke van Aelst see Elizabeth Cleland, *Grand Design: Pieter Coecke van Aelst and Renaissance Tapestry*, exh. cat., Metropolitan Museum, New York (New Haven, CT, and London, 2014).
7 On Bruegel in the contest between vernacular and classicizing traditions see David Freedberg, 'Allusion and Topicality in the Work of Pieter Bruegel: The Implications of a Forgotten Polemic', in *The Prints of Pieter Bruegel the Elder*, ed. David Freedberg, exh. cat., Bridgestone Museum of Art, Tokyo (1989), pp. 53–65.

8 James D. Tracy, *Erasmus of the Low Countries* (Berkeley and Los Angeles, CA, 1996), pp. 189–91.

9 Katharine Park, 'The Organic Soul', in *The Cambridge History of Renaissance Philosophy*, ed. Charles Schmitt et al. (Cambridge, 1988), pp. 464–7; see also Andrew Cunningham, Sachiko Kusukawa and Gregor Reisch, *Natural Philosophy Epitomised: Books 8–11 of Gregor Reisch's 'Philosophical Pearl' (1503)* (Farnham and Burlington, VT, 2010).

10 Desiderius Erasmus, *Adages*, in *Collected Works*, ed. R.A.B. Mynors, trans. Margaret Mann Phillips (Toronto, Buffalo and London, 1982), vol. XXXII, pp. 62–3.

11 Ibid., p. 57.

12 Important recent contributions to the study of this work include Bret Rothstein, 'The Problem with Looking at Pieter Bruegel's Elck', *Art History*, XXVI/2 (2003), pp. 143–73; Ethan Matt Kavaler, *Pieter Bruegel: Parables of Order and Enterprise* (Cambridge, 1999), pp. 77–90; and see Nadine M. Orenstein, ed., *Pieter Bruegel the Elder: Drawings and Prints*, exh. cat., Metropolitan Museum, New York (New Haven, CT, and London, 2001), pp. 166–70.

13 John Jeffries Martin, *Myths of Renaissance Individualism* (Basingstoke and New York, 2004), especially pp. 30–38.

14 Cornelis Augustijn, *Erasmus: His Life, Works, and Influence*, trans. J. C. Grayson (Toronto, Buffalo and London, 1991), pp. 44–6.

15 Desiderius Erasmus, *Enchiridion militis christiani/The Handbook of the Christian Soldier*, trans. Charles Fantazzi, in *Collected Works*, ed. John W. O'Malley (Toronto, Buffalo and London, 1988), vol. LXVI, p. 40.

16 Ibid., p. 44.

17 Ibid., p. 41.

18 Charles Trinkaus, *In Our Image and Likeness: Humanity and Divinity in Italian Humanist Thought* (Chicago, IL, 1970), Introduction.

19 Giles Constable, 'The Ideal of the Imitation of Christ', in *Three Studies in Medieval Religious and Social Thought* (Cambridge, 1995), p. 244.

20 Giovanni Pico della Mirandola, 'On the Dignity of Man' [1486], in *The Renaissance Philosophy of Man*, ed. Ernst Cassirer, Paul Oskar Kristeller and John Herman Randall, trans. Elizabeth Livermore Forbes (Chicago, IL, 1948), p. 225.

21 Agnes Heller, *Renaissance Man*, trans. Richard E. Allen
    (London, 1978), pp. 428–32.
22 Cunningham, Kusukawa and Reisch, *Natural Philosophy Epitomised*, p. 81.
23 Ibid., p. 240.
24 On these see Nina Serebrennikov, 'Pieter Bruegel the Elder's
    Series of "Virtues" and "Vices"'(unpublished doctoral dissertation,
    University of North Carolina, 1986), and Orenstein, *Pieter Bruegel
    the Elder*, pp. 144–62 and 177–93; on their relation to Erasmus
    see Irving L Zupnick 'The Influence of Erasmus' *Enchiridion* on
    Bruegel's *Seven Virtues*' *De Gulden Passer*, 47 (1969), pp. 225–35.
25 Tracy, *Erasmus of the Low Countries*, p. 43; on the utility of proverb
    collections in general see Mark Meadow, 'On the Structure of
    Knowledge in Bruegel's Netherlandish Proverbs', *Volkskundig Bulletin*,
    XVIII/2 (1992), pp. 141–69.
26 Erasmus, *Adages*, in *Collected Works*, vol. XXXI, pp. 4, 5, 14.
27 Ibid., pp. 19–20.
28 Erasmus, *Adages*, in *Collected Works*, vol. XXXIII, p. 196.
29 Ibid., p. 252
30 Margaret Carroll, *Painting and Politics in Northern Europe* (State
    College, PA, 2008), pp. 47–9.
31 On this painting, three important recent works in English are:
    Margaret Sullivan, 'Bruegel's Proverbs: Art and Audience in the
    Northern Renaissance', *Art Bulletin*, LXXIII/3 (1991), pp. 431–66;
    Mark Meadow, *Pieter Bruegel the Elder's Netherlandish Proverbs and the
    Practice of Rhetoric* (Zwolle, 2002); and Walter S. Gibson, *Figures of
    Speech: Picturing Proverbs in Renaissance Netherlands* (Berkeley and Los
    Angeles, CA, 2010). An earlier work that initiated much of the
    later debate is Carl Gustaf Stridbeck, *Bruegelstudien* (Stockholm,
    1956).
32 On the copies after Bruegel's painting, and also the question of the
    number of proverbs shown, see Klaus Ertz, *Pieter Brueghel der Jüngere
    (1564–1637/36)* (Lingen, 2000), pp. 24–75.
33 For details of the contents of this and the other *Virtues* prints
    see H. Arthur Klein, *The Graphic Worlds of Pieter Bruegel the Elder*
    (New York, 1963), pp. 120–33.
34 Erasmus, *Enchiridion*, p. 45, using frugality and avarice as one
    example of this phenomenon.

2 Mankind in the Cosmos

1 For Bruegel's trip to Italy and the larger context of Flemish artists journeying there see Nils Büttner, '"Quid siculas sequeris per mille pericula terras?" Ein Beitrag zur Biographie Pieter Bruegels d.Ä. und zur Kulturgeschichte der niederländischen Italienreise', *Marburger Jahrbuch für Kunstwissenschaft*, 27 (2000), pp. 209–42.

2 Manfred Sellink in Nadine M. Orenstein, ed., *Pieter Bruegel the Elder: Drawings and Prints*, exh. cat., Metropolitan Museum, New York (New Haven, CT, and London, 2001), p. 104.

3 Karel van Mander, *The Lives of the Illustrious Netherlandish and German Painters*, 6 vols (Doornspijk, 1994), vol. I, p. 190.

4 For the idea of Bruegel's early landscapes as inviting imagined itineraries see Joseph Leo Koerner, 'The Printed World', in *The Printed World of Pieter Bruegel the Elder*, ed. Barbara Butts and Joseph Leo Koerner, exh. cat., Saint Louis Art Museum, St Louis, MO (1995), pp. 24–5.

5 Christopher White, '"The Rabbit Hunters" by Pieter Bruegel the Elder', in *Pieter Bruegel und seine Welt*, ed. Otto von Simson and Matthias Winner (Berlin, 1979), pp. 187–8.

6 On the evolution of this closed-system view into our modern sense of the infinite see Alexandre Koyre, *From the Closed World to the Infinite Universe* (Baltimore, MD, 1968); S. K. Heninger Jr, *The Cosmographical Glass: Renaissance Diagrams of the Universe* (San Marino, CA, 1977), p. 48.

7 Agnes Heller, *Renaissance Man*, trans. Richard E. Allen (London, 1978), pp. 385–6; Heninger, *Cosmographical Glass*, pp. 108–10.

8 Desiderius Erasmus, *Enchiridion militis christiani/The Handbook of the Christian Soldier*, in *Collected Works*, ed. John W. O'Malley, trans. Charles Fantazzi (Toronto, Buffalo and London, 1988), vol. LXVI, p. 42.

9 See E.M.W. Tillyard, *The Elizabethan World Picture* (London, 1960); Arthur O. Lovejoy, *The Great Chain of Being* (New York, 1936).

10 Albrecht Classen, 'The Discovery of the Mountain as an Epistemological Challenge', in *The Book of Nature and Humanity in the Middle Ages and the Renaissance*, ed. David Hawkes and Richard G. Newhauser (Turnhout, 2013), pp. 11–12.

11 Jan Muylle, 'Pieter Bruegel en Abraham Ortelius: Bijdrage tot de Literaire Receptie van Pieter Bruegels Werk', in *Archivum artis*

Lovaneniense: Bijdragen tot de geschiedenis van de kunst der Nederlanden: Opgedragen aan Prof. Dr. J. K. Steppe, ed. Maurits Smeyers (Leuven, 1981), pp. 319–37.

12 Marcel van den Broecke, *Ortelius Atlas Maps: An Illustrated Guide*, 2nd edn (Houten, 2011), p. 69.

13 Giovanni Pico della Mirandola, 'On the Dignity of Man' [1486], in *The Renaissance Philosophy of Man*, ed. Ernst Cassirer, Paul Oskar Kristeller and John Herman Randall, trans. Elizabeth Livermore Forbes (Chicago, IL, 1948), p. 225.

14 On Erasmus see Barbara Pitkin, 'Erasmus, Calvin, and the Faces of Stoicism in Renaissance and Reformation Thought', in *The Routledge Handbook of the Stoic Tradition*, ed. John Sellars (London and New York, 2016), pp. 145–59; on Bruegel, Justus Müller Hofstede, 'Zur Interpretation von Pieter Bruegels Landschaft: Ästhetischer Landschaftsbegriff und stoische Weltbetrachtung', in *Pieter Bruegel und seine Welt*, ed. Otto von Simson and Matthias Winner (Berlin, 1979), pp. 73–142.

15 Denis Cosgrove, 'Globalism and Tolerance in Early Modern Geography', *Annals of the Association of American Geographers*, XCIII/4 (2003), pp. 860–63.

16 Heller, *Renaissance Man*, pp. 104–6.

17 Cosgrove, 'Globalism and Tolerance', pp. 863–4.

18 Antoni Maczak, *Travel in Early Modern Europe*, trans. Ursula Phillips (Cambridge, 1995), p. 24.

19 Iain Buchanan, 'The Collection of Niclaes Jongelinck II: The "Months" by Pieter Bruegel the Elder', *Burlington Magazine*, CXXXII/1049 (1990), p. 541.

20 Claudia Goldstein, 'Artifacts of Domestic Life: Bruegel's Paintings in the Flemish Home', *Nederlands Kunsthistorisch Jaarboek*, 51 (2000), pp. 173, 180.

21 Desiderius Erasmus, *The Colloquies of Erasmus*, trans. Craig R. Thompson (Chicago, IL, and London, 1965), p. 48.

22 Heninger, *Cosmographical Glass*, p. 154; on the development of weather imagery in the seventeenth century see R. L. Falkenburg, '"Schilderachtig weer" bij Jan van Goyen', in *Jan van Goyen*, ed. Christiaan Vogelaar, exh. cat., Stedelijk Museum de Lakenhal, Leiden (1996), pp. 60–69.

23 Hans J. van Miegroet, '"The Twelve Months" Reconsidered: How a Drawing by Pieter Stevens Clarifies a Bruegel Enigma', *Simiolus*, 16 (1986), pp. 29–35; Yvette Bruijnen, 'Over de Twelf Maendekens en de Vier Tyden's Jaers: De Maanden en Jaargetijden in de Kunst van de Nederlanden circa 1500 tot 1750', in *De vier jaargetijden in de kunst van de Nederlanden 1500–1750*, ed. Yvette Bruijnen and Paul Huys Janssen (Zwolle, 2002), pp. 51–71; Heninger, *Cosmographical Glass*, p. 113.

24 Walter S. Gibson, *'Mirror of the Earth': The World Landscape in Sixteenth-century Flemish Painting* (Princeton, NJ, 1989), p. 71.

25 On the bird trap/ice parallel see Linda and George Bauer, 'Winter Landscape with Skaters and Bird Trap by Pieter Bruegel the Elder', *Art Bulletin*, LXVI/1 (1984), pp. 145–50; Bertram Kaschek, *Weltzeit und Endzeit: Die 'Monatsbilder' Pieter Bruegels d.Ä.* (Munich, 2012), pp. 13–15.

26 On the concepts of fortune and chance in this period see Jessen Kelly, *Material Culture and Games of Chance in the Early Modern Netherlands* (Kalamazoo, MI, forthcoming).

27 Kaschek, *Weltzeit und Endzeit*, 150–55; Walter S. Gibson, 'Pieter Bruegel the Elder and the Flemish World Landscape of the Sixteenth Century', in *Bruegel and Netherlandish Landscape Painting from the National Gallery, Prague*, exh. cat., National Museum of Western Art, Tokyo, and National Museum of Modern Art, Kyoto (1990), pp. 11–23.

28 Reindert L. Falkenburg, 'Pieter Bruegel's Series of the Seasons: On the Perception of Divine Order', in *Liber amicorum Raphael de Smedt: 2 artium historia*, ed. Joost Vander Auwera, Miscellanea Neerlandica, XXIV (Leuven, 2001), pp. 253–76.

29 On the virtue of peasant labour see Ethan Matt Kavaler, 'Pieter Bruegel's Fall of Icarus and the Noble Peasant', *Jaarboek van het Koninklijk Museum voor Schone Kunsten, Antwerpen* (1986), pp. 83–98; Robert Baldwin, 'Peasant Imagery and Bruegel's "Fall of Icarus"', *Konsthistorisk Tidskrift*, LV/3 (1986), pp. 101–14; Elizabeth Alice Honig, *Painting and the Market in Early Modern Antwerp* (New Haven, CT, and London, 1998), pp. 56–7.

30 A. J. Gurevich, *Categories of Medieval Culture* (London, 1985), pp. 42, 51–2.

31 Buchanan, 'The Collection of Niclaes Jongelinck', p. 541.

32 On the dynamics of Christ's positioning see Joseph F. Gregory,
    'Toward the Contextualization of Pieter Bruegel's Procession to
    Calvary', *Nederlands Kunsthistorisch Jaarboek*, 47 (1996), p. 214.

33 On Bruegel and paradox see Jürgen Müller, *Das Paradox als Bildform*
    (Munich, 1999).

34 Cicero, *De re publica;* see Cosgrove, 'Globalism and Tolerance',
    p. 860.

35 On different ways of depicting time in Flemish art in general see
    Brigitte Dekeyzer et al., 'Het Sprokkelen van de Tijd: Sporen van
    het Middeleeuwse Tijds- en Wereldbeeld in Zuid-Nederlandse
    Kalenderminiaturen', in *De Vier Jaargetijden in de Kunst van de
    Nederlanden 1500–1750*, ed. Yvette Bruijnen (Zwolle, 2002),
    pp. 25–35; for time in Bruegel, see Kaschek, *Weltzeit und Endzeit*.

36 On the mill see especially Michael Francis Gibson, *The Mill and the
    Cross: Pieter Bruegel's 'Way to Calvary'* (Lausanne, 2000), pp. 62–71;
    Larry Silver, *Pieter Bruegel* (New York and London, 2011), p. 24.

37 For time and anachronism in Bruegel see Mark Meadow, 'Bruegel's
    "Procession to Calvary", Aemulatio, and the Space of Vernacular
    Style', *Nederlands Kunsthistorisch Jaarboek*, 47 (1996), pp. 181–205;
    Joseph F. Gregory, *Contemporization as Polemical Device in Pieter Bruegel's
    Biblical Narratives* (Lewiston, NY, 2005).

38 Margaret Sullivan, 'Bosch, Bruegel, Everyman and the Northern
    Renaissance', *Oud Holland*, CXXI/2–3 (2008), pp. 117–46; Yona
    Pinson, 'Hieronymus Bosch: Homo Viator at a Crossroads: A New
    Reading of the Rotterdam Tondo', *Artibus et historiae*, 26 (2005),
    pp. 57–84.

39 Reindert L. Falkenburg, *Joachim Patinir: Landscape as an Image of
    the Pilgrimage of Life*, trans. Michael Hoyle (Amsterdam and
    Philadelphia, PA, 1988).

3 Ambition and Authority

1 Jacobus de Voragine, *The Golden Legend: Readings on the Saints*, trans.
   William Granger Ryan, 2 vols (Princeton, NJ, 1993), p. 119.
   On Paul's pride see Leo Steinberg, *Michelangelo's Last Paintings*
   (London, 1975), p. 26.

2 'Hovardye werdt van godt boven al ghehaet', or, 'pride is hated above all by God.' Erasmus agrees on this point in *Enchiridion militis christiani/The Handbook of the Christian Soldier*, trans. Charles Fantazzi, in *Collected Works*, ed. John W. O'Malley (Toronto, Buffalo and London, 1988), vol. LXVI, p. 123.

3 Erasmus, *Enchiridion*, pp. 113–27. See too Lester K. Little, 'Pride Goes before Avarice: Social Change and the Vices in Latin Christendom', *American Historical Review*, LXXVI/1 (1971), pp. 16–49.

4 Desiderius Erasmus, *Adages*, in *Collected Works*, ed. R.A.B. Mynors, trans. Margaret Mann Phillips (Toronto, Buffalo and London, 1982), vol. XXXI, p. 234; *Enchiridion* pp. 99–100.

5 Niccolò Machiavelli, *Discourses on Livy*, trans. Harvey C. Mansfield and Nathan Tarcov (Chicago, IL, and London, 1996), p. 19.

6 *Abrahami Ortelii . . . epistulae*, ed. Jan Hendrik Hessels (Cambridge, 1887), No. 23, cited by Larry Silver, *Pieter Bruegel* (New York and London, 2011), p. 304.

7 M. J. Rodriguez-Salgado, 'King, Bishop, Pawn? Philip II and Granvelle in the 1550s and 1560s', in *Les Granvelle et les anciens Pays-Bas*, ed. Krista de Jonge and Gustaf Janssens (Leuven, 2000), pp. 105–34.

8 Ibid., pp. 120–21.

9 Ibid., pp. 106–7, 122–3; Martin van Gelderen, *The Political Thought of the Dutch Revolt, 1555–1590* (Cambridge, 1992), pp. 110–15.

10 *Refereynen ende Liedekens van diversche Rhetoricienen wt Brabant/Vlaenderen/ Hollant/en Zeelant. Ghelesen en Ghesonghen op de Corenbloeme Camere binnen Bruessele/Op haer izerlijcxse Prinsfeeste* (Brussels, 1563). See on this Ethan Matt Kavaler, *Pieter Bruegel: Parables of Order and Enterprise* (Cambridge, 1999), pp. 64–5; Tine Luk Meganck, *Pieter Bruegel the Elder: Fall of the Rebel Angels* (Milan, 2014), pp. 136–8.

11 For instance *Refereynen*, Nos 6, 19, 30, 54.

12 Van Gelderen, *Political Thought*, Chapter Three, 'Religion and Resistance'.

13 E. H. Kossmann and A. F. Mellink, eds, *Texts concerning the Revolt of the Netherlands* (Cambridge, 1974), pp. 59–61.

14 Alastair Duke, 'Salvation by Coercion: The Controversy surrounding the "Inquisition" in the Low Countries on the Eve

of the Revolt', in *Reformation Principle and Practice*, ed. Peter Newman Brooks (London, 1980), pp. 135–56.

15 Ibid., pp. 141–2; Van Gelderen, *Political Thought*, pp. 71–2.

16 Van Gelderen, *Political Thought*, p. 75.

17 Duke, 'Salvation by Coercion', pp. 139–40.

18 Nina Serebrennikov, 'Pieter Bruegel the Elder's Series of "Virtues" and "Vices"' (unpublished doctoral dissertation, University of North Carolina, 1986), p. 153.

19 See Little, 'Pride Goes before Avarice'.

20 On this painting see most recently and usefully Meganck, *Pieter Bruegel*.

21 Lucifer and the rebel angels are mentioned in *Refereynen*, Nos 15, 40, 48, 54 and 68.

22 Giovanni Pico della Mirandola, 'On the Dignity of Man' [1486], in *The Renaissance Philosophy of Man*, ed. Ernst Cassirer, Paul Oskar Kristeller and John Herman Randall, trans. Elizabeth Livermore Forbes (Chicago, IL, 1948), p. 227; see too Ficino in Charles Trinkaus, *In Our Image and Likeness: Humanity and Divinity in Italian Humanist Thought* (Chicago, IL, 1970), vol. II, p. 491; and Robert Payne, *Hubris: A Study of Pride* (New York, 1960), pp. 79–84.

23 Meredith J. Gill, *Angels and the Order of Heaven in Medieval and Renaissance Italy* (Cambridge, 2014), pp. 204–5.

24 See Anne T. Woollett 'Hitting the Mark: Strategies of Display in the Altarpieces of the Antwerp Militia Guilds', in *Rekonstruktion der Gesellschaft aus Kunst*, ed. Eckhard Leuschner (Petersberg, 2016), pp. 89–100.

25 On the style conflict between these artists see David Freedberg, 'Allusion and Topicality in the Work of Pieter Bruegel: The Implications of a Forgotten Polemic', in *The Prints of Pieter Bruegel the Elder*, ed. David Freedberg, exh. cat., Bridgestone Museum of Art, Tokyo (1989), pp. 53–65.

26 On Bruegel as a Bosch imitator see Larry Silver, 'Second Bosch: Family Resemblance and the Marketing of Art', *Nederlands Kunsthistorisch Jaarboek*, 50 (1999), pp. 31–56; Silver, *Pieter Bruegel*, Chapter Five, pp. 139–78.

27 See Joseph Koerner, 'Impossible Objects: Bosch's Realism', *RES: Anthropology and Aesthetics*, 46 (2004), pp. 73–97.

28 On the very uncertain dating of the *Icarus*, see Kavaler, *Pieter Bruegel*,
    p. 59.

29 The story is told in *Metamorphoses* VIII: 183–235.

30 Lyckle de Vries, 'Bruegel's "Fall of Icarus": Ovid or Solomon?',
    Simiolus, XXX/1–2 (2003), pp. 7–8.

31 Desiderius Erasmus, *De copia*, trans. Betty I. Knott, in *Collected
    Works*, ed. Craig R. Thompson (Toronto, Buffalo and London,
    1978), vol. XXIV, p. 611.

32 Kavaler, *Pieter Bruegel*, pp. 57–76; Ethan Matt Kavaler, 'Pieter
    Bruegel's Fall of Icarus and the Noble Peasant', *Jaarboek van het
    Koninklijk Museum voor Schone Kunsten, Antwerpen* (1986), pp. 83–98.

33 See Larry Silver, 'Pieter Bruegel in the Capital of Capitalism',
    Nederlands Kunsthistorisch Jaarboek, 47 (1996), pp. 125–53.

34 Christopher Heuer, 'Disappearing into the Green', unpublished
    manuscript. My thanks to Christopher Heuer for allowing me to
    read this work in progress.

35 Michel de Montaigne, *The Complete Essays of Montaigne*, trans. Donald
    M. Frame (Stanford, CA, 1965), pp. 478–9, 489; Little, 'Pride Goes
    before Avarice', pp. 21–3.

36 S. A. Mansbach, 'Pieter Bruegel's Towers of Babel', *Zeitschrift für
    Kunstgeschichte*, XLV/1 (1982), p. 44.

37 Elizabeth Cleland, *Grand Design: Pieter Coecke van Aelst and Renaissance
    Tapestry*, exh. cat., Metropolitan Museum, New York (New Haven,
    CT, and London, 2014), pp. 198–200.

38 On Bruegel and Clovio see Charles de Tolnay, 'Newly Discovered
    Miniatures by Pieter Bruegel the Elder', *Burlington Magazine*,
    CVII/744 (1965), p. 113 and n. 9.

39 For a suggestion about the relationship between this pair of works
    see Joseph Leo Koerner, *Bosch and Bruegel: From Enemy Painting to
    Everyday Life* (Princeton, NJ, and Oxford, 2016), p. 302.

40 Edward Snow, 'The Language of Contradiction in Bruegel's
    "Tower of Babel"', *RES: Anthropology and Aesthetics*, 5 (1983), pp. 40–48.

41 On the tower's materials see Koerner, *Bosch and Bruegel*, p. 300.

42 Joris van Grieken, Ger Luijten and Jan van der Stock, eds,
    Hieronymus Cock: The Renaissance in Print, exh. cat., M-Museum Leuven
    and Fondation Custodia, Paris (New Haven, CT, and London,
    2013), pp. 89–123.

43 Erasmus, *Enchiridion*, p. 37.
44 Erich Auerbach, 'Saul's Pride', *Modern Language Notes*, LXIV/4 (1949),
    pp. 267–9.
45 Seneca, *Naturales quaestiones*, trans. John Clarke; see
    naturalesquaestiones.blogspot.nl, Preface to Book I.
46 Marcel van den Broecke, *Ortelius Atlas Maps: An Illustrated Guide*,
    2nd edn (Houten, 2011), pp. 75–6.

4 Triumph of War: Humanity in a World of Chaos

1 For an extended interpretation on this basis see 'Bruegel's *Triumph
   of Death*: A Secular Apocalypse', in Walter S. Gibson, *Pieter Bruegel the
   Elder: Two Studies* (Lawrence, KS, 1991), pp. 53–86.
2 Hélène M. Verougstraete and Roger A. van Schoute, 'The
   Triumph of Death by Pieter Bruegel the Elder and Pieter Brueghel
   the Younger', in *The Triumph of Death by Pieter Brueghel the Younger*,
   ed. and trans. James I. W. Corcoran (Antwerp, 1993), p. 38.
3 For the German prints see J. R. Hale, *Artists and Warfare in the
   Renaissance* (New Haven, CT, and London, 1990); on the Conquest
   of Tunis series see Iain Buchanan in Elizabeth Cleland, ed.,
   Grand Design: Pieter Coecke van Aelst and Renaissance Tapestry, exh. cat.,
   Metropolitan Museum, New York (New Haven, CT, and London,
   2014), pp. 320–31.
4 For example Larry Silver, 'Ungrateful Dead: Bruegel's Triumph
   of Death Re-examined', in *Excavating the Medieval Image*, ed. David S.
   Areford and Nina A. Rowe (Aldershot and Burlington, VT, 2004),
   p. 269.
5 Idan Sherer, *Warriors for a Living: The Experience of the Spanish Infantry
   in the Italian Wars, 1494–1559* (Leiden and Boston, MA, 2017),
   pp. 160–72.
6 Cited in Julius R. Ruff, *Violence in Early Modern Europe, 1500–1800*
   (Cambridge, 2001), p. 60.
7 J. R. Hale, 'Sixteenth-century Explanations of War and Violence',
   in *Renaissance War Studies* (London, 1983), pp. 335–58.
8 Desiderius Erasmus, *Adages*, in *Collected Works*, ed. R.A.B. Mynors,
   trans. Margaret Mann Phillips (Toronto, Buffalo and London,
   1982), vol. XXXV, pp. 401–2, 406; also in Erasmus, 'A Complaint

of Peace Spurned and Rejected by the Whole World' [1516], in *Collected Works*, ed. Betty Radice (Toronto, Buffalo and London, 1986), vol. XXVII, p. 295.

9 Seneca, 'De ira'/'On Anger', in *Moral and Political Essays*, ed. John M. Cooper and J. F. Procope (Cambridge, 1995), p. 23.

10 Ernst Cassirer, *The Individual and the Cosmos in Renaissance Philosophy* (New York and Evanston, IL, 1964), pp. 99–122.

11 Thomas More, *Utopia* [1516], ed. Edward Sturtz (New Haven, CT, and London, 1964), p. 118.

12 Ibid., p. 124.

13 Desiderius Erasmus, 'On the War against the Turks'/'De bello turcico', in *The Erasmus Reader*, ed. Erika Rummel (Toronto, Buffalo and London, 1990), pp. 317, 321.

14 Erasmus speaks frequently, here and elsewhere, of the horrors of Christians killing other Christians, but for 'atrocities' see ibid., p. 318. On the evils of a pope urging war see especially 'Julius Excluded from Heaven' in *The Erasmus Reader*, pp. 216–38.

15 The term is from Gibson, 'Bruegel's *Triumph of Death*'.

16 Nina Serebrennikov, 'Pieter Bruegel the Elder's Series of "Virtues" and "Vices"' (unpublished doctoral dissertation, University of North Carolina, 1986), pp. 20–21.

17 Hale, 'Sixteenth-century Explanations', p. 345.

18 Desiderius Erasmus, *Enchiridion militis christiani*/*The Handbook of the Christian Soldier*, trans. Charles Fantazzi, in *Collected Works*, ed. John W. O'Malley (Toronto, Buffalo and London, 1988), vol. LXVI, p. 125.

19 Seneca, 'De ira', p. 17; see there n. 1 for many other ancient texts that echo his concept of anger as a 'brief insanity'.

20 Carol Thomas Neely, *Distracted Subjects: Madness and Gender in Shakespeare and Early Modern Culture* (Ithaca, NY, and London, 2004), pp. 3–4; Carol Thomas Neely, 'Recent Work in Renaissance Studies', *Renaissance Quarterly*, XLIV/4 (1991), p. 778.

21 Terms from Irina Metzler, *Fools and Idiots? Intellectual Disability in the Middle Ages* (Manchester, 2016), p. 82.

22 Described in More's *Apology* as cited in Paromita Chakravarti, 'Natural Fools and the Historiography of Renaissance Folly', *Renaissance Studies*, XXV/2 (2011), p. 210.

23 Desiderius Erasmus, *Praise of Folly* [1511], ed. A.H.T. Levi, trans.
Betty Radice, in *Collected Works* (Toronto, Buffalo and London,
1986), vol. XXVII, p. 111.

24 Seneca, 'De ira', pp. 17, 80.

25 See Margaret Sullivan, 'Madness and Folly: Peter Bruegel the
Elder's Dulle Griet', *Art Bulletin*, LIX/1 (1977), pp. 62–3.

26 Karel van Mander, *Den grondt der edel vry schilder-const* [1604],
trans. Hessel Miedema (Utrecht, 1973), pp. 192–3.

27 Jan Grauls, *Volkstaal en volksleven in het werk van Pieter Bruegel* (Antwerp
and Amsterdam, 1957), pp. 32–3.

28 Walter S. Gibson, 'Bruegel, Dulle Griet, and Sexist Politics in the
Sixteenth Century', in *Pieter Bruegel und seine Welt*, ed. Otto von
Simson and Matthias Winner (Berlin, 1979), pp. 9–15; Natalie
Zemon Davis, 'Women on Top', in *Society and Culture in Early Modern
France* (Stanford, CA, 1965), pp. 124–51.

29 On representing chaos see Martin Meisel, *Chaos Imagined: Literature,
Art, Science* (New York, 2016), pp. 31–9.

30 Geoffrey Parker, 'Early Modern Europe', in *The Laws of War*,
ed. Michael Howard, George J. Andreopoulos and Mark R. Shulman
(New Haven, CT, and London, 1994), p. 47; Ruff, *Violence in Early
Modern Europe*.

31 Justus Lipsius, *On Constancy*, ed. John Sellars, trans. Sir John
Stradling (Exeter, 2006), pp. 71, 37.

32 Mark Morford, *Stoics and Neostoics* (Princeton, NJ, 1991), pp. 162–3.

33 On this painting in the context of war see Jane Fishman,
*Boerenverdriet: Violence between Peasants and Soldiers in Early Modern
Netherlandish Art* (Ann Arbor, MI, 1979), pp. 19–30, and David
Kunzle, 'Spanish Herod, Dutch Innocents: Bruegel's Massacres
of the Innocents in Their Sixteenth-century Political Contexts',
Art History, XXIV/1 (2001), pp. 51–82.

34 Desmond Shawe-Taylor and Jennifer Scott, *Bruegel to Rubens: Masters
of Flemish Painting* (London, 2007), pp. 88–91.

35 Sherrer, *Warriors for a Living*, Chapter Four, 'The Experience of the
Sack', pp. 144–74, Parker, 'Early Modern Europe', pp. 41, 45–6.

36 See More, *Utopia*, pp. 128–9, for an exception.

37 Geoffrey Parker, 'The "Military Revolution", 1560–1660 – a Myth?',
Journal of Modern History, XLVIII (1976), pp. 206–7.

38 Van Mander, *Grondt*, p. 174.

39 Jan Muylle, 'Ethos en Pathos: De literaire appreciatie van expressie in het werk van Metsijs en Bruegel', *Nederlands Kunsthistorisch Jaarboek*, 60 (2010), pp. 19–33.

5 Inside and Out: Natural Languages of Human Nature

1 My account follows the Dutch/German version of the tale, the oldest that survives, as summarized by Arthur Dickson, *Valentine and Orson: A Study in Late Medieval Romance* (New York, 1929), pp. 13–21.

2 On the wild man see Richard Bernheimer, *Wild Men in the Middle Ages* (New York, 1970); Paul Vandenbroeck, *Beeld van de andere, vertoog over het zelf* (Antwerp, 1987), pp. 7–21.

3 These descriptions of layers of the self roughly follow John Jeffries Martin, *Myths of Renaissance Individualism* (Basingstoke and New York, 2004); see Chapter One of this book.

4 Pierre Charron, 'De la sagesse' [1541], cited by Agnes Heller, *Renaissance Man*, trans. Richard E. Allen (London, 1978), p. 207.

5 'Of Presumption', in Michel de Montaigne, *The Complete Essays of Montaigne*, trans. Donald M. Frame (Stanford, CA, 1965), p. 491.

6 Martin Porter, *Windows of the Soul: Physiognomy in European Culture, 1470–1780* (Oxford, 2005), p. 173.

7 Desiderius Erasmus, *Adages*, in *Collected Works*, ed. and annotated R.A.B. Mynors, trans. Margaret Mann Phillips (Toronto, Buffalo and London, 1982), vol. XXXIII, p. 191; Michael W. Kwakkelstein, *Leonardo da Vinci as a Physiognomist* (Leiden, 1994), p. 56.

8 Martin, *Myths of Renaissance Individualism*, p. 29.

9 Guy Marchant, *The Kalendar and Compost of Shepherds* [1493; Eng. trans. 1518] (London, 1931), p. 152; Richard Roussat, *The Most Excellent, Profitable, and Pleasant Booke of the Famous Doctour and Expert Astrologian Arcandam . . . with the Addition of Phisiognomie Very Pleasant to Reade*, trans. William Warde (London, 1564), n.p.

10 For example Karel van Mander, *Den Grondt der edel vry schilder-const* [1604], trans. Hessel Miedema (Utrecht, 1973), p. 169.

11 Marchant, *Kalendar and Compost*, p. 150; Roussat, *Most Excellent, Profitable, and Pleasant Booke*, Conclusion.

12 See above, Chapter Four of this book.

13 Jan Muylle, 'Tronies toegeschreven aan Pieter Bruegel: Fysionomie en expressie', *De zeventiende eeuw*, XVII/2 (2001), pp. 174–204, and XVIII/2 (2002), pp. 115–48.

14 Marchant, *Kalendar and Compost*, p. 153.

15 Magdi Toth-Ubbens, *Verloren beelden van miserabele bedelaars* (Ghent, 1987), p. 77.

16 Hans Belting, *Face and Mask: A Double History*, trans. Thomas S. Hansen and Abby J. Hansen (Princeton, NJ, and Oxford, 2017), was helpful in thinking about faces and mask types.

17 Joseph Leo Koerner, *Bosch and Bruegel: From Enemy Painting to Everyday Life* (Princeton, NJ, and Oxford, 2016), p. 317.

18 Herman Pleij, *Dreaming of Cockaigne: Medieval Fantasies of the Perfect Life*, trans. Diane Webb (New York, 2001), p. 151.

19 See Koerner, *Bosch and Bruegel*, p. 313.

20 On disability terminology see Irina Metzler, *Disability in Medieval Europe* (London and New York, 2006), pp. 4–5.

21 J. L. Vives, *De subventione pauperum*, ed. and trans. C. Matheeussen and C. Fantazzi (Leiden, 2002), p. 25.

22 Larry Silver and Henry Luttikhuizen, 'The Quality of Mercy: Representations of Charity in Early Netherlandish Art', *Studies in Iconography*, 29 (2008), p. 216.

23 Ben Wuyts, *Over narren, kreupelen, doven en blinden. Leven met een handicap. Van de Oudheid tot Nu* (Leuven, 2005), pp. 76–7.

24 Paul Slack, *Poverty and Policy in Tudor and Stuart England* (London and New York, 1988); Vandenbroeck, *Beeld van de andere*, p. 117.

25 Vives, *De subventione pauperum*, p. 29; see too pp. 91, 95.

26 Tom Nichols, *The Art of Poverty: Irony and Ideal in Sixteenth-century Beggar Imagery* (Manchester, 2007), pp. 32–3, 71–2.

27 Famously, Nicholas Jennings of London, as described and illustrated in Thomas Harman, 'A Caveat or Warning for Commen Cursitors, Vulgarly Called Vagabonds' [1566], in *The Elizabethan Underworld*, ed. A. V. Judges (New York, 1930), pp. 85–90.

28 Meltzer, *Disability in Medieval Europe*, p. 55.

29 Francis Bacon, 'On Deformity', in *The Essays or Counsels Civil and Moral* (Oxford, 1999), p. 99.

30 Ruth Melinkoff, *Outcasts: Signs of Otherness in Northern European Art of the Late Middle Ages*, 2 vols (Berkeley and Los Angeles, CA, 1993), vol. I, p. 114; Meltzer, *Disability in Medieval Europe*, p. 41.

31 Toth-Ubbens, *Verloren beelden*, pp. 76–9.

32 See Erving Goffman, *Stigma: Notes on the Management of Spoiled Identity* (New York, London and Toronto, 1986), pp. 5–6.

33 On leprosy and its representations see Saul Nathaniel Brody, *The Disease of the Soul: Leprosy in Medieval Literature* (Ithaca, NY, and London, 1974), and Christine M. Boeckl, *Images of Leprosy: Disease, Religion, and Politics in European Art* (Kirksville, MO, 2011).

34 R. I. Moore, *The Formation of a Persecuting Society* (Oxford, 1987), p. 51; Brody, *Disease of the Soul*, pp. 65–75.

35 Boeckl, *Images of Leprosy*, pp. 131, 150.

36 Brody, *Disease of the Soul*, p. 31.

37 Toth-Ubbens, *Verloren beelden*, pp. 75–6.

38 Paul Vandenbroeck, *Jheronimus Bosch: Tussen volksleven en stadscultuur* (Berchem, 1987), pp. 339–41.

39 Yemi Onafuwa, 'Bruegel's Cripples and Early Modern Humor', *Athanor*, 25 (2007), pp. 49–57.

40 Vives, *De subventione pauperum*, p. 107; Thomas More, *Utopia* [1516], ed. Edward Sturtz (New Haven, CT, and London, 1964), p. 113.

41 Otto Kurz, 'Tapestries after Hieronymus Bosch', *Journal of the Warburg and Courtauld Institutes*, 30 (1967), p. 157; see too Wuyts, *Over narren*, p. 65. On this 'entertainment' in the Middle Ages see Edward Wheatley, *Stumbling Blocks before the Blind: Medieval Constructions of a Disability* (Ann Arbor, MI, 2014), pp. 1–3; on laughing at the blind, see his Chapter Four, 'Humoring the Sighted', pp. 90–128.

42 Roger H. P. Marijnissen et al., *Bruegel: Tout l'oeuvre peint et dessiné* (Antwerp and Paris, 1988), pp. 365–8.

43 Kahren Jones Hellerstedt, 'The Blind Man and His Guide in Netherlandish Painting', *Simiolus*, XIII/3–4 (1983), pp. 163–81.

44 This was suggested to me in conversation with Jess Bailey. On identifying the types of blindness shown in Bruegel see Tony M. Torrilhon, 'La pathologie chez Bruegel' (dissertation, Faculté de medicine, Paris, 1957), and Zeynel A. Karcioglu, 'Ocular Pathology in the Parable of the Blind Leading the Blind and Other

Paintings by Pieter Bruegel', *Survey of Ophthalmology*, XLVII/1 (2002), pp. 55–62. My thanks to Odilia Bonebakker for these references.
45 Marchant, *Kalendar and Compost*, p. 154.
46 Belting, *Face and Mask*, p. 7; Donald D. Kirtley, *The Psychology of Blindness* (Chicago, IL, 1975), p. 20.

6 Laughing Man

1 Karel van Mander, *Den grondt der edel vry schilder-const* [1604], trans. Hessel Miedema (Utrecht, 1973), p. 190. On this topic in general the important recent work is Walter S. Gibson, *Pieter Bruegel and the Art of Laughter* (Berkeley and Los Angeles, CA, 2006).
2 M. A. Screech, *Rabelais* (Ithaca, NY, 1979), p. 1.
3 Karel van Mander, *The Lives of the Illustrious Netherlandish and German Painters*, 6 vols (Doornspijk, 1994), vol. I, p. 193.
4 See Mikhail Bakhtin, *Rabelais and His World*, trans. Helene Iswolsky (Bloomington, IN, 1984), pp. 68–9; Jacques Le Goff, 'Laughter in the Middle Ages', in *A Cultural History of Humour from Antiquity to the Present Day*, ed. Jan Bremmer and Herman Roodenburg (Cambridge and Oxford, 1997), p. 43; Quentin Skinner, 'Why Laughing Mattered in the Renaissance', *History of Political Thought*, XXII/3 (2001), pp. 425–6.
5 Skinner, 'Why Laughing Mattered', pp. 435, 438–40.
6 Bakhtin, *Rabelais and His World*, pp. 66–7.
7 Desiderius Erasmus, *De civilitate morum puerilium/On Good Manners for Boys*, trans. Brian McGregor, in *Collected Works*, ed. J. K. Sowards (Toronto, Buffalo and London, 1985), vol. XXV, pp. 275–6.
8 Baldesar Castiglione, *The Book of the Courtier*, trans. George Bull (London, 1967), p. 155.
9 Bakhtin, *Rabelais and His World*, pp. 11–12.
10 Gerard Rooijakkers, *Rituele repertoires: Volkscultuur in oostelijk Noord-Brabant 1559–1853* (Nijmegen, 1994), pp. 395–8.
11 Lodovico Guicciardini, *Beschryvinghe van alle de Neder-Landen* [1567], trans. Cornelius Kiliaan (Amsterdam, 1612), p. 30.
12 A. Monballieu, 'De "Kermis van Hoboken" bij P. Bruegel, J. Grimmer en G. Mostaert', *Jaarboek van het Koninklijk Museum voor Schone Kunsten, Antwerpen* (1974), pp. 141–2.

13 Ibid., p. 146; Gibson, *Pieter Bruegel and the Art of Laughter*, p. 81.

14 Desiderius Erasmus, *Praise of Folly*, ed. A.H.T. Levi, trans. Betty Radice, in *Collected Works* (Toronto, Buffalo and London, 1986), vol. XXVII, p. 109.

15 Nadine M. Orenstein, ed., *Pieter Bruegel the Elder: Drawings and Prints*, exh. cat., Metropolitan Museum, New York (New Haven, CT, and London, 2001), p. 198.

16 Sandra Hindman, 'Pieter Bruegel's Children's Games, Folly, and Chance', *The Art Bulletin*, LXIII/3 (1981), pp. 447–75, with references to earlier literature and a key identifying each game.

17 On the division of stages of childhood see Barbara Hanawalt, 'Medievalists and the Study of Childhood', *Speculum*, LXXVII/2 (2002), pp. 447–50.

18 Erasmus, *De civilitate*, pp. 288–9.

19 Hindman, 'Pieter Bruegel's Children's Games', p. 469.

20 James D. Tracy, *Erasmus of the Low Countries* (Berkeley and Los Angeles, CA, 1996), pp. 47, 71–3.

21 Leah Sinanoglou Marcus, *Childhood and Cultural Despair: A Theme and Variations in Seventeenth-century Literature* (Pittsburgh, PA, 1978), p. 25.

22 Elizabeth Alice Honig, 'Country Folk and City Business', *The Art Bulletin*, LXXVIII/3 (1996), p. 511.

23 Yona Pinson, 'Folly and Childishness Go Hand in Hand: Hans Holbein's "Dixit Insipiens"', *Source: Notes in the History of Art*, XXII/3 (2003), pp. 1–7.

24 Erasmus, *Praise of Folly*, p. 91.

25 Irina Metzler, *Fools and Idiots? Intellectual Disability in the Middle Ages* (Manchester, 2016), pp. 119–25.

26 Paul Vandenbroeck, *Beeld van de andere, vertoog over het zelf* (Antwerp, 1987), pp. 40–60.

27 Erasmus, *Praise of Folly*, p. 110.

28 Ibid., pp. 106, 108.

29 All quotations here from Van Mander, *Lives*, vol. 1, p. 190. I have made a few adjustments to the translation provided there.

30 Svetlana Alpers, 'Bruegel's Festive Peasants', *Simiolus*, VI/3–4 (1972), pp. 167–8; Margaret Carroll, 'Peasant Festivity and Political Identity in the Sixteenth Century', *Art History*, X/3 (1987),

pp. 297–9; Stephanie Porras, *Pieter Bruegel's Historical Imagination* (University Park, PA, 2016), pp. 32–53.

31 Claudia Goldstein, *Pieter Bruegel and the Culture of the Early Modern Dinner Party* (Farnham and Burlington, VT, 2013), pp. 37, 49.

32 Bakhtin, *Rabelais and His World*, p. 9.

33 On the satirical genre of the peasant wedding, see Paul Vandenbroeck, 'Verbeeck's Peasant Weddings', *Simiolus*, X IV/2 (1984), pp. 79–124, and Alison G. Stewart, *Before Bruegel: Sebald Beham and the Origins of Peasant Festival Imagery* (Aldershot and Burlington, VT, 2008), pp. 189–217; on dances, Hans Joachim Raupp, *Bauernsatiren: Entstehung und Entwiklung des bäuerlichen Genres in der deutschen und niederländischen Kunst ca. 1470–1570* (Niederzier, 1986), pp. 165–94; Walter S. Gibson, 'Festive Peasants before Bruegel: Three Case Studies and Their Implications', *Simiolus*, XXXI/4 (2004), pp. 292–309.

34 Many thanks to Sarah R. Cohen and Lorraine Ratajczak for their suggestions about the dance being performed in this painting.

35 Castiglione, *Book of the Courtier*, p. 64.

36 Herman Roodenburg, *The Eloquence of the Body: Perspectives on Gesture in the Dutch Republic* (Zwolle, 2004), pp. 28–9.

37 Erasmus, *De civilitate*, pp. 273–4; see too Jacques Revel, 'The Uses of Civility', in *A History of Private Life*, ed. Jacques Chartier (London, 1989), pp. 168–71.

38 Erasmus, *De civilitate*, p. 277, repeated on p. 281.

39 Ibid., pp. 274, 283.

40 Stewart, *Before Bruegel*, p. 112.

41 Anna Bryson, *From Courtesy to Civility: Changing Codes of Conduct in Early Modern England* (Oxford, 1998), pp. 82–4.

42 Aileen Ribeiro, *Dress and Morality* (New York, 1986), pp. 59–64; Jeffery C. Persels, 'Bragueta Humanistica, or Humanism's Codpiece', *Sixteenth Century Journal*, XXVIII (1997), pp. 79–99.

43 Gibson, *Pieter Bruegel and the Art of Laughter*, p. 91.

44 Erasmus, *De civilitate*, pp. 280–86.

45 Goldstein, *Pieter Bruegel*, pp. 37, 56.

46 Vandenbroeck, 'Verbeeck's Peasant Weddings'; Walter S. Gibson, 'Verbeeck's Grotesque Wedding Feasts: Some Reconsiderations', *Simiolus*, XXI/1–2 (1992), pp. 29–39.

47 Gibson, *Pieter Bruegel and the Art of Laughter*, pp. 102–5.

48 Paul Freedman, *Images of the Medieval Peasant* (Stanford, CA, 1999), pp. 214–17.

49 On children as imitative see Steven Ozment, *Ancestors: The Loving Family in Old Europe* (Cambridge, MA, and London, 2001), pp. 68–9.

Conclusion: Speaking Truth

1 For a good overview see David Cressy, *Dangerous Talk: Scandalous, Seditious, and Treasonable Speech in Pre-modern England* (Oxford, 2010), pp. 1–6.

2 Desiderius Erasmus, 'Lingua'/'The Tongue', ed. Elaine Fantham and Erika Rummel, trans. Elaine Fantham, in *Collected Works* (Toronto, Buffalo and London, 1989), vol. XXIX, pp. 269–93.

3 Ibid., p. 328. On the importance of reputation see Thelma Fenster and Daniel Lord Smail, eds, *Fama: The Politics of Talk and Reputation in Medieval Europe* (Ithaca, NY, and London, 2003), pp. 3, 9–10; Cressy, *Dangerous Talk*, pp. 23–4.

4 Erasmus, 'Lingua', p. 357.

5 Hessel Miedema's commentary on Karel van Mander, *The Lives of the Illustrious Netherlandish and German Painters*, 6 vols (Doornspijk, 1994), vol. III, p. 252.

6 Van Mander, *Lives*, vol. I, p. 193.

7 Ibid., vol. I, p. 194.

8 Henk van Nierop, '"And Ye Shall Hear of Wars and Rumors of Wars." Rumor and the Revolt of the Netherlands', in *Public Opinion and Changing Identities in the Early Modern Netherlands*, ed. Judith Pollmann (Leiden, 2006), p. 72.

9 Martin van Gelderen, *The Political Thought of the Dutch Revolt, 1555–1590* (Cambridge, 1992), p. 40.

10 Pieter Spierenburg, *The Spectacle of Suffering: Executions and the Evolution of Repression* (Cambridge, 2008), pp. 8–9; Alastair Duke, 'Salvation by Coercion: The Controversy Surrounding the "Inquisition" in the Low Countries on the Eve of the Revolt', in *Reformation Principle and Practice*, ed. Peter Newman Brooks (London, 1980), pp. 143–4.

11 Gerrit Voogt, *Constraint on Trial: Dirck Volckertsz. Coornhert and Religious Freedom*, Sixteenth-century Essays and Studies (Kirksville, MO, 2000), vol. LII, p. 34.

12 Roger H. Marijnissen et al., *Bruegel: Tout l'oeuvre peint et dessiné* (Antwerp and Paris, 1988), pp. 372–3; Ethan Matt Kavaler, *Pieter Bruegel: Parables of Order and Enterprise* (Cambridge, 1999), pp. 223–4.

13 Paul Oskar Kristeller, 'The Unity of Truth', in *Renaissance Concepts of Man and Other Essays* (New York, 1972), pp. 53–9.

14 Martin van Gelderen *The Political Thought of the Dutch Revolt, 1555–1590* (Cambridge, 1992), pp. 65–6.

15 Desiderius Erasmus, *Praise of Folly*, ed. A.H.T. Levi, trans. Betty Radice, in *Collected Works* (Toronto, Buffalo and London, 1986), vol. XXVII, p. 118.

16 Michiel Plomp in Nadine M. Orenstein, ed., *Pieter Bruegel the Elder: Drawings and Prints*, exh. cat., Metropolitan Museum, New York (New Haven, CT, and London, 2001), pp. 234–6.

17 J. Denucé, *Kunstuitvoer in de 17e eeuw te Antwerpen: De firma Forchoudt*, Bronnen voor de geschiedenis van de Vlaamsche kunst, I (Antwerp, 1931), p. 115.

18 See David Cast, *The Calumny of Apelles: A Study in the Humanist Tradition* (New Haven, CT, and London, 1981); Stephanie Porras, *Pieter Bruegel's Historical Imagination* (University Park, PA, 2016), pp. 117–23.

19 Cast, *Calumny of Apelles*, p. 45. Botticelli's famous painting is somewhat exceptional in this regard: Truth is clothed in most of the images illustrated by Cast.

BIBLIOGRAPHY

Allmand, Christopher, 'War and the Non-combatant in the Middle
 Ages', in *Medieval Warfare*, ed. Maurice Keen (Oxford, 1999),
 pp. 253–72
Alpers, Svetlana, 'Bruegel's Festive Peasants', *Simiolus*, VI (1972),
 pp. 163–76
Arnade, Peter, *Beggars, Iconoclasts, and Civic Patriots: The Political Culture of the
 Dutch Revolt* (Ithaca, NY, 2008)
Auerbach, Erich, 'Saul's Pride', *Modern Language Notes*, LXIV/4 (1949),
 pp. 267–9
Augustijn, Cornelis, *Erasmus: His Life, Works, and Influence*, trans. J. C.
 Grayson (Toronto, Buffalo, NY, and London, 1991)
Bacon, Francis, 'On Deformity', in *The Essays or Counsels Civil and Moral*
 (Oxford, 1999), pp. 99–100
Bakhtin, Mikhail, *Rabelais and His World*, trans. Helene Iswolsky
 (Bloomington, IN, 1984)
Bakker, Boudewijn, *Landscape and Religion from Van Eyck
 to Rembrandt*, trans. Diane Webb (Farnham and Burlington,
 VT, 2012)
Baldwin, Robert, 'Peasant Imagery and Bruegel's "Fall of Icarus"',
 Konsthistorisk Tidskrift, LV/3 (1986), pp. 101–14
Bastiaensen, Jean, 'Bouwsteenen voor de biografie van Pieter Bruegel
 de Oude', *Jaarboek van het Felix Timmermans-Genootschap*, 41 (2013),
 pp. 97–114
—, 'De verloving van Pieter Bruegel de Oude. Nieuwe licht op de
 Antwerpse verankering', *Openbaar Kunstbezit Vlaanderen*, LI/1 (2013),
 pp. 26–7

Bauer, Linda, and George Bauer, 'Winter Landscape with Skaters and
    Bird Trap by Pieter Bruegel the Elder', *Art Bulletin*, LXVI/1 (1984),
    pp. 145–50
Belting, Hans, *Face and Mask: A Double History*, trans. Thomas S. Hansen
    and Abby J. Hansen (Princeton, NJ, and Oxford, 2017)
Bernheimer, Richard, *Wild Men in the Middle Ages* (New York, 1970)
Boeckl, Christine M., *Images of Leprosy: Disease, Religion, and Politics in
    European Art* (Kirksville, MO, 2011)
Brody, Saul Nathaniel, *The Disease of the Soul: Leprosy in Medieval Literature*
    (Ithaca, NY, and London, 1974)
Broecke, Marcel van den, *Ortelius Atlas Maps: An Illustrated Guide*, 2nd edn
    (Houten, 2011)
Bruijnen, Yvette, 'Over de twelf maendekens en de vier tyden's jaers:
    De maanden en jaargetijden in de kunst van de Nederlanden
    circa 1500 tot 1750', in *De vier jaargetijden in de kunst van de Nederlanden
    1500–1750*, ed. Yvette Bruijnen and Paul Huys Janssen (Zwolle,
    2002), pp. 51–71
Bryson, Anna, *From Courtesy to Civility: Changing Codes of Conduct in Early
    Modern England* (Oxford, 1998)
Buchanan, Iain, 'The Collection of Niclaes Jongelinck II: The
    "Months" by Pieter Bruegel the Elder', *Burlington Magazine*,
    CXXXII/1049 (1990), pp. 541–50
Burke, Peter, *Popular Culture in Early Modern Europe* (London, 1978)
Büttner, Nils, *Die Erfindung der Landschaft: Kosmographie und Landschaftskunst
    im Zeitalter Bruegels* (Göttingen, 2000)
—, '"Quid siculas sequeris per mille pericula terras?" Ein Beitrag zur
    Biographie Pieter Bruegels d.Ä. und zur Kulturgeschichte der
    niederländischen Italienreise', *Marburger Jahrbuch für Kunstwissenschaft*,
    27 (2000), pp. 209–42
Carroll, Margaret, *Painting and Politics in Northern Europe* (State College,
    PA, 2008)
—, 'Peasant Festivity and Political Identity in the Sixteenth Century',
    Art History, X/3 (1987), pp. 289–314
Cassirer, Ernst, *The Individual and the Cosmos in Renaissance Philosophy*
    (New York and Evanston, IL, 1964)
Cast, David, *The Calumny of Apelles: A Study in the Humanist Tradition*
    (New Haven, CT, and London, 1981)

Castiglione, Baldassare, *The Book of the Courtier*, trans. George Bull (London, 1967)

Chakravarti, Paromita, 'Natural Fools and the Historiography of Renaissance Folly', *Renaissance Studies*, xxv/2 (2011), pp. 208–27

Classen, Albrecht, 'The Discovery of the Mountain as an Epistemological Challenge', in *The Book of Nature and Humanity in the Middle Ages and the Renaissance*, ed. David Hawkes and Richard G. Newhauser (Turnhout, 2013)

Cleland, Elizabeth, ed., *Grand Design: Pieter Coecke van Aelst and Renaissance Tapestry*, exh. cat., New York, Metropolitan Museum (New Haven, CT, and London, 2014)

Constable, Giles, 'The Ideal of the Imitation of Christ', in *Three Studies in Medieval Religious and Social Thought* (Cambridge, 1995), pp. 145–248

Cosgrove, Denis, 'Globalism and Tolerance in Early Modern Geography', *Annals of the Association of American Geographers*, 93 (2003), pp. 852–70

Cressy, David, *Dangerous Talk: Scandalous, Seditious, and Treasonable Speech in Pre-modern England* (Oxford, 2010)

Cunningham, Andrew, Sachiko Kusukawa and Gregor Reisch, *Natural Philosophy Epitomised: Books 8–11 of Gregor Reisch's 'Philosophical Pearl' (1503)* (Farnham and Burlington, VT, 2010)

Davis, Natalie Zemon, 'Women on Top', in *Society and Culture in Early Modern France* (Stanford, CA, 1965), pp. 124–51

Dekeyzer, Brigitte, Bert Cardon and An Kenens, 'Het sprokkelen van de tijd: Sporen van het middeleeuwse tijds- en wereldbeeld in Zuid-Nederlandse kalenderminiaturen', in *De vier jaargetijden in de kunst van de Nederlanden 1500–1750*, ed. Yvette Bruijnen and Paul Huys Janssen (Zwolle, 2002), pp. 25–35

Denucé, J., *Kunstuitvoer in de 17e eeuw te Antwerpen: De firma Forchoudt*, Bronnen voor de geschiedenis van de vlaamsche kunst, I (Antwerp, 1931)

Dickson, Arthur, *Valentine and Orson: A Study in Late Medieval Romance* (New York, 1929)

Duke, Alastair, 'Salvation by Coercion: The Controversy Surrounding the "Inquisition" in the Low Countries on the Eve of the Revolt', in *Reformation Principle and Practice*, ed. Peter Newman Brooks (London, 1980), pp. 135–56

Elias, Norbert, *The Civilizing Process*, vol. I: *The History of Manners*,
    trans. Edmund Jephcott (New York, 1978)
Erasmus, Desiderius, *Adages*, ed. R.A.B. Mynors and John N. Grant,
    trans. Margaret Mann Phillips and Denis L. Drysdall, in
    Collected Works (Toronto, Buffalo, NY, and London, 1982),
    vols XXXI–XXXV
— 'A Complaint of Peace Spurned and Rejected by the Whole World'
    [1516], in *Collected Works*, ed. Betty Radice (Toronto, Buffalo, NY,
    and London, 1986), vol. XXVII, pp. 289–322
—, *The Colloquies of Erasmus*, trans. Craig R. Thompson (Chicago, IL,
    and London, 1965)
—, 'De bello turcico'/'On the War against the Turks', in *The Erasmus
    Reader*, ed. Erika Rummel (Toronto, Buffalo, NY, and London,
    1990), pp. 315–33
—, *De civilitate morum puerilium*/*On Good Manners for Boys*, in *Collected Works*,
    ed. J. K. Sowards, trans. Brian McGregor (Toronto, Buffalo, NY,
    and London, 1985), vol. XXV, pp. 269–89
—, *De copia*, trans. Betty I. Knott, in *Collected Works*, vol. XXIV (Toronto,
    Buffalo, NY, and London, 1978), pp. 279–659
—, *Enchiridion militis christiani*/*The Handbook of the Christian Soldier*, in
    Collected Works, ed. John W. O'Malley, trans. Charles Fantazzi
    (Toronto, Buffalo, NY, and London, 1988), vol. LXVI, pp. 1–127
—, 'Lingua'/'The Tongue', ed. Elaine Fantham and Erika Rummel,
    trans. Elaine Fantham, in *Collected Works* (Toronto, Buffalo, NY,
    and London, 1989), vol. XXIX, pp. 250–412
—, *Praise of Folly*, ed. A.H.T. Levi, trans. Betty Radice, in *Collected Works*
    (Toronto, Buffalo, NY, and London, 1986), vol. XXVII, pp. 77–153
Ertz, Klaus, *Pieter Brueghel der Jüngere (1564–1637/30)* (Lingen, 2000)
Falkenburg, Reindert L., *Joachim Patinir: Landscape as an Image of
    the Pilgrimage of Life*, trans. Michael Hoyle (Amsterdam and
    Philadelphia, PA, 1988)
—, 'Pieter Bruegels Kruisdraging: een proeve van "close-reading"',
    Oud Holland, CVII (1993), pp. 17–33
—, 'Pieter Bruegel's *Series of the Seasons*: On the Perception of Divine
    Order', in *Liber amicorum Raphael de Smedt. 2 Artium Historia*, ed. Joost
    Vander Auwera, Miscellanea Neerlandica, XXIV (Leuven, 2001),
    pp. 253–76

—, '"Schilderachtig weer" bij Jan van Goyen', in *Jan van Goyen*, ed. Christiaan Vogelaar, exh. cat., Leiden, Stedelijk Museum de Lakenhal (Leiden, 1996), pp. 60–69

Fenster, Thelma, and Daniel Lord Smail, eds, *Fama: The Politics of Talk and Reputation in Medieval Europe* (Ithaca, NY, and London, 2003)

Fishman, Jane, *Boerenverdriet: Violence between Peasants and Soldiers in Early Modern Netherlandish Art* (Ann Arbor, MI, 1979)

Freedberg, David, 'Allusion and Topicality in the Work of Pieter Bruegel: The Implications of a Forgotten Polemic', in *The Prints of Pieter Bruegel the Elder*, ed. David Freedberg, exh. cat., Tokyo, Bridgestone Museum of Art (Tokyo, 1989), pp. 53–65

Freedman, Paul, *Images of the Medieval Peasant* (Stanford, CA, 1999)

Gelderen, Martin van, *The Political Thought of the Dutch Revolt, 1555–1590* (Cambridge, 1992)

Gibson, Michael Francis, *The Mill and the Cross: Pieter Bruegel's 'Way to Calvary'* (Lausanne, 2000)

Gibson, Walter S., 'Bruegel, Dulle Griet, and Sexist Politics in the Sixteenth Century', in *Pieter Bruegel und seine Welt*, ed. Otto von Simson and Matthias Winner (Berlin, 1979), pp. 9–15

—, 'Festive Peasants before Bruegel: Three Case Studies and Their Implications', *Simiolus*, XXXI/4 (2004), pp. 292–309

—, *Figures of Speech: Picturing Proverbs in Renaissance Netherlands* (Berkeley and Los Angeles, CA, 2010)

—, 'Mirror of the Earth': The World Landscape in Sixteenth-century Flemish Painting* (Princeton, NJ, 1989)

—, *Pieter Bruegel and the Art of Laughter* (Berkeley and Los Angeles, CA, 2006)

—, 'Pieter Bruegel the Elder and the Flemish World Landscape of the Sixteenth Century', in *Bruegel and Netherlandish Landscape Painting from the National Gallery, Prague*, exh. cat., Tokyo, National Museum of Western Art; Kyoto, National Museum of Modern Art (Tokyo and Kyoto, 1990), pp. 11–23

—, *Pieter Bruegel the Elder: Two Studies* (Lawrence, KS, 1991)

—, 'Verbeeck's Grotesque Wedding Feasts: Some Reconsiderations', *Simiolus*, XXI/1–2 (1992), pp. 29–39

Gill, Meredith J., *Angels and the Order of Heaven in Medieval and Renaissance Italy* (Cambridge, 2014)

Goffman, Erving, *Stigma: Notes on the Management of Spoiled Identity*
    (New York, London and Toronto, 1986)
Goldstein, Claudia, 'Artifacts of Domestic Life: Bruegel's Paintings
    in the Flemish Home', *Nederlands Kunsthistorisch Jaarboek*, 51 (2000),
    pp. 173–93
—, *Pieter Bruegel and the Culture of the Early Modern Dinner Party* (Farnham
    and Burlington, VT, 2013)
Grauls, Jan, *Volkstaal en volksleven in het werk van Pieter Bruegel* (Antwerp
    and Amsterdam, 1957)
Gregory, Joseph F., *Contemporization as Polemical Device in Pieter Bruegel's
    Biblical Narratives* (Lewiston, NY, 2005)
—, 'Toward the Contextualization of Pieter Bruegel's Procession
    to Calvary', *Nederlands Kunsthistorisch Jaarboek*, 47 (1996),
    pp. 207–21
Grieken, Joris van, Ger Luijten and Jan van der Stock, eds, *Hieronymus
    Cock: The Renaissance in Print*, exh. cat., Leuven, M-Museum, and
    Paris, Fondation Custodia (New Haven, CT, and London, 2013)
Grossmann, Fritz, *Bruegel: The Paintings* (London, 1955)
Guicciardini, Lodovico, *Beschryvinghe van alle de Neder-Landen* [1567],
    trans. Cornelius Kilian (Amsterdam, 1612)
Gurevich, A. J., *Categories of Medieval Culture* (London, 1985)
Hale, J. R., *Artists and Warfare in the Renaissance* (New Haven, CT,
    and London, 1990)
—, 'Sixteenth-century Explanations of War and Violence', in
    Renaissance War Studies (London, 1983), pp. 335–58
Hanawalt, Barbara, 'Medievalists and the Study of Childhood',
    Speculum, LXXVII/2 (2002), pp. 440–60
Harman, Thomas, 'A Caveat or Warning for Commen Cursitors,
    Vulgarly Called Vagabonds' [1566], in *The Elizabethan Underworld*,
    ed. A. V. Judges (New York, 1930), pp. 61–118
Heller, Agnes, *Renaissance Man*, trans. Richard E. Allen (London, 1978)
Hellerstedt, Kahren Jones, 'The Blind Man and His Guide in
    Netherlandish Painting', *Simiolus*, XIII/3–4 (1983), pp. 163–81
Heninger, S. K., *The Cosmographical Glass: Renaissance Diagrams of the Universe*
    (San Marino, CA, 1977)
Heuer, Christopher, 'Disappearing into the Green: Pieter Bruegel
    and the Sea' (unpublished manuscript)

Hindman, Sandra, 'Pieter Bruegel's Children's Games, Folly, and
 Chance', *Art Bulletin*, LXIII/3 (1981), pp. 447–75
Honig, Elizabeth Alice, 'Country Folk and City Business', *Art Bulletin*,
 LXXVIII/3 (1996), pp. 511–26
—, *Painting and the Market in Early Modern Antwerp* (New Haven, CT,
 and London, 1998)
Jeanneret, Michel, *A Feast of Words: Banquets and Table Talk in the
 Renaissance*, trans. Jeremy Whiteley and Emma Hughes
 (Chicago, IL, 1991)
Karcioglu, Zeynel A., 'Ocular Pathology in the Parable of the Blind
 Leading the Blind and Other Paintings by Pieter Bruegel',
 Survey of Ophthalmology, XLVII/1 (2002), pp. 55–62
Kaschek, Bertram, *Weltzeit und Endzeit: Die 'Monatsbilder' Pieter Bruegels d.Ä.*
 (Munich, 2012)
Kavaler, Ethan Matt, *Pieter Bruegel: Parables of Order and Enterprise*
 (Cambridge, 1999)
—, 'Pieter Bruegel's Fall of Icarus and the Noble Peasant', *Jaarboek van
 het Koninklijk Museum voor Schone Kunsten, Antwerpen* (Antwerp, 1986),
 pp. 83–98
Kelly, Jessen, *Material Culture and Games of Chance in the Early Modern
 Netherlands* (Kalamazoo, MI, forthcoming 2020)
Kilinski, Karl II, 'Bruegel on Icarus: Inversions of the Fall', *Zeitschrift
 Für Kunstgeschichte*, 67 (2004), pp. 91–114
Kirtley, Donald D., *The Psychology of Blindness* (Chicago, IL, 1975)
Klein, H. Arthur, *The Graphic Worlds of Pieter Bruegel the Elder*
 (New York, 1963)
Koerner, Joseph Leo, *Bosch and Bruegel: From Enemy Painting to Everyday Life*
 (Princeton, NJ, and Oxford, 2016)
—, 'Impossible Objects: Bosch's Realism', *RES: Anthropology and Aesthetics*,
 46 (2004), pp. 73–97
—, 'The Printed World', in *The Printed World of Pieter Bruegel the Elder*,
 ed. Barbara Butts and Joseph Leo Koerner, exh. cat., Saint Louis
 Art Museum (St Louis, MO, 1995), pp. 20–34
—, 'Unmasking the World: Bruegel's Ethnography', *Common Knowledge*,
 X/2 (2004), pp. 220–51
Kossmann, E. H., and A. F. Mellink, eds, *Texts concerning the Revolt of the
 Netherlands* (Cambridge, 1974)

Koyre, Alexandre, *From the Closed World to the Infinite Universe*
    (Baltimore, MD, 1968)
Kristeller, Paul Oskar, 'The Unity of Truth', in *Renaissance Concepts
    of Man and Other Essays* (New York, 1972), pp. 43–63
Kunzle, David, 'Spanish Herod, Dutch Innocents: Bruegel's *Massacres
    of the Innocents* in Their Sixteenth-century Political Contexts',
    Art History, XXIV/1 (2001), pp. 51–82
Kurz, Otto, 'Tapestries after Hieronymus Bosch', *Journal of the Warburg
    and Courtauld Institutes*, 30 (1967), pp. 150–62
Kwakkelstein, Michael W. *Leonardo da Vinci as a Physiognomist*
    (Leiden, 1994)
Le Goff, Jacques, 'Laughter in the Middle Ages', in *A Cultural History
    of Humour*, ed. Jan Bremmer and Herman Roodenburg
    (Cambridge, 1997), pp. 40–53
Lipsius, Justus, *On Constancy*, ed. John Sellars, trans. Sir John Stradling
    (Exeter, 2006)
Little, Lester K., 'Pride Goes before Avarice: Social Change and the
    Vices in Latin Christendom', *American Historical Review*, LXXVI/1
    (1971), pp. 16–49
Lovejoy, Arthur O., *The Great Chain of Being* (New York, 1936)
Machiavelli, Niccolò, *Discourses on Livy*, trans. Harvey C. Mansfield
    and Nathan Tarcov (Chicago, IL, and London, 1996)
Maczak, Antoni, *Travel in Early Modern Europe*, trans. Ursula Phillips
    (Cambridge, 1995)
Mander, Karel van, *Den grondt der edel vry schilder-const* [1604], trans.
    Hessel Miedema (Utrecht, 1973)
—, *The Lives of the Illustrious Netherlandish and German Painters*, ed. Hessel
    Miedema, trans. Jacqueline Pennial-Boer and Charles Ford, 6 vols
    (Doornspijk, 1994)
Mansbach, S. A., 'Pieter Bruegel's Towers of Babel', *Zeitschrift Für
    Kunstgeschichte*, XLV/1 (1982), pp. 43–56
Marchant, Guy, *The Kalendar and Compost of Shepherds* [1493; English trans.
    1518] (London, 1931)
Marcus, Leah Sinanoglou, *Childhood and Cultural Despair: A Theme and
    Variations in Seventeenth-century Literature* (Pittsburgh, PA, 1978)
Marijnissen, Roger H., et al., *Bruegel: Tout l'oeuvre peint et dessiné*
    (Antwerp and Paris, 1988)

Martin, John Jeffries, *Myths of Renaissance Individualism* (Basingstoke and New York, 2004)

Meadow, Mark, 'Bruegel's *Procession to Calvary*, Aemulatio and the Space of Vernacular Style', *Nederlands Kunsthistorisch Jaarboek*, 47 (1996), pp. 181–205

—, 'On the Structure of Knowledge in Bruegel's Netherlandish Proverbs', *Volkskundig Bulletin*, XVIII/2 (1992), pp. 141–69

—, *Pieter Bruegel the Elder's Netherlandish Proverbs and the Practice of Rhetoric* (Zwolle, 2002)

Meganck, Tine Luk, *Pieter Bruegel the Elder: Fall of the Rebel Angels* (Milan, 2014)

Meisel, Martin, *Chaos Imagined: Literature, Art, Science* (New York, 2016)

Melinkoff, Ruth, *Outcasts: Signs of Otherness in Northern European Art of the Late Middle Ages*, 2 vols (Berkeley and Los Angeles, CA, 1993)

Metzler, Irina, *Disability in Medieval Europe* (London and New York, 2006)

—, *Fools and Idiots? Intellectual Disability in the Middle Ages* (Manchester, 2016)

Middleton, Thomas, *The Works of Thomas Middleton*, ed. Alexander Dyce, 5 vols (London, 1840)

Miegroet, Hans J. van, '"The Twelve Months" Reconsidered: How a Drawing by Pieter Stevens Clarifies a Bruegel Enigma', *Simiolus*, XVI/1 (1986), pp. 29–35

Monballieu, A., 'De "Kermis van Hoboken" bij P. Bruegel, J. Grimmer en G. Mostaert', *Jaarboek van het Koninklijk Museum voor Schone Kunsten, Antwerpen* (1974), pp. 139–69

Montaigne, Michel de, *The Complete Essays of Montaigne*, trans. Donald M. Frame (Stanford, CA, 1965)

Moore, R. I., *The Formation of a Persecuting Society* (Oxford, 1987)

More, Thomas, *Utopia* [1516], ed. Edward Sturtz (New Haven, CT, and London, 1964)

Morford, Mark, *Stoics and Neostoics* (Princeton, NJ, 1991)

Müller Hofstede, Justus, 'Zur Interpretation von Pieter Bruegels Landschaft: Ästhetischer Landschaftsbegriff und stoische Weltbetrachtung', in *Pieter Bruegel und seine Welt*, ed. Otto von Simson and Matthias Winner (Berlin, 1979), pp. 73–142

Müller, Jürgen, *Das Paradox als Bildform* (Munich, 1999)

Muylle, Jan, 'Ethos en pathos: De literaire appreciatie van expressie in
     het werk van Metsijs en Bruegel', *Nederlands Kunsthistorisch Jaarboek*,
     60 (2010), pp. 19–33
—, 'Pieter Bruegel en Abraham Ortelius: Bijdrage tot de literaire
     receptie van Pieter Bruegels werk', in *Archivum artis Lovaneniense:
     Bijdragen tot de geschiedenis van de kunst der Nederlanden: Opgedragen
     aan Prof. Dr. J. K. Steppe*, ed. Maurits Smeyers (Leuven, 1981),
     pp. 319–37
—, 'Tronies toegeschreven aan Pieter Bruegel: Fysionomie en expressie
     (1)', *De zeventiende eeuw*, XVII/2 (2001), pp. 174–204
—, 'Tronies toegeschreven aan Pieter Bruegel: Fysionomie en expressie
     (2)', *De zeventiende eeuw*, XVIII/2 (2002), pp. 115–48
Neely, Carol Thomas, *Distracted Subjects: Madness and Gender in Shakespeare
     and Early Modern Culture* (Ithaca, NY, and London, 2004)
—, 'Recent Work in Renaissance Studies', *Renaissance Quarterly*, XLIV/4
     (1991), pp. 776–91
Neubauer, Hans-Joachim, *The Rumour: A Cultural History* (London and
     New York, 1999)
Nichols, Tom, *The Art of Poverty: Irony and Ideal in Sixteenth-century Beggar
     Imagery* (Manchester, 2007)
Nierop, Henk van, '"And Ye Shall Hear of Wars and Rumors of Wars."
     Rumor and the Revolt of the Netherlands', in *Public Opinion and
     Changing Identities in the Early Modern Netherlands*, ed. Judith Pollmann
     (Leiden, 2006), pp. 69–86
Onafuwa, Yemi, 'Bruegel's Cripples and Early Modern Humor',
     Athanor, 25 (2007), pp. 49–57
Orenstein, Nadine M., ed., *Pieter Bruegel the Elder: Drawings and Prints*,
     exh. cat., New York, Metropolitan Museum (New Haven, CT,
     and London, 2001)
Ozment, Steven, *Ancestors: The Loving Family in Old Europe* (Cambridge,
     MA, and London, 2001)
Parker, Geoffrey, 'Early Modern Europe', in *The Laws of War*, ed.
     Michael Howard, George J. Andreopoulos and Mark R. Shulman
     (New Haven, CT, and London, 1994), pp. 40–58
—, 'The "Military Revolution", 1560–1660 – a Myth?', *Journal of Modern
     History*, XLVIII/2 (1976), pp. 195–214
Payne, Robert, *Hubris: A Study of Pride* (New York, 1960)

Persels, Jeffery C., 'Bragueta humanistica, or Humanism's Codpiece',
    Sixteenth-century Journal, XXVIII/1 (1997), pp. 79–99
Pico della Mirandola, Giovanni, 'On the Dignity of Man' [1486],
    in *The Renaissance Philosophy of Man*, ed. Ernst Cassirer, Paul Oskar
    Kristeller and John Herman Randall, trans. Elizabeth Livermore
    Forbes (Chicago, IL, 1948), pp. 215–54
Pinson, Yona, 'Folly and Childishness Go Hand in Hand: Hans
    Holbein's "Dixit Insipiens"', *Source: Notes in the History of Art*, XXII/3
    (2003), pp. 1–7
—, 'Hieronymus Bosch: Homo Viator at a Crossroads: A New
    Reading of the Rotterdam Tondo', *Artibus et Historiae*, XXVI/52
    (2005), pp. 57–84
Pitkin, Barbara, 'Erasmus, Calvin, and the Faces of Stoicism in
    Renaissance and Reformation Thought', in *The Routledge Handbook
    of the Stoic Tradition*, ed. John Sellars (London and New York, 2016),
    pp. 145–59
Pleij, Herman, *Dreaming of Cockaigne: Medieval Fantasies of the Perfect Life*,
    trans. Diane Webb (New York, 2001)
Porras, Stephanie, *Pieter Bruegel's Historical Imagination* (University Park,
    PA, 2016)
Porter, Martin, *Windows of the Soul: Physiognomy in European Culture,
    1470–1780* (Oxford, 2005)
Raupp, Hans Joachim, *Bauernsatiren. Entstehung und Entwiklung des
    bäuerlichen Genres in der deutschen und niederländischen Kunst ca. 1470–1570*
    (Niederzier, 1986)
*Refereynen ende Liedekens van diverse Rhetoricienen wt Brabant/Vlaenderen/
    Hollant/en Zeelant. Ghelesen en Ghesonghen op de Corenbloeme Camere binnen
    Bruessele/op haer izerlijcxse Prinsfeeste* (Brussels, 1563)
Revel, Jacques, 'The Uses of Civility', in *A History of Private Life*, ed.
    Jacques Chartier (London, 1989), pp. 167–205
Ribeiro, Aileen, *Dress and Morality* (New York, 1986)
Richardson, Todd M., *Pieter Bruegel the Elder: Art Discourse in the Sixteenth-
    century Netherlands* (Farnham and Burlington, VT, 2011)
Rodriguez-Salgado, M. J., 'King, Bishop, Pawn? Philip II and
    Granvelle in the 1550s and 1560s', in *Les Granvelle et les anciens
    Pays-Bas*, ed. Krista de Jonge and Gustaf Janssens (Leuven, 2000),
    pp. 105–34

Roodenburg, Herman, *The Eloquence of the Body: Perspectives on Gesture in the Dutch Republic* (Zwolle, 2004)

Rooijakkers, Gerard, *Rituele Repertoires. Volkscultuur in Oostelijk Noord-Brabant 1559–1853* (Nijmegen, 1994)

Rothstein, Bret, 'The Problem with Looking at Pieter Bruegel's Elck', *Art History*, XXVI/2 (2003), pp. 143–73

Roussat, Richard, *The Most Excellent, Profitable, and Pleasant Booke of the Famous Doctour and Expert Astrologian Arcandam . . . with the Addition of Phisiognomie Very Pleasant to Reade*, trans. William Warde (London, 1564)

Ruff, Julius R., *Violence in Early Modern Europe, 1500–1800* (Cambridge, 2001)

Schmitt, Charles, et al., eds, *The Cambridge History of Renaissance Philosophy* (Cambridge, 1988)

Schoute, Roger van, and Hélène Verougstraete, 'A Painted Wooden Roundel by Pieter Bruegel the Elder', *Burlington Magazine*, CXLII/1164 (2000), pp. 140–46

Screech, M. A., *Rabelais* (Ithaca, NY, 1979)

Sellink, Manfred, *Bruegel: The Complete Paintings, Drawings, and Prints* (Ghent, 2007)

Seneca, 'De ira'/'On Anger', in *Moral and Political Essays*, ed. John M. Cooper and J. F. Procope (Cambridge, 1995), pp. 1–116

—, *Naturales Quaestiones*, trans. John Clarke, see naturalesquaestiones. blogspot.nl, accessed February 2018

Serebrennikov, Nina, 'Pieter Bruegel the Elder's Series of "Virtues" and "Vices"' (unpublished doctoral dissertation, University of North Carolina, 1986)

Shawe-Taylor, Desmond, and Jennifer Scott, *Bruegel to Rubens: Masters of Flemish Painting* (London, 2007)

Sherer, Idan, *Warriors for a Living: The Experience of the Spanish Infantry in the Italian Wars, 1494–1559* (Leiden and Boston, MA, 2017)

Silver, Larry, *Pieter Bruegel* (New York and London, 2011)

—, 'Pieter Bruegel in the Capital of Capitalism', *Nederlands Kunsthistorisch Jaarboek*, 47 (1996), pp. 125–53

—, 'Second Bosch: Family Resemblance and the Marketing of Art', *Nederlands Kunsthistorisch Jaarboek*, 50 (1999), pp. 31–56

—, 'Ungrateful Dead: Bruegel's Triumph of Death Re-examined', in *Excavating the Medieval Image*, ed. David S. Areford and Nina A. Rowe (Aldershot and Burlington, VT, 2004), pp. 265–83

Silver, Larry, and Henry Luttikhuizen, 'The Quality of Mercy:
    Representations of Charity in Early Netherlandish Art',
    Studies in Iconography, 29 (2008), pp. 216–48
Skinner, Quentin, 'Why Laughing Mattered in the Renaissance',
    History of Political Thought, XXII/3 (2001), pp. 418–47
Slack, Paul, *Poverty and Policy in Tudor and Stuart England* (London and
    New York, 1988)
Snow, Edward, 'The Language of Contradiction in Bruegel's "Tower
    of Babel"', *RES: Anthropology and Aesthetics*, 5 (1983), pp. 40–48
Spierenburg, Pieter, *The Spectacle of Suffering: Executions and the Evolution
    of Repression* (Cambridge, 2008)
Steinberg, Leo, *Michelangelo's Last Paintings* (London, 1975)
Stewart, Alison G., *Before Bruegel: Sebald Beham and the Origins of Peasant
    Festival Imagery* (Aldershot and Burlington, VT, 2008)
Stridbeck, Carl Gustaf, *Bruegelstudien* (Stockholm, 1956)
Sullivan, Margaret, 'Bosch, Bruegel, Everyman and the Northern
    Renaissance', *Oud Holland*, CXXI/2–3 (2008), pp. 117–46
—, 'Bruegel's Proverbs: Art and Audience in the Northern
    Renaissance', *Art Bulletin*, LXXIII/3 (1991), pp. 431–66
—, 'Madness and Folly: Peter Bruegel the Elder's Dulle Griet',
    Art Bulletin, LIX/1 (1977), pp. 55–66
Tillyard, E.M.W., *The Elizabethan World Picture* (London, 1960)
Tolnay, Charles de, 'Newly Discovered Miniatures by Pieter Bruegel
    the Elder', *Burlington Magazine*, CVII/744 (1965), pp. 110–15
Torrilhon, Tony M., 'La pathologie chez Bruegel' (thesis, Faculté de
    medicine, Paris, 1957)
Toth-Ubbens, Magdi, *Verloren beelden van miserabele bedelaars* (Ghent, 1987)
Tracy, James D., *Erasmus of the Low Countries* (Berkeley and Los Angeles,
    CA, 1996)
Trinkaus, Charles, *In Our Image and Likeness: Humanity and Divinity in Italian
    Humanist Thought*, 2 vols (Chicago, IL, 1970)
Vandenbroeck, Paul, *Beeld van de andere, vertoog over het zelf*, Koninklijk
    Museum voor Schone Kunsten (Antwerp, 1987)
—, *Jheronimus Bosch: Tussen volksleven en stadscultuur* (Berchem, 1987)
—, 'Verbeeck's Peasant Weddings', *Simiolus*, XIV/2 (1984), pp. 79–124
Veldman, Ilja M., *Maarten van Heemskerck and Dutch Humanism in the
    Sixteenth Century*, trans. Michael Hoyle (Maarssen, 1977)

Verougstraete, Hélène M., and Roger A. van Schoute, 'The Triumph of Death by Pieter Bruegel the Elder and Pieter Brueghel the Younger', in *The Triumph of Death by Pieter Bruegel the Younger*, ed. and trans. James I. W. Corcoran (Antwerp, 1993), pp. 35–53

Vigarello, Georges, 'The Upward Training of the Body from the Age of Chivalry to Courtly Civility', in *Fragments for a History of the Human Body*, ed. Michel Feher (New York, 1989), II, pp. 149–99

Vives, J. L., *De subventione pauperum*, ed. C. Matheeussen and C. Fantazzi (Leiden, 2002)

Voogt, Gerrit, *Constraint on Trial: Dirck Volckertsz. Coornhert and Religious Freedom*, Sixteenth-century Essays and Studies (Kirksville, MO, 2000), vol. LII

Voragine, Jacobus de, *The Golden Legend: Readings on the Saints*, trans. William Granger Ryan, 2 vols (Princeton, NJ, 1993)

Vries, Lyckle de, 'Bruegel's "Fall of Icarus": Ovid or Solomon?', *Simiolus*, XXX/1–2 (2003), pp. 4–18

Wheatley, Edward, *Stumbling Blocks before the Blind: Medieval Constructions of a Disability* (Ann Arbor, MI, 2014)

White, Christopher, '"The Rabbit Hunters" by Pieter Bruegel the Elder', in *Pieter Bruegel und seine Welt*, ed. Otto von Simson and Matthias Winner (Berlin, 1979), pp. 187–91

Woollett, Anne T., 'Hitting the Mark: Strategies of Display in the Altarpieces of the Antwerp Militia Guilds', in *Rekonstruktion der Gesellschaft aus Kunst*, ed. Eckhard Leuschner (Petersberg, 2016), pp. 89–100

Wuyts, Ben, *Over narren, kreupelen, doven en blinden. Leven met een handicap. Van de oudheid tot nu* (Leuven, 2005)

Yeoman, Victoria, 'Speaking Plates: Text, Performance, and Banqueting Trenchers in Early Modern Europe', *Renaissance Studies*, XXXI/5 (2017), pp. 755–79

Zupnick, Irving L., 'The Influence of Erasmus' *Enchiridion* on Bruegel's Seven Virtues', *De Gulden Passer*, 47 (1969), pp. 225–35

ACKNOWLEDGEMENTS

My first thanks are to Michael Leaman and François Quiviger for inviting me to contribute a book on Pieter Bruegel to the Renaissance Lives
series, and for then supporting my own decisions about what kind of
book it would be. My previous two studies circled around Bruegel: this
one allowed me to take him on directly, but from an angle that I found
particularly interesting. Also thanks to Svetlana Alpers, who told me that
I needed to write about a really great artist. She was right; it has been
hugely fun.

My book on Pieter Bruegel's son Jan Brueghel took too much time
to write; this one has taken perhaps too little. I thank Gary Schwartz for
insisting that I could indeed write a book this fast, and for giving me
some suggestions on how to do it. My rush to write was greatly aided by
three seminars that I taught at Berkeley: 'Bruegel's Renaissance', 'Insiders
and Outsiders in the Age of Bruegel' and especially a graduate seminar
on 'Human Nature' that I co-taught with Beate Fricke. The last of these
oriented me toward the relevant material and connected my early
modern ideas to their medieval roots, and I am most grateful to Beate
and all the students in that stimulating class. A semester spent at the
department of Art History at Utrecht University gave me the space to
think and write about this material, and I very much appreciated the
exceptionally warm welcome I received from everybody there, not to
mention the extremely light teaching load and the gorgeous office that
Thijs Weststeijn allowed me to use.

When you work on a great artist, I discovered, there is an equal
amount of great scholarship to contend with, and I feel certain that I
have not done justice to all of those who paved the way in this field. Two

recent contributors to the Bruegel literature, Stephanie Porras and Larry Silver, have given me tips and guideposts (and roadside crosses) when I needed them. Other scholars have shared their ideas and sometimes unpublished work with me: Al Acres, Jean Bastiaensen, Odilia Bonebakker, Jessica Buskirk, Sarah Cohen, Margie Ferguson, Christopher Heuer, Bertram Kaschek, Machteld Löwenstein, Elizabeth McFadden, Tine Meganck, Lori Ratajczak, Paul Vandenbroeck and Victoria Yeoman. Sabine Penot allowed me to spend some quality time in the conservation studio at the Kunsthistorisches Museum with Bruegel's *Christ Carrying the Cross*, a great gift. I first researched the material in Chapter Six long ago when I was working at the (then) Amsterdams Historisch Museum, and I thank Renée Kistemaker for that opportunity, as well as the Fulbright and AAUW grants that funded it.

Katy Longshore, Eva Allan and especially Jess Bailey gave me extremely helpful feedback on drafts of all the chapters. Amy Salter at Reaktion answered unreasonable numbers of e-mailed questions. And Rebecca Levitan did a fantastic job of obtaining all the permissions even while doing her own archaeological work in Greece.

Finally I need to thank my family for tolerating my singular focus on this book over the period when I spent five months off in the Netherlands, and then read and wrote like a maniac for the following five. The house was not terribly tidy and I attended to nobody's games, performances, college applications, graduations etc., but I note that there was always good food, because this was a Bruegel household. I especially thank Deb for overseeing three children, two dogs, two cats and four chickens in my real and virtual times of absence. For all her love and support through two entire books and beyond, this one is dedicated to her.

PHOTO ACKNOWLEDGEMENTS

The author and publishers wish to express their thanks to the below sources of illustrative material and/or permission to reproduce it. Some locations of artworks are also given below, in the interests of brevity:

Albertina, Vienna: 53; Alte Pinakothek, Munich: 45; British Museum, London: 10, 68; Fine Arts Museum of San Francisco: 5; Gemäldegalerie, Berlin: 6, 7, 8; Hessisches Landesmuseum, Darmstadt: 67; Institute of Fine Arts, Detroit: 62, 63; Koninklijk Museum voor Schone Kunsten, Antwerp: 28; Kunsthistorisches Museum, Vienna: 14, 15, 19, 20, 21, 22, 23, 31, 33, 34, 47, 48, 49, 50, 51, 59, 60, 61, 64, 65, 66; Library of Congress, Washington, DC: 13; Lobkowicz Collection, Prague: 17; Metropolitan Museum of Art, New York: 4, 9, 11, 12, 16, 18, 24, 25, 30, 38, 44, 56, 57, 58; Musée du Louvre, Paris: 52; Museo Nazionale di Capodimonte, Naples: 54; Museum Boijmans-van Beuningen, Rotterdam: 32; Museum Mayer van den Bergh, Antwerp: 1, 2, 3, 39, 40; National Gallery, London: 46; Patrimonio Nacional, Madrid: 37; Museo del Prado, Madrid: 35, 36; Rijksmuseum, Amsterdam: 55; Royal Collection: 41, 42, 43; Royal Museum of Fine Arts, Brussels: 26, 27, 29.

INDEX